Argumentation: Critical Thinking in Action

SECOND EDITION

Argumentation: Critical Thinking in Action

SECOND EDITION

David Lapakko, Ph.D.

iUniverse, Inc.
New York   Bloomington

iUniverse books may be ordered through booksellers or by contacting:

iUniverse
1663 Liberty Drive
Bloomington, IN 47403
www.iuniverse.com
1-800-Authors (1-800-288-4677)

Because of the dynamic nature of the Internet, any Web addresses or links contained in this book may have changed since publication and may no longer be valid. The views expressed in this work are solely those of the author and do not necessarily reflect the views of the publisher, and the publisher hereby disclaims any responsibility for them.

ISBN: 978-1-4401-6838-3 (sc)
ISBN: 978-1-4401-6839-0 (dj)
ISBN: 978-1-4401-6840-6 (ebook)

Printed in the United States of America

iUniverse rev. date: 10/20/09

For Helen, Tony, and Jamee—
the three most important people in my life.

Table of Contents

PREFACE

I have long been fascinated with issues related to argumentation, critical thinking, and advocacy. My formal connection with this world began as a junior in high school, when I signed up for the debate team. I was then extensively involved in contest debate for my last two years of high school and my first two years of college. After graduating from Macalester College in St. Paul, I became a high school teacher and served as a head debate coach. And during that time, for six summers I was a staff member at the Macalester Summer High School Debate Institute.

As a graduate student at the University of Minnesota in the 1980s, I taught many sections of SPCH 1-313, Analysis of Oral Argument. Since my arrival at Augsburg College in Minneapolis in the fall of 1986, I have taught dozens of sections of COM 351, Argumentation, as well as several sections of Comm 1650, Argumentation and Advocacy, at Hamline University in St. Paul.

In all those years of teaching, I adopted textbooks that were usually quite good. However, I was never able to find a text that met all of my ideal criteria. First, I kept finding "holes" in the texts—i.e., topics that did not receive sufficient attention, or any attention at all. This text is my attempt to provide a more comprehensive view of the subject. Second, I found that the explanations of certain concepts were not quite accurate or correct; this text is my effort to say things in a way that makes the most sense—at least, to me! Finally, I think that many argumentation texts tend to be on the "dry and stuffy" side—not "user-friendly" for undergraduate students. *Argumentation: Critical Thinking in Action* represents my attempt to speak to a student audience in a more informal and down-to-earth manner. You will find that the language is generally quite "oral" in tone, even a little "chatty." That colloquial style is intentional, and I hope that it makes the material more approachable.

FEATURES NEW TO THIS EDITION

Whenever a textbook comes out in a new edition—in this case, the 2nd edition—one can legitimately ask if there is any justification for it. Although the "basics" from the 1st edition of this book remain, in nearly the same form, I have tried to expand and enhance the study of argument in several ways.

All 12 chapters now include a list of "specialized terms to know"—that is, academic terms that are not "common knowledge" and have a specialized technical meaning. Chapter 1 now includes an explanation and discussion of Bloom's Taxonomy, perhaps the best-known framework related to critical thinking. Chapter 1 also includes a deeper discussion of the ethical issues connected to argument. Chapter 6 now features a "fallacy quiz" to test your knowledge of the various fallacies. Chapter 8 features a more detailed discussion of dramatism—especially the section dealing with symbolic convergence theory, as well as Burke's pentad. And chapter 10 now includes five common judging paradigms that are employed when people evaluate debates. Also, in many places, I have provided additional examples, striving for more clarity and depth, including more recent news items that are relevant to the ideas in this text.

ACKNOWLEDGMENTS

I owe a great debt to many people who are responsible for whatever merits this work may have. At the most general level, I am indebted to my father and mother, Victor and Tobey Lapakko, who raised me in an environment where information and ideas were ever-present; their commitment to my education was immense and will never be forgotten.

As a student and debater at Macalester, I learned many critically important things from W. Scott Nobles, for many years the Director of Forensics, and a mentor to me and countless others. His wisdom about many topics is reflected throughout this book. And as a graduate student at the University of Minnesota, I am grateful to have had Robert L. Scott as both a teacher and a dissertation advisor; he was and is a role model for anyone with scholarly interests. Additionally, as noted in chapter 8 of this text, I feel fortunate to know J. Vernon Jensen, himself a successful argumentation textbook author whose ideas are present here.

While writing working drafts of this text, my colleagues at Augsburg College also deserve to be recognized. Deborah Redmond has an eagle eye and was amazingly quick at catching typos and unclear passages. Kristen Chamberlain was kind enough to provide helpful feedback to an outline of the book. And Robert Groven provided specific suggestions for that part of chapter 11 dealing with the legal sphere of argument. Finally, my good friend and disciplinary colleague from Hamline University, George Gaetano, provided some helpful feedback on the section of chapter 8 dealing with symbolic convergence theory. Finally, I want to thank my many argumentation students over the years, who have helped me understand what is easy and what is difficult for them to grasp; their questions and comments have helped me better determine how to explain many ideas in this book.

Chapter 1

ORIENTATION TO ARGUMENTATION

After reading this chapter, you should understand:

- The benefits of studying argument
- How argumentation differs from "arguing," "logic," "debate," and "persuasion"
- How argumentation has been defined
- How argumentation has been criticized as having a cultural or gender bias
- How a field-invariant approach to argument differs from a field-variant approach
- The three elements that are always present in argumentation
- Bloom's Taxonomy as a framework for critical thinking
- What critical thinking involves, and what traits it promotes
- Some basic ethical issues connected to argumentation

Specialized terms to know:

- descriptive approach
- prescriptive approach
- ethos
- pathos
- logos
- left-brain analytical thinking
- dualistic thinking
- field invariant
- field variant
- factual claims
- value claims
- policy claims

WHY STUDY ARGUMENT?

Here's a troubling way to start: I am not sure of your mindset as you are reading this sentence. You might have opened this book "kicking and screaming"—maybe it's required for a course in argu-

1

mentation or critical thinking, and you are reading it only because it's assigned. Or, maybe you have a genuine interest in the subject and would devour these pages even if you didn't have to. Whatever the case, an initial question obviously becomes, why in the world should you study argument? What possible value could it have? Both the apathetic reader and the enthusiastic reader deserve an answer.

Perhaps I'm biased ("perhaps" may be a slight understatement!), but the study and practice of argument can be immensely valuable. I learned about argument by "doing," mainly through contest debate in high school and college. I spent the better part of four school years going to debate tournaments on weekends; in many ways, I couldn't get enough of the activity—it was a challenge, but an enjoyable and stimulating one. I am certainly not alone in that regard. In the preface to his text on critical thinking and argument, Jay Verlinden (2005, xv) writes,

> I believe that I was very fortunate to have grown up in a school system that introduced me to interscholastic debate and to have attended a college that allowed me to participate in intercollegiate debate. I believe that my experience as a debater did more than anything else in my educational experience to teach me how to analyze ideas, think critically, find published information, evaluate evidence, consider alternative explanations, organize and present ideas clearly, and construct sound arguments. And it was fun!

I suspect that Verlinden's experience was similar to my own. In some ways, we both learned argumentation "backwards"—first we were involved in "doing" it, and then, much later, we actually studied it and wrote about it in a more formal way. But whether you go from "theory" to "practice" or the reverse, being involved in the world of argumentation offers several benefits.

First, by studying argument, you get to learn about a variety of important issues. People have to argue about *something*. It may be gun control, it may be mass transit, it may be stem cell research, it may be U.S. policy in the Middle East, it may be what kind of car to buy, it may be whether UFOs are "for real," but whatever it is, it occurs in a context—it involves "subject matter." Therefore, you have the opportunity to learn what people have said about these and other issues, and how you personally may feel about them.

Equally important, you will learn that almost all issues have two or more "sides" to them—that issues are more complex than you might have realized. Learning about the world and its various controversies is a critical part of being well-educated, and a study of argument promotes such awareness.

Second, a course in argument can make you a more effective advocate. During your life, you will find yourself in a variety of situations where you will have to convince somebody of something. That "something" may be an essay for school, it may be an analysis of a business plan, it may be a letter to the editor of your local newspaper, or it may be an attempt to convince your best friend to purchase the "right" computer. How do you suppose you need to proceed in such situations? In this text, you will discover ways to enhance your ability to communicate an idea. Some of those ways involve the hard content of your message, and others involve the "soft" elements that relate to style, form, and establishing credibility.

Third—and to me, most important—learning about argumentation can help make you a better thinker. I can think of nothing more valuable than that. Studying argument means "cutting through the crap"—understanding the nature of claims, the evidence that supports them, and the assumptions behind each point. It means being able to carefully analyze a message, understand how it is constructed, judge its strengths and weaknesses, and respond coherently to it. That clarity of thought, if you can achieve it here, has value beyond the price of this book, or the price of the course in which it may be required reading. You don't want to spend the rest of your life as an "airhead," and the formal study of argument and critical thinking will help you avoid that nasty affliction.

MATTERS OF DEFINITION

Another obvious question to start would be, "How do you define argumentation?" As you might imagine, there are lots of definitions out there—check any texts of this sort and you'll readily find them. Before providing a more formal definition, I'd like to begin by defining the term through what is usually called defining by negation—that is, what argumentation is *not*.

- **Argumentation is not the same as "arguing."**

I wish I had a nickel for every student I've had who, in the first few days of the term, tells me, "My mother/father/sister/spouse/roommate/best friend (choose the most relevant relationship) wonders whether I should even be in this class to begin with—we argue like crazy, and I usually get my way!" What these people seem to think is that argumentation is an emotional, hostile activity, something like the arguments they have with their friends around the refrigerator/water cooler/dining room table (again, choose your venue). Although people who study and make arguments are not robots, argumentation, by its nature, is tied more to good *reasons* than strong *emotions*. It is not really a study of human relationships, but a study of ideas and how they are developed. So, when we discuss "arguing a point" in this book, it's not an exhibition of personal animosity.

Argumentation scholar Daniel O'Keefe (1977) made a similar distinction when he wrote about the difference between **making** an argument (the focus of this textbook) and **having** an argument (that is, "fighting" with someone else). When we **make** arguments, we are concerned with supporting ideas with strong evidence and sound reasoning; when we **have** arguments, we are usually a little "hot under the collar" and are engaged in a type of interpersonal warfare. Clearly, these two senses of argument can overlap, but our main concern here is to examine how a good argument is constructed.

- **Argumentation is not the same as "logic."**

If you ever take a course in logic, you will find yourself in an interesting—if confusing—little world. Logic textbooks in many ways resemble math textbooks, complete with answers at the end of the book for the even-numbered problems in each chapter. Logicians are quite comfortable with statements such as "All As are B, all Cs are A; therefore, all Cs are B." (As you will learn later in more detail in chapter 5, what you are looking at here are the major premise, minor premise, and conclusion for a categorical syllogism.) Because logic operates at a very abstract level, often putting symbols in place of words or ideas, it is in some ways devoid of content—in the example above, it doesn't really matter what "A," "B," and "C" are, as long as the information is plugged into the proper place. In argumentation, however, the content of what's being advanced is of critical importance, and if the content is weak, then the argument will be weak. So, argumentation pays more attention to content than does the study of logic.

Second, as implied above, in logic courses, there is usually one "correct" answer—it can be found in the back of the book. However, if you look in the back of *this* book, you will only find a glossary of key terms. In the world of logic, there are definite answers. For example:

Major premise: Citrus fruits have vitamin C.
Minor premise: Oranges are a citrus fruit.
Conclusion: Therefore, oranges have vitamin C.

In this example, if indeed the major premise and the minor premise are "true," then the conclusion HAS to be true—it's a rule of logic. Now, it's not as though many of the principles of logic have no relevance to argument, but if you are making a case that we should reform U.S. immigration policy, I think you can see how this would be difficult to reduce to a simple syllogism. "Real world" arguments don't always fit into the tidy world of logic, and "real world" arguments do not have a universally-accepted "right" answer. **Indeed, I am going to try to discourage you from using three words: TRUTH, FACT, and PROVE.** Now of course, it's not that you can never speak these words—there's a place for everything. But these three words suggest something that is not normally possible, at least in any absolute sense. What is the truth? What is a fact? What can you prove? In each case, the burden is very great. Even things that we take for granted as "the truth" or "facts" can be and are challenged. The planet Earth is a sphere, right? Well, yes and no—it's generally spherical in shape, but current science would say that it's not a perfect sphere. The speed of light is one constant in the universe, right? Well, physicists have been able to manipulate the speed of light by sending it through various substances. In short, just about anything can be challenged.

- **Argumentation is not the same as "debate."**

As I mentioned at the start of this chapter, some people have had extensive experience in contest debate. Among our teachers, attorneys, TV reporters, and public officials there are more "former debaters" than you might realize! Of course, debate is a form of argumentation, but it is just one particular form; "argumentation" is a much broader term. "Debate" is a more narrow label because:
  - most debates are "formal" events (not "water cooler discussions");

- most debates have a definite format and definite rules—for example, "constructive" speeches of x-number of minutes, "rebuttal" speeches of x-number of minutes;
- most debates are judged by one individual (a judge) or a small panel of individuals who render a formal decision and are supposed to have particular qualifications to make such a decision;
- debates are explicitly competitive, because one team "wins" and the other "loses"; and
- in contest debate, there are a variety of "unwritten rules" about appearance, demeanor, and the specific duties of each speaker that make debate a "specialized" form of argument. Indeed, if you have never witnessed a traditional academic debate, you might find it to be horribly confusing, as people tend to talk very fast, read a lot of evidence cards, and use "debate jargon" (such as, "In 2NC we showed that both PMAs still apply and the affirmative plan spikes will not solve for them"). (Say what?)

Overall, like any rhetorical situation, contest debate is a rhetorical situation with rather specific rules and expectations. Although it is an interesting little world, it reflects only one relatively narrow form of argument.

Also, just so you know, we often deal these days with "Presidential debates." These "debates" are substantially different than academic debate. Although Presidential debates always have some sort of format—for example, a panel of reporters might ask each candidate certain questions, alternating between the various candidates—many of us who are schooled in academic debate find these events to be a form of "debate lite," or not even a "debate" in "the true sense of the word." What I mean is that unlike academic debate, the candidates don't examine each other's cases in intricate detail. In academic debate, "direct clash" is expected; each team has to examine the other team's case point-by-point, and in many academic debate formats, the members of each team formally cross-examine their "opponents" and force them to defend the specifics of their case. Unlike academic debate, the candidates can often avoid the reporters' questions, or at least steer them in a different direction without an opponent "calling them" on it. And unlike academic debate, there are no rigorous standards for evaluating arguments. Rather, the issues tend to become: Who looked better? Who didn't put their foot in their mouth? And who did opinion polls say did the better job? So, Presidential "debates" can be a useful forum for voters to get a sense about those who aspire to high office, but they lack the depth of analysis that characterizes academic debate. And, for better or for worse, they look and sound *way* different from the more specialized world of contest speaking in our high schools and colleges.

- **Argumentation is not the same as "persuasion."**

The distinction between argumentation and persuasion is a difficult one. Part of the reason is that the two clearly do overlap: a good persuader should also strive to seem logical, but by the same token, a good arguer should realize that argument is not and cannot be a totally rational activity. So when we do differentiate between argumentation and persuasion, the distinction is to some extent arbitrary. And to some extent, the distinction is an "academic" one—most departments of communication studies offer both a course in persuasion and one in argumentation, so there has to be a way to differentiate them. Here are at least a few ways in which we might make such a distinction, even if some of those distinctions are a bit simplistic:

Persuasion is descriptive; argumentation is prescriptive

Persuasion often concerns itself with the world as it is—it merely **describes** the way that influence occurs, good, bad, or otherwise. If, for example, an advertiser knows that its sales will increase by putting an attractive model next to the product, then they will likely do so. It doesn't matter that this is a "bad" or illogical reason to buy the product; all that matters is that it *works*. In this sense, the study of persuasion can be a little amoral—not that ethical issues are irrelevant, but the initial focus is on what will elicit a change. On the other hand, argumentation pays more attention to what should be—it **prescribes** that a "good" argument needs to have certain characteristics. Even if the attractive model "works" for many people, from an argumentation standpoint, it's a silly reason to buy anything. (Isn't it?) Argumentation focuses more on what *should* be a sound reason to do or believe something. In that sense, argumentation does promote what you might call a "higher standard" for good reasons. Therefore, by reading this text, I would hope that you'd become a connoisseur of "good" arguments, just as a good restaurant reviewer will not accept a dish simply because it looks good or feels filling. In short, in argumentation, we are not merely concerned with what **can** work; we prefer to deal in what **should** work, given an intelligent, reflective audience.

Persuasion is one-way; argumentation is more interactive

Persuasion is often a "stimulus-response" type of activity. In persuasion, we send out a message (for example, an ad campaign or a political spot) and see how people respond. Often, the receivers don't have the opportunity to question or critique the message; they simply "consume" the messages. Much of the study of persuasion is built around one-way messages, with an active sender and a passive receiver. On the other hand, an important premise of argumentation is that people should be able to *defend* their point of view in light of opposing refutation. In fact, in an ideal world, arguers should *welcome* such scrutiny. So, argumentation stresses the need to examine each other's claims, with the unstated premise that such examination will lead us to the "right" or "best" answer.

Persuasion deals more with ethos and pathos; argumentation deals more with logos

Our old friend Aristotle, often considered a founding figure in communication studies, believed that there were three sources of influence. One, **ethos**, is built around the person presenting the message. Do we believe this person because of who they are or how they come across? That's ethos in action. And as countless studies have shown, the exact same message presented by supposedly "different" people will lead receivers to evaluate the message differently. For example, in a classic study by Franklyn Haiman (1949), three randomly-selected groups each heard an identical tape-recorded speech on national health insurance. One group was told that the speech was given by the Surgeon General of the United States. The second group was told that it was a speech by the Secretary-General of the Communist Party of America. And the third group was told that the speech was given by a university sophomore. Not surprisingly, those who *thought* they were listening to the Surgeon General were influenced most significantly, even though the speeches themselves were identical. Many other studies have arrived at the same conclusion.

Second, **pathos** involves those parts of the message that tap into our needs, drives, and emotions. For example, if you decide to attend State U because most of your friends are going there and want you to go also, then you may decide to go because their appeal is connected to your need to conform. Or maybe you decide to go to State U because it will enable you to maximize your potential—then you are going to address your need for achievement or mastery. Finally, **logos**—those parts of the message that appeal to our intellect—is the third source of belief, according to Aristotle.

Because persuasion deals with the psychology of influence in ways that argumentation does not, it should not surprise you, therefore, that persuasion puts more emphasis on ethos and pathos. And viewed in what could be considered its least flattering light, a lot of modern persuasion boils down to having a credible or likeable spokesperson (say, Tiger Woods) leaving us with a good feeling about a product (in this case, a Buick, or Nike, or American Express). Students of argument, however, would not want to be overly impressed by Tiger Woods, or for that matter, Paris Hilton or Queen Latifah. That's because we have no substantive reason to buy the product; we would want to know about its features, not merely what famous person or what "pretty face" endorsed it.

Persuasion deals with the verbal and the nonverbal messages; argumentation tends to focus only on the verbal.

It is common for a persuasion textbook to address language as a means of persuasion, but persuasion texts also examine the nonverbal dimensions of influence. For example, there is some interesting research on touch—it turns out that merely touching another person on the shoulder can have an impact on how much they are willing to do for you. Similarly, persuasion texts will consider gestures, physical appearance, and visual images as a source of influence. In other words, they consider all forms of messages, whether they be in words or not. On the other hand, the study of argument tends to confine itself to language—the verbal message. It's not that visual/nonverbal messages cannot have an impact—surely they can—but in some ways, the nonverbal aspects of communication are a sort of "window dressing." From an argumentation standpoint, it should not matter whether an advocate is a "mesomorph" (athletic and muscular in build), an "ectomorph" (someone who is more thin and frail), or an "endomorph" (someone who is fat and round)—what should matter is the quality of their ideas and how they express them with words. Nonetheless, academic research indicates, for example, that endomorphs are "less likely to get jobs, less likely to earn high salaries, and less likely to be accepted into colleges than thinner people with the same IQ" (Gass and Seiter, 2007, 181). I hope we can agree that even if "fat and round" people can be at a competitive disadvantage in some persuasive situations, that a "higher standard" of evaluation would involve their actual communication—their language and their ideas—which is the more exclusive domain of argumentation.

Argumentation defined

Well, we've looked at what argumentation is not, and how it differs from other topics and other intellectual pursuits, but the question remains, what is it? I would be the first to tell you that I am not a big fan of formal definitions. Why? Because a definition can never fully capture an idea. I still remember my 10th grade vocabulary lessons. We had to memorize the definition of ten words each week. One week our teacher, David Coleman, included a word he said we'd never forget. Along with all the other "fancy" terms on the list was the word "kiss," and the definition provided was: "an anatomical juxtaposition of the obicularis oris muscles in a state of contraction." Is that what a kiss means to you? With this example, we see that definitions include some things and exclude others, and sometimes neither is a good idea. For instance, the definition of "kiss" that I have provided is very good at describing the physical aspects of a kiss, but it kind of misses the emotional or romantic dimensions. Similarly, a "romantic" definition would be accurate in one sense but limited in other senses. In the same way, any definition of "argumentation" is going to include some aspects of the concept yet slight others. Nonetheless, people like the security of definitions, and so I shall offer the following:

Argumentation is the process of advancing, examining, and responding to claims, primarily through the use of reasoned discourse.

Notice that this definition regards argumentation as a *process*—it is ongoing and interactive. Notice that we are dealing with *claims*—not "proven facts." Notice that we advance claims, we examine and analyze claims, and we respond to other people's claims, all mainly through the use of reasoned messages.

In **Table 1.1**, you will find some other definitions of "argumentation" from various books in the field. If you are interested in even more ways to define argumentation, I encourage you to check other sources, many of which are cited throughout this book.

Argumentation as a "white male, Western" mode of thinking

It's worth a paragraph or two of your time to consider that some people regard traditional argumentation courses as reflecting a "white male, Western" mode of thinking. If by this label they mean that argumentation stresses left-brain, analytical thinking, they are probably right. That is, courses in argument try to "break down" an argument into its various parts—e.g., the claim, the data, the reasoning. Just as chemical analysis involves breaking down a chemical compound into its various parts (e.g., water is two parts hydrogen, one part oxygen) so too do students of argument with the claims they encounter. From a traditional standpoint, one should be able to break things down in this way—it's not enough to say, "That's a great argument because I feel it in my gut," or "That's a weak argument, but I can't explain why." Providing the reasons either way is definitely a "left-brain" activity.

Now, does that mean that argumentation courses are "sexist" or "racist" or "ethnocentric" in some way? I guess I would say that regardless of one's cultural background, there is potential value in left-brain analytical thinking. And as far as that goes, I think everyone can benefit from an analytical study of argument, regardless of race or gender—analysis is simply a skill that everyone ought to learn. Having said that does not mean that there isn't a place for "holistic" or "intuitive" thinking in human inquiry—not at all. It just means that we haven't figured out where those other ways of thinking fit into the study of argument—but I hope someone will help with that! Finally, some object to argumentation because they believe it is by nature "competitive" and should promote cooperative dialogue, not domination of one person or group over another. As I shall contend in many places, a "good" argument need not and probably should not be nasty and competitive—the best arguments are presented in a way that makes the arguer likeable and trustworthy, not overbearing, and show respect for their opponent(s) and their audience.

TABLE 1.1:
SOME COMMON DEFINITIONS OF "ARGUMENTATION"

"Argumentation is a form of instrumental communication relying on reasoning and proof to influence a belief or behavior through the use of spoken or written messages."

- Karyn Charles Rybacki and Donald J. Rybacki, Advocacy and Opposition: An Introduction to Argumentation, 5th ed. (Boston: Pearson, 2004)

"Argumentation is the communicative process of advancing, supporting, criticizing, and modifying claims so that appropriate decision makers, defined by relevant spheres, may grant or deny adherence."

- Richard D. Rieke, Malcolm O. Sillars, and Tarla Rai Peterson, Argumentation and Critical Decision Making, 6th ed. (Boston: Pearson, 2005)

"In this text, argumentation usually refers to a form of communication in which at least one person explicitly or implicitly puts forth a claim and provides support for that claim with evidence and reasoning."

- Jay Verlinden, Critical Thinking and Everyday Argument (Thomson Wadsworth, 2005)

"Reason giving in communicative situations by people whose purpose is the justification of acts, beliefs, attitudes, and values."

- Austin J. Freely and David L. Steinberg, Argumentation and Debate: Critical Thinking for Reasoned Decision Making, 11th ed. (Belmont, CA: Wadsworth, 2005)

"Argumentation is the process of making arguments intended to justify beliefs, attitudes, and values so as to influence others."

- Edward S. Inch, Barbara Warnick, and Danielle Endres, Critical Thinking and Communication: The Use of Reason in Argument, 5th ed. (Boston: Pearson, 2006)

"Argumentation is a language-based social phenomenon that enables us to discover what beliefs and actions are reasonable in any social context and that is concerned with the selection and organization of ideas to justify particular positions."

- George W. Ziegelmueller, Jack Kay, and Charles A. Dause, Argumentation: Inquiry and Advocacy, 2nd ed. (Englewood Cliffs, NJ: Prentice-Hall, 1990)

Argumentation as field-invariant or field-variant

You should appreciate that there are two basic ways to study argument. One, the field-invariant approach, is more "generic" in nature. This approach pays no real attention to the context of the argument. Most of this book is field-invariant in nature—that is, it examines the various types of claims, the various types of evidence, and the various types of reasoning, but only in a general sense, without paying much attention to where the argument appears. On the other hand, a field-variant approach says that one must consider where the argument is being made. Is this argument being presented at an academic conference? In a church? At a legislative hearing? In a court of law? As you might imagine, what constitutes a "good" argument will change, depending on what "sphere" of argument you are in. A field-variant approach tries to identify what makes arguments "different" in different spheres. For example, in a court of law, the rules of evidence tend to be very strict. Therefore, "hearsay" evidence (reporting what someone told you happened, even though you didn't actually see it), is inadmissible in court; so too is evidence which is obtained illegally. In a religious context, it might be appropriate to cite a story or parable to make your point—but in a business context, the same story might be regarded as rather odd! In politics, it might be helpful to cite that the majority of Americans favor your proposal, but in an academic argument, public opinion is not nearly as important or influential. If you think about it, a field-variant approach is a little closer to "persuasion" than a field-invariant approach in the sense that it asks us to consider the audience and the occasion. Fortunately, there is no need to choose between these two approaches. Although much of this text is field-invariant, we will spend some time (in chapter 11 specifically) on the need to consider arguments in various spheres.

THREE ELEMENTS ALWAYS PRESENT IN ARGUMENT

Whenever and wherever we encounter arguments, we can always depend on three things. These three elements, if they aren't immediately present, will *be* present as an argument is examined in more depth. They are (1) **claims**, (2) **data**, and (3) **assumptions**, or a reasoning process.

Claims: Factual, value, and policy

FACTUAL CLAIMS involve the question, "Is it true or false?" One thing which distinguishes factual claims is that they can be *verified* in some way. For example, if I claim that the high temperature yesterday in Tucson, Arizona was 94 degrees, I can call the National Weather Service and verify the claim. (Or, if I live in Tucson, I can have a thermometer in my back yard and take the temperature measurements myself.) Statements such as these are factual in nature:

- Jefferson City is the capital of Missouri.
- The unit of currency in Malaysia is the ringgit.
- The Chicago Bulls won the 1996 NBA title.

Please remember that a factual claim may or may not be "true." Each of these claims is factual *in nature*:

- The moon is made of moldy provolone cheese.
- President Gerald R. Ford was 3 feet, 10 inches tall.
- The main ingredient in pizza is pitted prunes.

Also remember that some factual claims are "predictive" in nature, and although they can't be verified right now, they can be verified at some point in the future. For example:

- The Philadelphia Eagles will win next year's Super Bowl.
- It's going to rain tomorrow.
- Global warming will continue through the year 2050.

VALUE CLAIMS deal with the issue, "Is it good or bad, right or wrong?" By nature, value claims, unlike factual claims, cannot be objectively verified. Why? Because value claims are based on matters of taste and judgment, and, needless to say, values. These are examples of value claims:

- Dustin Hoffman is a better actor than Robert DeNiro.
- Of all the nuts, cashews are the tastiest.
- It is better to be rich than to be intelligent.

Claims connected to "ethics" or "morals" are also value claims, which may be one reason why we continue to debate the morality of many different practices—these are value issues and ultimately not capable of being resolved or verified. Does that mean that any one value claim is as "good" as any other value claim? Of course not. When making a value claim, one still has the burden to make a convincing argument. I can't say that "opera sucks" or "welfare is a lousy way to spend public money" and then just sit down; I would need to provide convincing reasons for such evaluations.

One point of agreement among most theorists when it comes to discussing value issues is that it helps to develop *criteria* or *standards* by which to evaluate them. For instance, if I'm going to contend that one restaurant is "better" than another, I would need to develop criteria to enable me to perform such an analysis. I might consider quality of the food, service, value, originality of the menu, or the ambiance or feel of the place—but in any event, there would be criteria that would guide my thinking. I would use these criteria to compare the various options. Or, if I were claiming that one state's prison system is better than another's, again I would need criteria—such as, which system better trains its inmates for new careers, which system has fewer problems with violence, which system is more cost-effective, and so on.

Needless to say, different people might have different criteria, or rank the same criteria in a different order—like any other matter, this process may lead to its own little "debates." Still, this seems like a reasonable way to proceed on value issues--but of course, there is no law that compels you to approach value questions in this manner.

POLICY CLAIMS deal with the question of "what should we do?" If the claim has the word "should" in it, chances are high that it's a policy claim. Policy claims would include the following:

- The U.S. should increase its financial support for the United Nations.
- The drinking age in all states should be lowered to 19.
- I should lose 15 pounds by Christmas.

(But of course, the word "should" doesn't *have* to be there—if I say, "We need more tax incentives to promote saving," that's policy, too. The issue always is, what is the purpose or function of the claim?)

Notice that a "policy" need not be a governmental action—"I should lose 15 pounds" is such an example. Even to say that one Hollywood star should marry another is a policy claim. (Since things in Hollywood can change so quickly, you'll note that I won't even *try* for an example here!)

One important aspect of policy claims is that they are, by nature, "broader" than factual and value claims. Policy issues are actually made up of a variety of "sub-issues" that relate to facts and values. For instance, take the issue which comes up in many larger communities: should we build a new baseball/football stadium in our town to keep the local teams happy? Within that policy issue are a variety of *factual* issues, including:

- How much would it cost to build a new stadium?
- What would be the net economic impact of a new stadium?
- How likely is it that the home team would move if we don't build a new stadium?

In addition, there would be a variety of value issues, such as:

- Do pro sports franchises deserve any sort of public money?
- How important is this pro team to our community?
- What is the best way to spend public tax dollars?

So, policy claims can be analyzed by trying to determine what factual and value questions are embedded within them.

A final note: some textbooks also include the notion of a *definitional* claim, as a separate type of claim. For example, "obesity will be defined as anyone having a BMI (body mass index) of greater than 30." However, I see no need for this separate category—it seems to me that most or all definitions are essentially "factual" claims, and will be considered as such here.

Caution: grey area alert

With respect to the various types of claims, it is worth stressing that sometimes, a claim will fall in that murky "grey area"—that is, different people might categorize a particular claim differently, and for good reason. (This idea—that in argumentation, "black" and "white" are hard to come by—is a recurring theme in this book!) For example, if the Pittsburgh Pirates finished their season with a record of 90 wins and 72 losses, qualified for the playoffs, and then got on a hot streak and won the World Series, we might be tempted to say that they are "the best team in baseball." Well, are they? They won in the playoffs, but in the regular season, other teams probably had more than 90 victories. So is this a value claim or a factual claim? I suppose if you pushed me on this, I'm inclined to call it a value claim, because it is a judgment about the quality of the team. However, just for the sake of argument, as they say, let's pretend that this Pittsburgh team went 162-0 in the regular season, and then won every game in the playoffs to finish with a (highly unlikely!) perfect record. In this situation, could a claim that they are the "best team" almost be considered "factual"? Maybe so. Or, if I say that "the current welfare system is an absolute failure," within such an ambiguous statement are all three types of claims—especially value (welfare is "bad") and policy (one must conclude that a change of some sort needs to be made). So again, "real life" may not line up with these categories in a nice, neat fashion—although usually, they should work for you.

Data: The evidence supporting the claim

Besides the claim itself, there will always be data or evidence to support the claim—if not initially, potentially. I say that if you're middle-aged and have a family history of heart disease, you should take a "baby aspirin" every day. So far, that's just a claim—you'd be well within your rights to say, "What evidence do you have to support that claim?" If I didn't have any, then my claim would be in trouble. But if I could summon up the research evidence that seems to demonstrate the effectiveness of those little 81 milligram aspirins, then my claim becomes stronger. As we will see later, in the chapter on evidence (chapter 3), there are basically four types of evidence that an arguer may use: examples, statistics, testimony, and objects.

Assumptions, or a reasoning process

Finally, the third component of *any* argument involves reasoning. Whenever someone makes a claim, they make it based on some sort of evidence and some type of thought process. Even if I say "the sun is shining today," I make certain assumptions—about the principles of astronomy, about our solar system, and about my own sense organs. In this case, these assumptions are fairly "innocent" and uncontroversial. But, of course, in many other situations the assumptions involved are more problematic. If, for instance, I say that we need capital punishment in order to deter crime, I am making certain assumptions about the nature of homicides, and the people who commit them. On the matter of deterrence, I would have to be assuming that people plan and calculate their homicides, and thus, if they know they will likely die if they murder someone, they will refrain from doing so. If this assumption has merit, then an argument for the deterrent effect of capital punishment can be made. On the other hand, if murder is a more "impulsive and irrational" act, then the deterrent effect of capital punishment may be limited because murderers are not thinking rationally about consequences. Obviously I am not here to get in the middle of this dispute—I only mean to say that embedded within all arguments are certain assumptions, and we would be wise to figure out what they are. Especially because, as we shall see later, people are often not even aware of what assumptions they are making in the first place—we as the critical receivers often need to determine what they are.

I have used the term "assumptions" here so far, but really, what people assume also reveals how they *reason*—that is, how they "go from point A to point B" in their minds and draw conclusions. When it comes to reasoning, we will discover in chapter 5 that there are five basic ways that people reason: inductively, deductively, by analogy, by sign reasoning, and by causal reasoning.

CRITICAL THINKING AND ARGUMENT

As you should have noticed by now, the subtitle of this book refers to argumentation as "critical thinking in action." And indeed, argumentation is a form of critical thinking—it is very much related to critical thinking. In some ways, the only real difference between "argumentation" and "critical thinking" is that argumentation tends to put more stress on the public *advocacy* of ideas—their presentation—along with the *response* to others' ideas, which involves refutation and rebuttal. In the field of Communication Studies, that means having students make argumentative cases, orally and in writing, on controversial public issues. Of course, in order to make such cases, students of argument need to be good critical thinkers as well. Many definitions of critical thinking are available; for our purposes, we could in general consider critical thinking as "a set of conceptual tools with associated intellectual skills and strategies useful for making reasonable decisions about what to do or believe" (Rudinow and Barry, 2008, 11). Or, we could define it as "the careful, deliberate determination of whether we should accept, reject, or suspend judgment about the truth of a claim or a recommendation to act in a certain way" (Reichenbach, 2001, 19).

BLOOM'S TAXONOMY

Easily the best-known framework for considering the skills involved in critical thinking is Bloom's Taxonomy, developed by Benjamin Bloom et al. (1956). Bloom believed that critical thinking can be divided into six different types of skills: knowledge, comprehension, application, analysis, synthesis, and evaluation.

1. knowledge
In Bloom's framework, knowledge involves the relatively simple ability to know facts, definitions, and other types of basic information. It could be something as simple as "St. Paul is the capital of Minnesota." Or, one might be able to recite a definition of "repression" as a psychoanalytic idea: repression is "a process by which unacceptable desires or impulses are excluded from consciousness and left to operate in the unconscious." Or, in the context of this book, I can say that argumentation can be studied from a "field variant" or a "field invariant" perspective, even I don't know exactly what those words mean. In general, the knowledge level involves what we might call "regurgitation"; it is a rather superficial level of mastery. For example, having taken chemistry many, many years ago, I can tell you what Avogadro's number is—6.02 x 10 to the 23rd power—but please don't ask me to say any more than that, because then I'm in big trouble! That's about as far as I can go; at best, I am at the "knowledge" level in Bloom's framework.

2. comprehension
On the other hand, comprehension involves actually *understanding* things—to be able to *explain* them, perhaps in your own words, and to show a grasp of what they *mean*. In the case of "repres-

sion," one would need to be able to explain that repression is a psychological way to mentally "bury" an unpleasant experience from the past because it is too painful to think about—childhood sexual abuse might be an example. Or if you know that St. Paul is the capital of Minnesota, comprehension involves whether you really understand what it means to *be* a capital city. (Believe it or not, there are those who don't! Some might mistakenly think that the capital city is the largest or most populous city in a state, which of course is not necessarily the case.) As it relates to chapter 1 of this book, I can demonstrate comprehension of the term "factual claim" by saying that it involves statements which are of a "true or false" nature and have the potential to be verified—for example, that water boils at 100 degrees centigrade. And I might also explain that in an uncertain world, even "factual" claims should not necessarily be regarded as "absolute truth."

3. application

The critical thinking skill of application involves being able to use the information that you understand in some way. It involves the ability to take ideas and "plug them in" to a particular situation. For example, with "repression," I might be able to use that idea to help discuss with a friend who is nervous around dogs whether there was a traumatic event in his childhood that explains the anxiety. If I was interested in living in a city where politics is important, I might use my knowledge of what a "capital" is to help determine where I might live. In short, I am able to take an idea and use it in another context. And as application relates to argument, I know and understand the principles of organization discussed in chapter 9 of this text, and I am able to actually use them to structure an argument that I am making. (Note to students: this skill is frequently a key concern for your instructors: can you take an idea and show how to use it?)

4. analysis

Analysis involves being able to break down a complex problem into its component parts. In analyzing a movie, for example, I could examine the various aspects of cinema—for example, acting, directing, editing, photography, special effects, and so on. With respect to "repression," analysis involves determining what parts of one's personality are reflected by things that are repressed, and what things are a part of one's conscious thoughts;

a Freudian analyst might even analyze a person's psyche in terms of the "ego," "id," and "super-ego." In the context of argument, one could analyze a speech in terms of the relative importance of ethos, pathos, and logos. As with application, analysis is a valued skill in the classroom—can you break an issue down into its various "pieces"?

5. synthesis

If analysis involves breaking something down to its parts, synthesis involves how you put things together to make a new whole, or to develop new insights. With the example of "repression" in mind, you are able to see connections between Freud's theory of repression and, say, Jung's theory of the "collective unconscious"—you may even develop a "new" theory that incorporates them both. With respect to state capitals, perhaps you can integrate ideas about making laws with ideas about scientific research, and how the two help us understand how humans make all sorts of decisions. Or, in the context of this textbook, you are able to "connect the dots" between arguments based on "reason" and arguments based on "emotion" and develop a "new" theory about how people are influenced. Or, one would hope, you could take a variety of ideas and information connected to a particular topic—say, for example, computer literacy —and develop your own original argument about how computer literacy should be developed in the schools. Synthesis is a creative process that enables a critical thinker to pull various ideas together into a new formulation. And with the classroom in mind, synthesis is one of those rather sophisticated skills that is prized by many in the academic world.

6. evaluation

Finally, evaluation involves some sort of judgment. Given all that I know, what is the best model, the most sensible conclusion? This skill typically involves applying various criteria to the issue in question. With "repression," one would ask, is this a "good" theory of human behavior? With state capitals, one could ask, is it better to live in a capital city than in another city? And with respect to this textbook, one could ask something like, should statistical evidence be considered better than testimonial evidence? Again, if you are a student and are asked to evaluate something—a theory, a political philosophy, a film, or an argument—you are being asked to render a judgment that reflects good awareness of the issues involved.

Those, then, are the six components of Bloom's Taxonomy. **But, now it is time for another "grey area alert."** In many situations, it is probably the case that more than one of these six critical thinking skills is relevant; in fact, I would contend that that's so in most cases. Still, the Bloom taxonomy offers a way to help understand the different components of critical thinking—to use Bloom's own vernacular, it's a nifty "analytical" tool!

Also, Bloom believed that these six skills are "hierarchical" in nature—that is, "knowledge" and "comprehension" are relatively simple skills, whereas "synthesis" and "evaluation" are relatively more sophisticated and complex. Although I would agree that that's often the case, I would encourage you not to think of this list as "neat and tidy" in that regard as well. For example, I would argue that evaluating one particular movie, for instance, is relatively easier than doing a synthesis of a dozen different movies. Similarly, I would contend that being able to apply a certain principle of personal computing may sometimes be easier than to really comprehend or explain it—i.e., I know how to make that particular software application work, but I can't explain why! Simply put, Bloom's taxonomy is not a simple "recipe book" that carves out "laws of the universe" into black and white categories; rather, it's a tool to help understand what types of thinking are involved in critical thinking—no more and no less.

TRAITS ASSOCIATED WITH GOOD CRITICAL THINKING

In my view, what is even more important than how we define the various critical thinking skills are the traits which are promoted within the critical thinking literature. Simply put, a good critical thinker thinks in certain ways, and these ways of thinking are also conducive to making good arguments. Elder and Elder (2007) have summarized some of these desirable critical thinking behaviors; among them they include:

• **Intellectual humility** (vs. intellectual arrogance) – as you've been told many times, the world is a complicated place; "truth" is elusive, and there are limits to what we know. Anyone who thinks they "know it all" is usually delusional. We must draw conclusions, but we must be aware of our limitations. A study of argument should force us to realize that we don't have all the answers, and that differing points of view can have merit, even if we disagree with them in the end. Also, as shall be discussed in sections of chapters 10 and 12, intellectual arrogance is not a desirable trait for arguers for purely "practical" reasons; to be blunt, most audiences don't react well to people who come off as "know-it-alls."

• **Intellectual courage** (vs. intellectual cowardice) – sometimes coming to your own conclusions will invite criticism from others, even ridicule. Critical thinkers have the courage of their convictions, and a reluctance to simply "follow along" because an idea is popular or expressed repeatedly. We live in a world where people like to "fit in," but sometimes we need to "call it as we see it" even if that means leaving us open to disapproval. We live in an age where once people give themselves a label (e.g., "conservative," "Democrat," "Christian") they sometimes feel constrained from having an opinion that is at odds with the groups of people to which they feel affiliated. Good critical thinkers are more "brave" than that. On a related note, as discussed in chapter 6, one fallacy in reasoning, *argumentum ad populum,* is based on the assumption that if most people believe something, then it must necessarily be "right" or "true." Although what the majority believes is worth considering, it should seldom be assumed that such a view is automatically correct.

• **Intellectual perseverance** (vs. intellectual laziness) – good critical thinkers really need to work at what they do. They have to do careful and extensive research. They have to spend time at it. As with physical exercise, good critical thinkers must "feel the burn" a little bit—"no pain, no gain." These days, with the pace of life being what it is, and people being stressed out in many ways, we all are tempted to "take shortcuts." Rather than carefully reading and thinking, we often wind up scanning a few headlines, glancing at a few websites, and consulting with a couple of friends and then regard that as "research."

• **Fairmindedness** (vs. intellectual unfairness) – we must be aware of our biases and be careful not to "prejudge" an issue based on those biases. We must be willing to consider alternative points of view, even if we end up disagreeing with them. And we must acknowledge that we all have a lot of "knee-jerk" reactions to opposing ideas that must be kept in check.

In addition to Elder and Elder's list, I would include the following as *obstacles* to good critical thinking:

• **Confusing labels with reality**. As discussed in chapter 8, words are not things—they merely attempt to represent reality. Just because you have a label for something—"victimless crime," for example—does not mean that you have fully captured its real meaning. We use a variety of labels—for example, "terrorist," "Republican," or "tax-and-spend liberal"—as if they are self-evident explanations of people or ideas. But we can be deceived by labels; the world is usually more complex than these labels would suggest.

• **Giving meaning to unrelated events**. As discussed in chapters 5 and 6, just because your mom sneezed at the moment you opened your textbook, that does not necessarily mean that mom is allergic to books. That's a silly example, but consider this one: just because the economy improved after so-and-so was elected President does not necessarily mean that the President was responsible for the improvement. Just because two things happen together in time, or in space, does not necessarily give them a causal relationship.

• **Wishful thinking**. We all wish that things could be a certain way. Will there be global warming? Will we see World War III? Can I afford that new laptop? In each case, our personal wishes and desires can cloud our judgment—we'd like to think that global warming won't ruin the planet, that World War III is out of the question, and that anything we want to buy will be affordable. But our wishes may conflict with "cold, hard reality." A variation of wishful thinking is called the "confirmation bias" in the field of psychology—that is, people often see what they want to see.

• **Either/or thinking**. Sometimes called "dualistic" thinking, this approach to looking at the world has a "black and white" orientation. Either you are "good" or "bad"; you either want "war" or "peace"; you are either "liberal" or "conservative"; you are either "part of the problem" or "part of the solution." Such simplistic orientations to the world again ignore the many complexities of an issue. And as explained in chapter 6, falsely assuming that something must be either "A" or "B" can lead to the fallacy in reasoning called a "false dilemma."

- **Unconscious assumptions and biases.** Many people are not even aware that they make assumptions, or have biases. We are so much a part of our own world—both personally and culturally—that we often cannot see what is right in front of us. As mentioned above, all arguments include assumptions and are based on certain values; therefore, we need to be aware of what these assumptions and biases are. For example (as discussed in more detail in chapter 11), many people in the U.S. are strongly "individualistic," believe in the value of self-reliance, and think that most anyone can be rich and successful provided that they work hard enough. If that is part of how we view the world, then you can imagine how such a view might influence one's arguments around issues such as poverty, welfare, and homelessness, to name just a few.

Overall, it would be tempting to believe that humans are "rational decision makers" who excel at thinking—after all, it's the ability to think and to symbolize that's supposed to differentiate us from the "animals." However, there is abundant evidence to suggest that we are far from perfect when it comes to reasoned or sensible decision-making. Indeed, if you have never made a "dumb decision" in your life—based on weak evidence, poor reasoning, or limited or careless evaluation of the issues involved—we would all like to meet you!

ETHICAL ISSUES IN ARGUMENTATION

Finally, an introduction to argumentation would not be complete without at least some concern for its ethical dimensions. By its very nature, all communication involves potential ethical issues. Why? Because communication involves *choices*, and if those choices can *affect* others in some way, then there is a potential ethical issue.

Of course, people are somewhat aware of ethics in other spheres of human life, such as the ethics of abortion, or cheating on one's taxes, or robbing a liquor store in order to feed your family. But the ethics of argumentation? What is there to know, and how could it possibly apply to me?

My answer is that ethical issues in communication and argumentation abound—they are issues that you and I face every day,
and they aren't limited to others who we read about in the newspaper. Simply put, ethical issues in communication involve all of
us. Equally important, I would contend that ethical issues in argumentation—indeed, like all ethical issues—are difficult to resolve.
Such issues are more complex than many people make them out
to be, and unfortunately, there are not many "pat answers" when
it comes to ethics. Because ethical issues involve questions of value—not "fact"—they cannot be objectively verified, and for that
reason, they can never be completely "resolved." Still, that hardly
means that we can ignore ethical issues, because they are relevant
whether we want them to be or not.

I would say that in the world of "persuasion," ethical issues may
be somewhat more troubling and ever-present. After all, as noted
earlier in this chapter, persuasion tends to deal more with the psychology of influence, and what "works," almost irrespective of ethics. The worlds of sales, advertising, and even politics can involve
some very sleazy appeals at times! However, argumentation, as
I have suggested, strives to set the bar higher and demand that
"good reasons" should dominate our efforts to influence others.
Still, argumentation will inevitably involve ethical issues. Let me
suggest a few of the most obvious ones:

• **Emotional appeals.** Are emotional appeals ever defensible
in argument? If I try to convince you to give money to a particular
charity because there are "all those suffering kids," is that fair? If
I argue that we need so-and-so to be our next President because
"those terrorists are plotting to get us and she can deal with them,"
is that an appropriate appeal? Although it is often difficult to separate "reason" from "emotion," arguments can play into a variety
of human needs, drives, and emotions—for example, our desires
for physical safety, emotional security, social approval, self-esteem,
and achievement. (Even a supposedly "unemotional" statistic—
say, the number of people who are killed by drunk drivers each
year—can have a dramatic, emotional undercurrent as well.) We
may need to conclude that if my only argument for tighter immigration laws is that "those illegal aliens are plotting to take over
major cities in the U.S," we should be aware that this is a "scare
tactic" that is not based on any recognized evidence; it merely plays
off of people's irrational fears. But again, to stress the complexity

of these issues, if I am concerned about worldwide nuclear proliferation and I present to you, in vivid detail, the gruesome horrors of nuclear war, would that be unethical? If such horrors are possible, couldn't I have an ethical *obligation* to get you a little emotionally invested in the problem?

- **One-sided messages.** Do I have an obligation to present both sides? If I am making a case for why our campus should build a windmill to generate electricity for the college, am I obligated to bring up possible drawbacks to it? If I want to convince my dad to buy me a new laptop, do I have to mention its weak points, and that my current model works just fine? If I am arguing that more nuclear power plants should be built in the United States, do I need to talk about "safety" concerns? In the short run, it might be possible to mislead people by presenting only one side of the issue, which may be what tempts arguers to use a one-sided message in the first place. But if there's any "good news," it is that over time, most people will learn about "opposing arguments" whether you want them to or not; therefore, for purely practical reasons, I would encourage dealing with competing views to yours, because not talking about them won't make them magically go away. Still, one could reasonably ask if there might be specific situations where a one-sided message would be ethically defensible. In cases where you believe that "the ends justify the means," perhaps one-sidedness could be condoned—for example, if you were making the argument that kids should not use "hard drugs," you might legitimately decide to ignore the notion that some famous writers and artists claim to have been inspired by their experiences while in drug-induced states! Chances are you'd want to focus almost exclusively on long-term health issues, even though one could argue (at least theoretically) that drugs could free up creative impulses.

- **Use of ambiguity.** Is intentional ambiguity ever ethically defensible in argument? If I call my new tax on cigarettes a "health fee," is that misleading? If I try to convince an employer to hire me but use a term such as "academic difficulties" as a way of saying I "flunked out," is that too deceptive? As discussed in more detail in chapter 7, arguers will often be intentionally ambiguous for strategic reasons—that is, they know that if they are "too clear," people might find their ideas or their proposal to be a little too controversial. So, they will "candy coat" things a bit in order to make them more palatable—for example, if our bombs kill innocent civilians, that becomes "collateral damage," a term which may be technically correct but is a little more murky.

- **Free speech issues**. Is it ever acceptable to use four-letter words in a speech? Is it ethically OK to argue that, say, African-Americans are genetically inferior to whites? To call for the violent overthrow of the U.S. government? To advocate the legalization of prostitution in all 50 states? Many people will say that they are in favor of "free expression," but that value can be tested in ways that sometimes make them want to re-consider. My own personal stance leads toward favoring the 1st Amendment to our Constitution, which promotes and protects freedom of speech, but I would contend that people are still responsible for the consequences of their words. Others, however, believe that some topics and some forms of expression should be stifled, legally or otherwise, and do not deserve to be heard in the first place.

- **Obligation to be knowledgeable**. If I know very little about the U.S. foreign aid program, but write an angry letter to my local newspaper, complaining about "federal giveaways to other nations," do I have any business trying to influence someone to begin with? Do I have to know something about the issue in order to advance an "ethical" argument? It's absolutely true that the First Amendment to the U.S. Constitution promotes and protects freedom of speech, but that may not mean that it's ethical for any person to try to influence others without some understanding of the issue.

- **Authorship issues**. To what extent can you borrow the words and the ideas of others in the process of constructing an argument? Although there are cultural differences with respect to what constitutes "plagiarism," you should be aware that in U.S. culture, "stealing" words, phrases, or ideas from other sources without proper attribution is a "big no-no" throughout the North American academic world. Using other people's words and ideas as your own is normally considered fraudulent and not within the bounds of acceptable academic conduct; indeed, you can and will be punished for plagiarism in American colleges and universities. And there is a fairly clear case against plagiarism—most notably, that it short-circuits your education. Part of what school is all about is developing the ability to think critically, analyze carefully, synthesize various ideas, and learn to present them with credibility. Plagiarism, by contrast, is simply an exercise in either typing or copying. Even outside of academia, such as the worlds of politics, literature, and journalism, people have paid heavy prices for plagiarism. (For example, in the 2008 Presidential campaign, Democratic Vice Presidential candidate Joe Biden was haunted, rightly or wrongly, by the charge that he had plagiarized part of one of his speeches given back in the late 1980s, some twenty years earlier!) So, even if you could in theory make a case to condone plagiarism, on this issue I must be more "moralistic" and simply say: don't do it. To plagiarize is to invite big problems into your life.

CONCLUSION

The study of argumentation and critical thinking is an important part of one's education. Argumentation has been defined in many ways, but at its core, it involves how we make, examine, and respond to claims, primarily through the use of reasoned discourse. Argumentation can be examined from a field-invariant or a field-variant perspective, and it always includes claims, evidence, and assumptions. The field of critical thinking promotes thinking habits that are essential to good argumentation. And like any other form of communication, argumentation can and does involve ethical issues.

REFERENCES

Bloom, Benjamin S., Max D. Engelhart, Edward J. Furst, Walker H. Hill, and David R. Krathwohl. *Taxonomy of educational objectives: the classification of educational goals.* New York: Longman, Green, and Co., 1956.

Elder, Paul and Linda Elder. *The miniature guide to critical thinking.* Dillon Beach, CA: Foundation for Critical Thinking Press, 2007.

Freeley, Austin J. and David L. Steinberg. *Argumentation and debate: Critical thinking for reasoned decision making,* 11th ed. Belmont, CA: Thomson-Wadsworth, 2005.

Gass, Robert and John Seiter. *Persuasion, social influence, and compliance gaining,* 3rd ed. Boston: Pearson, 2007.

Haiman, Franklyn S. 1949. An experimental study of the effects of ethos in public speaking. *Speech Monographs* 16: 190-202.

Inch, Edward S., Barbara Warnick, and Danielle Endres. *Critical thinking and communication: The use of reason in argument*, 5th ed. Boston: Pearson, 2006.

O'Keefe, Daniel. 1977. Two concepts of argument. *Journal of the American Forensic Association* 13: 121-128.

Reichenbach, Bruce. *Introduction to critical thinking.*   Boston: McGraw-Hill, 2001.

Rieke, Richard., Malcolm O. Sillars, and Tarla Rai Peterson. *Argumentation and critical decision making.* 6th ed. Boston: Pearson, 2005.

Rudinow, Joel and Vincent Barry. *Invitation to critical thinking.* Belmont, CA: Thomson-Wadsworth, 2008.

Rybacki, Karyn Charles and Donald J. Rybacki. *Advocacy and opposition: An introduction to argumentation.* Boston: Pearson, 2005.

Verlinden, Jay. *Critical thinking and everyday argument.* Belmont, CA: Thomson-Wadsworth, 2005.

Ziegelmueller, George W., Jack Kay, and Charles A. Dause. *Argumentation: Inquiry and advocacy*, 2nd ed. Englewood Cliffs, NJ: Prentice-Hall, 1990.

Chapter 2

FUNDAMENTAL CONCEPTS OF ARGUMENT

After reading this chapter, you should understand:

- What the concepts of "presumption" and "burden of proof" involve
- What "stock issues" are, and how they relate to policy, value, and factual propositions
- The nature and components of the Toulmin model of argument

Specialized terms to know:

- presumption
- burden of proof
- ill/significance
- blame/inherency
- structural barrier
- attitudinal barrier
- cure/solvency
- cost/desirability
- warrant
- backing
- qualifier
- reservation
- major triad
- minor triad

Now that you have some idea of how argumentation can be defined and what its basic components are, we must now deal with other fundamental concepts that are commonly used in the study of argument. At the top of that list we would have to put: presumption, burden of proof, and stock issues, along with what is easily the best-known model of argument, the Toulmin model.

Presumption

If you think about it, arguments have to "start" someplace. We need a decision-making principle—how do we know whether to believe what we already believe, or whether we should believe something else? Well, presumption is one approach to that. Like any other idea, you don't have to *agree* with the concept of presumption, but you should certainly *understand* what it involves. And, like any other idea, someone had to "invent" it. In this case, the inventor is Bishop Richard Whately, who, in 1828, published the book *Elements of Rhetoric* in which he explained his notions of presumption.

Basically, Whately believed that presumption lies with the **status quo**, a fancy Latin term for the current situation. That is to say, the "starting point" for any discussion lies with the status quo. Whately contended that presumption is applicable in three different situations:

(1) There is a presumption in favor of traditional values and beliefs. It's "debatable" what constitutes a "traditional" value or belief, but most people would say that living is better than dying, love is better than hate, promoting happiness is better than promoting misery, and so on. Most of us would presume that it's good to be educated, it's better to be healthy than to be sick, wealth is preferable to poverty, and the like.

(2)   There is a presumption in favor of majority opinion. Of course, the majority can be "wrong," but our initial posture might well consider what most people think. If most people think that the Earth revolves around the sun, maybe I ought to lean in that direction until someone "proves" otherwise.

(3)   There is a presumption in favor of existing institutions. Some people have said that the U.S. health care system is a mess, and that we need to adopt the Canadian system instead. Presumption would dictate that we stay with what we have until something clearly "better" can be established. Does that mean that the current system (of health care, of mass transit, of education—whatever is being discussed) is performing "well" or is the "best"? Absolutely NOT. **Presumption is not necessarily a ringing endorsement of the status quo (although it CAN be)—it simply means that we should keep what we've got for now until someone clearly demonstrates otherwise.** Ziegelmueller, Kay, and Dause (1990, 17) make this same point when they write:

> Presumption makes no judgment concerning the wisdom of present beliefs or policies. Although presumption may have the effect of causing present beliefs or policies to continue, this occurs by default—because what already exists continues to exist—and not because present beliefs or policies have been necessarily been justified.

In many ways, presumption is more of a cautious, "conservative" posture than a daring, "liberal" concept. Especially with regard to policy matters, presumption is saying, be careful! With change comes risk and uncertainty, and so before we make a change, we should be darn sure of what we're doing. Again, you don't have to agree with this idea—maybe you're a person who just likes to try new policies impulsively, on the spur of the moment. You have that right, but presumption operates differently.

Of course, you are probably most familiar with presumption in the legal context—the idea that someone is presumed innocent until the State can prove beyond a reasonable doubt that they are guilty. This type of presumption is sometimes called "artificial" presumption because it's a made-up rule, so to speak. But, in my opinion, it's a good one—imagine if people were presumed to be guilty and had to prove that they were innocent! On the other hand, what is sometimes called "natural" presumption is just the commonsensical idea that we shouldn't, for instance, assume that the President of the U.S. is an alien invader unless we have some awfully good evidence to support such a bizarre claim. It's not an institutional "rule," here—just a good idea. Similarly, it makes sense to assume that schools should continue to offer physical education programs until someone can definitely show that we should not; after all, the concept of "sound mind, sound body" goes all the way back to ancient Greece. So even though presumption was "invented" by Bishop Whately, it is really a way of thinking that we are all drawn to and have used at some time or another.

Keep in mind, however, that people do not always agree on where presumption lies—that too can be a focal point for argument. I think that most of us would presume that the Earth revolves around the sun, but can we presume that "education" is preferable to "ignorance"? Most of us would say yes, but the answer is not *completely* self-evident. Some would regard "global warming" as a claim that needs to be "proven," while others believe that the evidence for global warming is so strong that it constitutes a presumptive position—the issue becomes, what should we *do* about it? Therefore, there may be times when arguers will need to explain and defend *why* presumption lies where they say it lies.

Burden of proof

Burden of proof is another commonly-cited idea in argument, and in some ways, it's the "companion" to presumption—that is, to overcome presumption, one must meet a burden of proof. Burden of proof refers to the arguer who wants to change the status quo needing to make a convincing case—one that is strong enough that presumption is in doubt, and a response is necessary. Another term that is often used in this context is another one of those funny Latin terms, **prima facie case**. Like any other term in argument, this one has been given a variety of definitions. For our purposes, let's just call a prima facie case one that is, on first hearing (literally, "first face"), strong enough that it requires a response.

In theory, if I can't make a prima facie case, I have not met my burden of proof and no response is necessary. If I were prosecuting Britney Spears for murder, and my evidence was:
- she was born on December 2, 1981 in McComb, Mississippi;
- she was raised in Kentwood, Louisiana as a southern Baptist;
- her father is a building contractor and her mother is a former grade school teacher;
- she has two children; and
- she has sold over 83 million records worldwide;

the defense could simply argue, "Even if everything he says is true, it does not add up to a reason to conclude that she's guilty of murder. So, for the lack of a prima facie case, the defense rests." (Britney's fans are elated!)

In essence, a prima facie case meets a certain threshold—it is sufficiently strong and convincing that presumption is in doubt and counterarguments must be provided. But as with the stock issue of ill/significance, people will disagree about whether an argument rises to this level. If you accused me of shoplifting because I was wearing a nice new sports coat, I don't think, in and of itself, that's enough for a conviction, but I still might be motivated to prove where I was on the night of November 27th! If you said that aspirin can cure AIDS because God told you so in a dream, I don't think that meets one's burden of proof; presumption would dictate that aspirin is not a cure for AIDS. Still, realistically, I might worry that *someone* would find the dream convincing, and so I might be inclined to respond in some way—all the while claiming that even if the dream felt "real" that it does not sufficiently meets one's burden of proof. The big idea is that arguers cannot simply assert a position—they must support it with sufficiently convincing evidence and reasoning that a response seems warranted.

Stock issues

There are issues, and there are stock issues. Issues are specific to a particular topic. If you want to analyze any controversy that's out there, framing as many specific issue-related questions as you can is a good first step. For example, with regard to the topic of legalizing marijuana, there are a number of issues. How many people smoke marijuana illegally? What are the health effects of marijuana? Is marijuana a "gateway drug" to other "harder" drugs? If marijuana were legalized, what would be the impact on marijuana use? And so on. These are all issues that are specific to this controversy—they are issues, but they are not framed as *stock* issues.

By contrast, stock issues are *not* unique to a particular subject. Stock issues are questions that come up *whenever* people deal with a topic, issue, or problem. They are *universal* in nature; they are "generic"; they can be used in *any* situation, to analyze *any* controversy. That of course is what makes them useful.

STOCK ISSUES FOR POLICY PROPOSITIONS

The best-known set of stock issues is the set dealing with matters of **policy**. As I will later discuss, people have also proposed stock issues for factual and value issues, but the stock issues for policy propositions are the most widely used and, frankly, the most instructive and helpful. There are four such issues: (1) ill, or significance; (2) blame, or inherency; (3) cure, or solvency; and (4) cost, or desirability.

Ill/significance

A natural and obvious question that comes up in any policy discussion will be, is there even a problem in the first place? That's what this stock issue is all about. Can you show people being hurt? Economic problems? Environmental dangers? Lack of efficiency or performance? To meet the demands of this stock issue, an advocate will need to find something that's going wrong. We have the old saying, "If it ain't broke, don't fix it," which is relevant here—from a stock issues perspective, if there isn't a problem, there isn't a reason to change. And there is often lively debate about whether there even *is* a significant problem: for example, some people see personal computers as the greatest invention of the 20ᵗʰ century, while others see them as machines that have made our daily lives more crazy and our interpersonal relationships more shallow. Some people believe that crime in our society is worse than ever, while others would contend that certain categories of serious crimes have been declining in recent years.

Blame/inherency

"Inherency" is an important concept in academic debate, but it's really no less important in the real world. Inherency deals with the question of whether the problem—even if it is significant—is of such a nature that we must change to a new policy in order to solve the problem. Put another way, one must demonstrate that the problem is inherent (built in) to the status quo. Arguers often establish inherency by trying to demonstrate that there are **barriers** to solving the problem within the status quo. One type of barrier is usually called a **structural** barrier—that means there is something tangible within the status quo (a law, a regulation, a policy) that prevents the status quo from effectively dealing with the problem. For instance, if you were arguing that all homeless people in the U.S. should be provided with minimal housing as a right of citizenship, you could simply say that there is no law currently which enables this to happen—it's not allowed in the status quo. That's a structural barrier to change—the current system simply cannot provide this type of housing. Or, if you were contending that mental health care should receive the same insurance coverage as "regular" medical care, you might be able to cite specific provisions in law or policy that currently prevent that from happening. Or, if you were advocating that someone not born in the U.S. (Arnold Schwarzenegger, for example) should be able to run for President of the United States, you could argue that this is impossible at the moment because it's prohibited by our Constitution. A structural barrier is anything within the structure of the status quo that prevents the problem from being addressed.

The other type of barrier is usually called an **attitudinal** barrier, and it's just what it sounds like—something less tangible or structural but still an obstacle. A classic example of an attitudinal behavior would be something like the "profit motive." You could argue, for example, that as long as the profit motive is part of our economy, there is no way that businesses will provide sufficient health care coverage for their employees—that is, businesses need to make a profit, and they will cut costs wherever possible in order to make that happen, including the cost of benefits for employees. (Of course, there are arguments "against" this idea, but that's the case with virtually *any* argument.) Other attitudinal behaviors could include "competition," "human nature," "the law of supply and demand," etc. For instance, I could argue that because people are by nature competitive and impatient, we cannot expect them to simply "get along" with every other driver on the freeway; therefore, we need tougher laws against "road rage" because human nature prevents us from solving this problem. Therefore, we need to change.

So, inherency deals with the issue of whether the status quo is to "blame" for the problem. Let's face it—there are many problems in the world, but some of them can be handled, at least in theory, within the current system. For instance, if you said that drunk driving is a significant problem, I could agree with you but say that we don't need any changes in the law—what we need is to enforce the current laws more aggressively. Or, if you argued that we need a new light rail transit system because our city's buses aren't sufficiently reliable, I could respond by saying that the bus system is not inherently unreliable, but can be made to operate more efficiently.

In the end, inherency is a very important issue in any situation where one is suggesting that only a significant change will address the problem at hand.

Cure/solvency

OK, you've shown a significant and inherent problem, so simply provide the solution, right? Not so fast! We first need to know if your solution will really cure the problem that you identified; this stock issue is often referred to as **solvency**. (Sometimes it is also referred to as the stock issue of "workability.") If you think about it, solvency is a very important issue, too—you simply can't assume that your solution will work. You need to demonstrate it. Take the issue of gun control, for instance. A lot of people are concerned about gun violence in the U.S. and consider it to be both a significant and inherent problem. But the issue then becomes, if someone proposes, say, a ban on handguns, will it work? Some skeptics will contend that even if there's a problem, such a solution simply won't have the desired effect. They would argue that "criminals" would never turn in their guns, as well as some "law-abiding" citizens. And so whether it's a good idea or not is kind of irrelevant. Indeed, they might continue to argue that if the goal of a handgun ban is to reduce crime, then such a ban would actually increase crime by making guns less available to the "good guys."

Another example of a solvency issue involves U.S. policy related to "illegal immigrants." Some have advocated that the U.S. should build a wall across the entire southern border of the nation to prevent illegal immigration from Mexico. But the question remains, even if that is a desirable goal, would such a wall actually prevent illegal immigration into the United States? Some proposals can be easily circumvented; in this case, an opponent to such a plan might argue that many illegal aliens could still find their way into the United States by some other means.

The last high school that I taught in (many years ago!) had what they believed to be a significant, inherent problem: the English students were not reading enough outside of class. And, perhaps, that was a problem, and certainly an inherent one—there was nothing in the curriculum that either required or guaranteed that students would read on their own, outside of class. The solution? Require all English students to read at least two books outside of class each term or they would automatically *flunk* English— regardless of how they did in class! Anyone with a reasonably vivid imagination can probably figure out what happened here. Some students read really short books. Some students relied on movies, or dust covers, or literature aids sold in bookstores. Some students reported on books that they had read the previous year. (In fact, the department had to develop a filing system just to keep track of the books students had previously read, just to nip this problem in the bud.) All of these problems are solvency problems, and so, in the end, the question remained as to whether students were really reading any more than they had read previously. So, solvency involves the issue of whether the proposed solution really can and will solve the problems that it is designed to address.

Cost/desirability

Finally, let's assume that you've shown a significant and inherent problem, and you have a solution that will actually deal with this problem. One question still remains: to solve this problem at what *price*? That's what the stock issue of "cost" or "desirability" is all about. For example, if you said that we needed a program of free tuition for all qualified students at public universities, it might solve some problems, but create others. Certainly such a program would have to be "paid for" in some way or another, so an opponent could argue that the economic impact of such a plan on our overall economy would be too harmful. Or, someone might advocate that we move away from nuclear power and toward coal power; in response, you might contend that such a shift would be bad for the environment, especially in terms of the "greenhouse effect." Or, I could advocate that we increase the speed limit on all interstate highways to 80 miles per hour—in response, you might say that this would increase our dependence on foreign oil and increase highway deaths as well.

The reality is this: in order to get something, you usually have to give up something. And so the stock issue becomes, is it worth the trade-off? The effects of a particular proposal could be economic, environmental, social, medical, educational—you name it. Because these effects can be significant—and often not carefully considered by those advocating change—many real-world policy proposals fail around the stock issue of desirability. Again, from a stock issues perspective, you need more than a demonstrated problem to "buy into" a proposal for change.

STOCK ISSUES FOR VALUE PROPOSITIONS

Are there stock issues for value questions as well? The basic answer is "yes," although stock issues for value propositions haven't been around as long—one could even say that theory surrounding this issue is still developing. However, the following questions seem to apply to any value issue:

1. By what set of criteria is the object of the proposition best evaluated? In other words, the first stock issue involves what standards we should use to arrive at a conclusion. For example, it I were to say that Arizona is a better place to live than Minnesota, then I would have some sort of criteria that I would use to support that claim, whether I consciously realized it or not. Maybe you believe that climate is an important consideration, or employment opportunities, or the quality of education, or the availability of leisure activities. But whatever criteria you employ, the first issue is always, what *are* they, and are they "good" criteria?

2. Do the value criteria truly support the claim being made? Once I have established my value criteria, I need to apply them to an analysis of the topic at hand. If, for instance, I contend that Burger Barn is better than McBurgerland, I might advance the criteria of "taste," "price," "speed of service," and "cleanliness." If indeed I thought these were the best criteria to use, I would need to show how Burger Barn "scores better" on each of them, so that my position is coherent and fully supported.

In the "old days" (read: 20 or 30 years ago), value propositions were not carefully examined in books on argument. As implied above, it is only recently that argumentation scholars have paid special attention to the nature of value propositions. Although our conception of them is still evolving, I think the two questions I have identified get to the heart of what we always want to know when it comes to resolving them.

STOCK ISSUES FOR FACTUAL PROPOSITIONS

If things are a little murky when it comes to stock issues for value propositions, I believe things are even murkier with respect to factual issues. Only a few texts in the field have even dared to suggest that there are stock issues for factual propositions. That doesn't mean there aren't any, but I think it does mean that they are more troublesome to identify. Not only that, but the ones I have seen don't seem to be nearly as instructive and helpful as the stock issues for policy propositions. However, the following two questions seem to always apply to factual matters, making them stock issues:

1. What does the proposition mean? Although this is a legitimate question for any claim—policy, value, or factual—it seems especially relevant here. Factual claims are the foundation for any type of argument—"facts" are the starting point in the process. Therefore, it seems important to determine, what is this factual claim actually saying? If I say that violent crime is decreasing in the U.S., what do I mean by "violent crime"? Or even what constitutes a "decrease"? If I argue that eating fiber reduces the risk of colon cancer, how should we define "fiber"? Issues involving definition are obviously relevant here, and a good critical thinker should be aware that arguers often choose definitions that best suit their purposes, even if they are potentially misleading or inaccurate.

2. Is there sufficient evidence to support the proposition? Since factual claims are built around evidence, this seems like the other obvious stock issue. Any claim that you might make must inevitably require *some* kind of evidentiary support. I simply can't assert that baby aspirin prevents heart attacks, or TV violence affects kids—I need to be able to support those claims with some form of evidence. (We will examine evidence in much more detail in chapters 3 and 4. For now, realize that there are four main types of evidence: examples, statistics, testimony, and objects.)

THE TOULMIN MODEL OF ARGUMENT

In 1958, a fellow named Stephen Toulmin published a book titled *The Uses of Argument*. Little did Toulmin probably realize at the time what impact he and his book would have on the study of argument. Indeed, it is safe to say that the Toulmin model is the single best-known model of studying argument, and if I did not include it in this text, I would be doing you a big disservice.

Signs of advancing age: the Toulmin model was actually relatively "new" when I was first exposed to it as a college student. At the time, I wasn't especially impressed with it, but I memorized the six components of the model and did all right on the exam. With the passage of time, however, I have come to better appreciate the model for its lucidity and its wisdom, and I hope you can come to appreciate its virtues as well.

Some initial observations about the Toulmin model:

1. It is very flexible. The Toulmin model can be used to analyze virtually any argument or claim, whether that claim be factual, value, or policy in nature. And the model can consider just about any type of "support material" or evidence—even, I would contend, "nonverbal" evidence such as the photos in print advertisements or videos of a particular event. Anytime someone is trying to get us to do or believe something, the model is potentially relevant.

2. The model describes—it does not evaluate. The Toulmin model is an analytical tool that can help you sort out what's going on in an argument. But in the end, the model itself does not "judge" the argument as being "good" or "bad." Now, you as a critic, of course, can make such judgments, based on what the model reveals—just remember that it is you who is making those judgments. (On a related note, students often want to analyze some famous person's speech by writing about how "the speaker used the Toulmin model," but to be precise, the *speaker* is not "using" the model—the student *critic* is using it as a way to help analyze the speech.)

3. The components of the model will appear in different sequences. Although I will have to start at some point in explaining the model, the reality is that there is no set "time order" for the components of the model. Sometimes people will state their claim first, sometimes they will start with the evidence, and sometimes they will start with what Toulmin calls the "reservation"—a situation under which the claim would be withdrawn. In any event, an argument may begin at *any* point in the model—there is no time order implied.

4. Not all six elements of the model are necessarily present or relevant. I've often given students a short message, such as a newspaper editorial or a letter to the editor, and asked them to do a Toulmin analysis of the message. Because the model has six parts, they often feel compelled to find all six—even if all six aren't there. Don't do that! You only use those parts of the model that are relevant. Some arguments, for example, don't have what Toulmin would call a "qualifier." Others don't really provide what Toulmin would call "backing." So don't find things that are not there.

5. Some interpretation on the part of the critic may be involved. Although some arguments are pretty "transparent" in how they are constructed, others can be more subtle or ambiguous. "Real" arguments are often more complicated than the examples you will see in this chapter. Therefore, some judgment and interpretation on the part of the critic may be involved. But, let's be clear about this: that doesn't mean that *any* Toulmin analysis is "correct," that they are all equally good. No, some interpretations will be more on the mark than others; your analysis still has to make sense.

OK, now it's time to look at the model itself and its six components: **data, claim, warrant, backing, qualifier,** and **reservation.** I will start with the data, since I have to start somewhere.

Data: What have you got to go on?

As mentioned previously, all arguments are based on some type of data or evidence or information. Toulmin acknowledges this fact with what he calls data or grounds for an argument. I will try to stick with "data," but "grounds" is also a very helpful term, insofar as evidence is often the "grounding point" for an argument or claim. Let's consider our good friend "Sara." (You know Sara, don't you? She's our imaginary friend created for purposes of illustration.) Let's suppose that Sara is a college student with a grade point average (GPA) of 3.97. By itself, that means nothing—it is simply information. But obviously, it can become a grounding point for lots of different claims. For example, from this one little bit of information, I might claim that:

- Sara is intelligent.
- Sara is a hard worker.
- Sara takes easy classes.
- Sara cheats on exams.
- Sara only has "book smarts."

Now, any of these claims is potentially relevant, but for purposes of illustration, let's stick with just one.

Claim: What do you want me to do or believe?

Sara has a 3.97 GPA. **From this information, I will conclude that she is *intelligent*.** And as we have already determined, claims can be factual, value, or policy in nature. To say that Sara is "intelligent" is probably best considered a "factual" claim, but it does have some "value" overtones as well.

Warrant: What does one have to do with the other?

As far as I am concerned, the warrant is the single most important and helpful part of the Toulmin model. **The warrant is essentially an assumption—an assumption that I am making** that enables me to make *that* claim from *that* information. Put another way, it is only *with* that assumption that the claim makes any sense, given the evidence that it's based upon. So, in the case of Sara, what key assumption are we making? What enables us to draw the conclusion that she is intelligent if she has a 3.97 GPA? We must be assuming something *about* GPA. In this case, the warrant could be stated as follows:

Since a high GPA is an indicator of intelligence.

Without that assumption, there would be no reason to conclude that Sara is intelligent; I must be assuming that GPA has something to do with intelligence. Now, about the warrant there is, unfortunately, more to say:

1. More often than not, the warrant is unstated or implied by the arguer. People do not walk around talking in full-blown sentences, "You know, since a high GPA is an indicator of intelligence, and Sara has a 3.97 GPA, therefore Sara is intelligent." No, real people are going to say, "Wow—Sara's got a 3.97 GPA— she must be really smart." So, one of the challenges for you the listener/reader/critic is to "read between the lines" and figure out what the warrant really is. As Toulmin (1958, 100) himself notes, "This is one of the reasons for distinguishing between data and warrants: data are appealed to explicitly, warrants implicitly." Although this distinction isn't always the case—that is, sometimes people do explicitly state their warrants—it is far more common that the warrant is either assumed or implied.

2. The warrant is NOT a simple re-statement of the claim, or the evidence. Using the "Sara" example, many students will initially want to say that the warrant is "That Sara has a high GPA which makes her intelligent." However, that is merely a re-statement of the data and the claim—to determine the warrant, you need to "get underneath" what's going on and see the big idea which links the data and the claim. For instance, if I say that "Those students at State Tech are so nerdy—my friend Sara goes there and she has a 3.97 GPA," I am assuming at least two important things: (a) that there is a direct correlation between GPA and "nerdiness," and (b) that Sara is a "typical" State Tech student—if I'm not assuming these things, then how or why would I conclude that all State Tech students are nerdy? I HAVE to be making such assumptions; otherwise, the argument would make no sense.

3. There is frequently more than one warrant in an argument. Not surprisingly, as implied in the example immediately above, arguments are not necessarily built around just one assumption. Even in the example of Sara being "intelligent," there are more "innocent" assumptions that are being made—for example, that Sara is indeed a student, that 3.97 is on a 4-point scale, that 3.97 is assumed to be a "high" GPA, and so on. These assumptions are all there, but the critical assumption is that a high GPA is associated with intelligence.

4. Think in terms of "if," "then," and "because." If this will help, think of the data as the "if" part, the claim as the "then" part, and the warrant as the "because" part. So, in our example,

IF Sara has a 3.97 GPA, (data)
THEN Sara is intelligent (claim)
BECAUSE a high GPA is an indicator of intelligence. (warrant)
These three parts of the Toulmin model (data, claim, and warrant) are often referred to as the "major triad" of the model. To get a little practice working with these three parts, please refer to **Table 2.1**, which provides sample claims for you to analyze. In each case, remember that the warrant is usually implied and unstated—in each of these examples, you will need to *infer* the warrant based on what is already there.

But now, we must consider the "minor triad" and the other three parts.

Backing: I still don't understand the connection

Remember our friend Sara. We have based our claim about her around a certain warrant: in this case, that a high GPA is an indicator of intelligence. But the question still remains, is this a "good" warrant? **"Backing" is Toulmin's term for anything the arguer uses to support the warrant.** If this is not too confusing, the backing is sort of like "data" to support the warrant—not the claim. Often, people don't need or want to provide backing for the warrant—in the case of Sara, if you believe that a high GPA indicates intelligence, we're done. But, what if you resist that premise? What if you are a little skeptical about that relationship? That's where the backing comes in.

TABLE 2.1
SAMPLE ARGUMENTS FOR TOULMIN ANALYSIS
IDENTIFY THE CLAIM, DATA, AND WARRANT(S) IN EACH.

1. It's been a balmy summer. Get ready for a warm winter!
2. The lottery has raised a lot of money for the state of Minnesota. It's bound to make lots of money for South Dakota, too.
3. Our fries were soggy, and the cheeseburger was cold. I'll never again eat at that sad excuse for a restaurant.
4. "CSI" is the best show on TV. It finished first in the Nielsen ratings almost every week.
5. Governor Bill Blowhard has done a terrible job so far. Since he took office, our nation has been attacked by terrorists, and gas prices have gone through the roof.
6. News Journal columnist Biff Hartman says the Vikings will win next year's Super Bowl, so I'm puttin' down a hundred bucks on "The Purple."
7. All these terrorist attacks have been orchestrated by Muslims. Clearly, Islam is the most violent religion in the world.

Suppose that you had to support the notion that GPA and intelligence are connected. What would you say? What support could you offer? Let's consider some hypothetical possibilities:

1. My friend Bill has a high GPA, and he's really smart.
2. A couple of my professors think that GPA and intelligence are related.
3. A study done at Harvard University demonstrated such a link.
4. Completing a course with an "A" obviously requires some degree of intelligence; you can't "fake your way through."

These and other such points exemplify backing. A strong argument ought to be able to provide substantial backing for the warrant, but sometimes arguers are incapable of supporting their own basic premise. Again, since the warrant is in many ways the foundation of an argument, it's essential to be able to support that warrant if you are challenged.

Qualifier: How Much Do You Want To Bet?

One of Toulmin's contributions to the study of argument is pointing out that arguers, when making claims, will often note their degree of certainty in the claim. **That "degree of certainty" part is what Toulmin called the qualifier.** It essentially answers the question, "How much do you want to bet?" Now in the case of our friend Sara, we've said that "Sara is intelligent." Trick question: what's the qualifier here? The answer is, there isn't one! It's just a statement: Sara…is….intelligent, period. So for something to function as a qualifier, it must show a degree of certainty. When textbooks discuss qualifiers, they will often use as their only examples the words "possibly" and "probably." And it's true that they are both qualifiers—to say that "Sara is probably intelligent" is to say, in essence, it's an uncertain world, I think this is a reasonable conclusion, but I want to "hedge my bets" just a bit. But of course, there are other words than "possibly" or "probably." Words or phrases such as the following also function as qualifiers:

> "I'm **pretty sure** Sara is intelligent."
> "**Chances are** that Sara is intelligent."
> "It's **very likely** that Sara is intelligent." And so on.

Not only that, but a qualifier may also be numerical. When your local weathercaster predicts a "**40 percent chance** of rain," he or she is using a qualifier. Or if I say, "the **odds are about 50-50** that the Twins will win the pennant," I'm also using a qualifier.

Like a lot of things in life, qualifiers have both a good side and a bad side. If you never use a qualifier ("Coffee will make you smarter," "Toothpaste causes mental illness") you run the risk of seeming a bit too sure of yourself. Intelligent people, shall we say, know that very few things are absolutely certain, so they will use qualifiers to acknowledge that fact. On the other hand, if you frequently use qualifiers ("There may possibly be, all else being equal, a slight causal connection between TV and kids' obesity") one may wonder if you even have a claim in the first place. So finding a "middle ground" is often worth considering.

I might add that there seem to be differences in the frequency of qualifier use depending on the context or sphere of argument. In politics, for example, it's not really common to see a lot of qualifiers—for better or worse, you usually won't hear a candidate say, "I think there's a pretty good chance I can help turn the economy around," apparently because such a statement seems to lack confidence. On the other hand, arguments in the academic arena are often riddled with qualifiers. Most academics—and their audiences—would consider it too "brash" to make claims with complete certainty. So we are often confronted with statements in the academic world such as, "If these findings are correct, there may be a reasonably significant correlation between the two variables."

Reservation: Any exceptions?

Our tour of the Toulmin model would not be complete without the sixth element: the reservation. (Some scholars, including Toulmin himself, often termed this the "rebuttal," but "reservation" is used in many circles and in my view better captures the idea behind this aspect of argument.) Again, not all arguments include a reservation, although many perhaps should. **A reservation is any circumstance or set of circumstances under which you would want to withdraw the claim.** Once again, take Sara. Let's assume that you still believe that Sara has a 3.97 GPA, and you still believe that GPA and intelligence are generally related. Even so, are there *any* circumstances under which you would not want to say that she's intelligent? Going back to the beginning of this chapter, let's consider some possibilities:

1. Maybe Sara only takes easy classes.
2. Maybe Sara cheats on exams.
3. Maybe other people write Sara's papers for her.
4. Maybe Sara is just good at "sucking up" to her professors.

In any of these situations, you would likely want to pull back a bit and withdraw your claim from consideration. That's what the reservation is all about. **Although a reservation does not have to use this word, if you can use the word "UNLESS" as a way**

to express the idea, you are probably dealing with a reservation. So, if I say, "Unless she only takes easy classes, Sara must
be intelligent because she has a 3.97 GPA," I have included a reservation at the beginning. If indeed she only takes easy classes,
I would want to hold back on my assessment of her intelligence.
But again, it's the way the idea *functions* in the argument that's
important. If I say, "Sara must be smart, although I haven't seen
whether she only takes easy classes," there is an implied reservation there, even if the word "unless" does not appear. But most
commonly, people will use that magic word: "*Unless* their relief
pitching falters, the Yankees will win it all this year," or "*Unless*
I'm crazy, we should have a good time tonight."

The complete argument regarding our friend Sara is diagrammed
in **Table 2.2**. Frequently, Toulmin analyses are visually portrayed in
such a fashion, but there is no one "best" or "right" way to do so.

Concluding thoughts about Toulmin

So there you have it—the six parts of the Toulmin model in all
their glory. At its best, the Toulmin model is not a recipe to follow,
but a tool to use in the analysis of an argument, and even a tool to
"play with" in a creative manner at times.

I want to once again stress the word *function*—how does something function in an argument? Going back—yes, once again to
Sara—let's suppose that I am trying to convince someone that she
is indeed intelligent, because she has a 3.97 GPA. But this someone
says, "I don't believe she even HAS a 3.97 GPA." With the Toulmin
model in mind, NOW where are we? Well, where we are is back at
the level of a claim. We were hoping that the 3.97 GPA would serve
as a grounding point for a conclusion about Sara's intelligence, but
instead, we're left with a statement that someone else is challenging. So, "Sara has a 3.97 GPA" is a statement that no longer functions as "data"—it is functioning at the moment as a claim that we
must "prove." That means we'll have to support this "new" claim
with data. Perhaps our data will be Sara's college transcript. If it is,
then the implied warrant would be "Since transcripts are credible,"
or something to that effect. Or we might say that "Sara's roommate
told me she has a 3.97 GPA"—certainly a riskier claim, since it is
based on the warrant that Sara's roommate is knowledgeable and
reliable. At any rate, we could go on from there and potentially see
the relevance of backing, reservations, and/or qualifiers. And then,

eventually, we hope, if we could convince our "someone" that Sara does indeed have a 3.97 GPA, then this information would function again as data for the claim that she is intelligent.

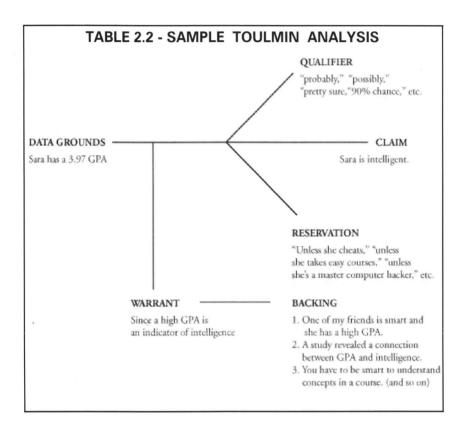

TABLE 2.2 - SAMPLE TOULMIN ANALYSIS

QUALIFIER
"probably," "possibly,"
"pretty sure,""90% chance," etc.

DATA GROUNDS
Sara has a 3.97 GPA

CLAIM
Sara is intelligent.

RESERVATION
"Unless she cheats," "unless
she takes easy courses," "unless
she's a master computer hacker," etc.

WARRANT
Since a high GPA is
an indicator of intelligence

BACKING
1. One of my friends is smart and
she has a high GPA.
2. A study revealed a connection
between GPA and intelligence.
3. You have to be smart to understand
concepts in a course. (and so on)

CONCLUSION

Any discussion of argument begins with the notion of presumption (what we currently assume is the case) and burden of proof (what is needed to overcome presumption). In considering what arguers need to demonstrate, certain standard stock issues are always relevant, and there are stock issues for policy, value, and factual claims. The Toulmin model, consisting of six parts or elements, can be used to analyze any type of claim. Now that we have an "overall" view of how arguments are constructed, we can begin to look at the specific components of any argument, and one of the key components is *evidence*—the focus of chapter 3.

REFERENCES

Toulmin, Stephen. *The uses of argument*. Cambridge, England: Cambridge University Press, 1964.

Whately, Richard. *Elements of rhetoric*. Carbondale, IL: Southern Illinois University Press, 1963.

Ziegelmueller, George W., Jack Kay, and Charles A. Dause. *Argumentation: Inquiry and advocacy*, 2nd ed. Englewood Cliffs, NJ: Prentice-Hall, 1990.

Chapter 3

CATEGORIES AND TYPES OF EVIDENCE

After reading this chapter, you should understand:

- Four different general categories of evidence
- Four specific types of evidence, and the keys to using each well
- Ten tests for evidence of any kind

Specialized terms to know:

- primary evidence
- secondary evidence
- direct evidence
- circumstantial evidence
- positive evidence
- negative evidence

- willing evidence
- reluctant evidence
- access
- external consistency
- internal consistency
- cumulativeness

As implied in previous chapters, evidence is in many ways the foundation for argument. Claims and beliefs need to be based on some sort of information. There's an old contest debate saying that "debates are won and lost in the library," and indeed, I spent a fair amount of my spare time in high school and college wandering around libraries, trying to find evidence that would, of course, decimate my future debate opponents! If you don't have the evidence to support your claims, you're often going to be in a vulnerable position, argumentatively. After all, why should you believe someone just because "they say so"? Occasionally, people will believe you without any evidence being provided; if I contend that "even modest exposure to the sun will cause skin cancer" and you immediately agree, there may not be a need to provide evidence. But normally, we want to know what information is available that can support such a claim; without such information, we are in a world of mere assertions, and people will often resist what you have to say.

To say that there is a lot of evidence out there these days is a gross understatement. With the advent of the Internet in particular, we have almost immediate access to thousands of websites and thousands of other references in print. For those who are not old enough to remember what finding evidence used to be like, suffice it to say that our research tools are incredibly more powerful than they used to be. In the "old days," one looked through a library card catalog, hoping to locate a couple of books on the subject in question, as well as a few indexes to magazines (such as the *Reader's Guide to Periodical Literature*), going through these annual indexes year by year, hoping to find at least a few magazine articles that would be appropriate. Now, with electronic search engines, one can suddenly be hooked up with, say, 263,000 "hits" in less than one second.

Of course, with that astronomical increase in the availability of evidence, the issues of "quality" and "credibility" become more important. If the Internet is a vast "ocean of information," that ocean is rather polluted! Anyone who wants to blog, or post, or write an entry for Wikipedia has that amazing opportunity in the 21st century. As a result, now, more than ever, one needs a way to sort through all the information we encounter and be able to analyze and assess it. That is the concern of this chapter.

GENERAL CATEGORIES OF EVIDENCE

There are a number of ways to sort out evidence. Let's start with four distinctions.

Primary or secondary evidence

If you find a medical study that appears in the *New England Journal of Medicine*, and you quote specific passages from the researchers who wrote this article—the actual study—you are making use of primary evidence. Primary evidence comes "straight from the horse's mouth," if you will—in other words, the original source. On the other hand, if I read about the same medical study in *Time* magazine, and the *Time* reporter is who I am reading, then I am relying on the reporter's interpretation of that study—in other words, I would be using a secondary source. Because I haven't seen the original study, I am depending on the *Time* reporter to give me an accurate accounting of things.

Obviously, we like to use primary evidence when we can. When you are using the original source, there is less chance that the evidence is distorted—it is in many ways more reliable and credible. The world is full of people who think they know what some writer believes but have never read the writer's original work. When I was in college, I took a course on Karl Marx. All I had ever heard was that he was a "Communist" and "wanted to take over the world." What a surprise it was to read Karl Marx "in the original"! Although some of his writing might be considered "revolutionary," I suppose, much of it was not too far from what any good labor union would say today about the challenges facing the working class. In short, it wasn't nearly as "wild and inflammatory" as I was expecting. I had been relying on the interpretations of others rather than going to the original source.

In a similar vein, the ABC news program "20/20" ran a segment some years ago (March 31, 1995) about a wide variety of "bogus research" that had been in circulation. One such "study," for example, was a list of the biggest problems in American schools in the 1940s (chewing gum, running in the halls, talking out of turn in class, etc.) compared to the biggest problems in the 1990s (drug abuse, gang violence, weapons in school, etc.) The segment showed a variety of well-known people who were citing this list as evidence that our schools were in disarray, including former first lady Barbara Bush and former Secretary of Education William Bennett. Well, John Stossel, the ABC reporter, tracked down the original source for this list—in other words, the primary source. Turns out it was a guy down in Texas (Texas oil executive T. Colin Davis) who had done no real "research" on this issue. He merely said, "I went to school in the '40s, so I know what the main problems were then, and I read the newspapers, so I know what the main problems are now." Oh my. In addition, this 20/20 segment mentioned that a March of Dimes study supposedly showed that domestic violence (read: spousal abuse) causes more birth defects than all other medical issues combined—but an investigation revealed that there simply was no such study ever conducted. In short, these days, with Internet searches being what they are, some "urban legends" are simply perpetuated because no one ever bothers to re-check the original source—the primary source—to see if the claim is actually "true."

With respect to primary evidence, a common questions is, **can you find primary evidence in your school library? The answer is an emphatic YES—original academic research, autobiographies, first-person accounts of events all qualify.** Sometimes students have too narrow a view of what constitutes primary evidence. They say, "Well, there *could* be primary evidence in our school library, if I was to personally witness a crime at the checkout desk." Although I suppose that is primary evidence, it's way too narrow—any published source (the source doesn't have to be you personally) where you are using the original accounting of things is primary. Anyway, strive to use the original source when you can.

Direct or circumstantial evidence

Some evidence relates directly to the claim. If I claimed the Earth had been visited by aliens, and I showed you the landing pod recovered from an alien-looking craft, we could call this direct evidence. Or, if someone saw this craft flying near downtown, that eyewitness account would also be direct evidence. On the other hand, circumstantial evidence relates indirectly to the claim. If I said that "the universe has *billions* of stars and *billions* of planets, so there must be intelligent life somewhere, and these life forms must have visited Earth at some point," I have circumstantial evidence at best.

Freeley and Steinberg (2005, 96) define circumstantial evidence (which they also call "presumptive" or "indirect" evidence) as "evidence that tends to show the existence of a fact in question by proving other, related facts—facts from which the fact in question may be inferred." In other words, by demonstrating "A," and perhaps even "B," we can reasonably infer that "C" is the case—it's just that the linkage is more indirect.

We are probably most familiar with the concept of circumstantial evidence in the world of crime and punishment. Did she commit that crime? Well, we found her fingerprints near the scene of the crime. She can't account for her whereabouts on that evening. And she has a past history of committing that type of crime. All of these supports are circumstantial in nature—not as convincing as, say, a videotape showing her breaking the law—but potentially pointing in the direction of the claim.

Now, unfortunately the line between direct and circumstantial evidence—like many other lines in this text—can be a little hard to draw clearly. In fact, in the larger world, there are famous cases where the key issue was, is the evidence direct or merely circumstantial? Certainly that was the case with the famous "Watergate" scandal of the 1970s—was President Nixon involved in this situation, or was it solely the work of his associates? Or, in the 1990s, did O.J. Simpson actually commit those murders, or was the evidence only circumstantial? In these and other cases, the metaphor that is often used is that of a "smoking gun." The "smoking gun" expression is meant to say, is there really direct evidence to support this claim? And again, people will have different ideas about what constitutes direct evidence. For example, during the Clinton administration, there were suspicions that the President was having a sexual relationship with intern Monica Lewinsky. Normally, "direct" evidence in a case like this might be some sort of eyewitness testimony, or an admission by one of the two people involved. In this case, the key piece of evidence that laid this issue to rest was Monica's blue dress, which contained a, well, "DNA stain" on it from the President. In some ways, this could be considered circumstantial—after all, there are in theory many ways stains can get places, but in this case, it seemed so direct as to be convincing. At any rate, we like to have direct evidence when we can get it, but sometimes all we have is indirect, circumstantial evidence.

Positive or negative evidence

Positive evidence is easy to explain: it's the presence of evidence. Is there evidence that smoking causes lung cancer? You betcha. Is there evidence that we may be in a period of global warming? Whether you buy into it or not, most definitely. Positive evidence is the presence of *some* sort of information that leads to the claim. It's probably safe to say that most evidence is positive in nature.

Negative evidence, on the other hand, is a little trickier to explain—it often throws people the first time around. But it's a very comprehensible idea. **Negative evidence is the *lack* of evidence, used *as* evidence.** Huh, you say? Consider a real-world example that you may even have experienced. In the workplace, most employees, when asked, will say they are doing a good job. Why do they believe they are doing a good job? The number one answer is this: "No one has told me that I'm doing a bad job, and no one has complained about my work." In other words, the absence of any complaints is being used as evidence for the claim that "I am doing a good job." This is negative evidence. In a similar vein, if one of your professors concludes that "my students are ready for the exam because there weren't any questions on the material," that too is negative evidence—the lack of any questions is used as evidence that the students are ready. (Probably a *dubious* assumption in many cases!) Or, on a more somber note, each year a certain number of people in the U.S. simply vanish. After some time, the unfortunate claim that we must make is that they are no longer living. How do we know? No one has seen them. There is no evidence that they have used their credit cards. No calls to relatives have been recorded. No police agencies have been contacted by this person. In other words, the lack of evidence is used as evidence. Of course, if we were to find their remains, or a person confessed to killing them, then we would be in the realm of positive evidence.

Obviously, we like to have positive evidence when we can get it. But sometimes all we have is the lack of evidence to make our point. I for one will continue to watch television without the fear of going blind, if only because I have never heard of a person going blind watching TV or a study which drew such a conclusion. Again, the lack of evidence is used to support my (mild) TV addiction in this case.

Willing or reluctant evidence

Much evidence is given willingly. People want to tell you that the President is doing a good or a poor job, that you should or should not buy a particular car, or that we should or should not endorse "conceal and carry" laws for handguns. Of course, the fact that people want you to believe certain things does not necessarily make it "bad" evidence by any means. But, we also need to remember that some people have a "vested interest"—even a downright bias—in what they have to say. So, if I quote the current Vice President, and he or she says that "the President is doing a great job," we need to remember the potential problem with this type of evidence—that it is given quite willingly. That is perhaps an extreme example, but we do need to keep this issue in mind.

On the other hand, some evidence seems quite different. Say for instance that you have a relative (let's call him "Fred") who works for the Fizzy Cola Company. Fred tells you, "As far as I'm concerned, Fizzy Cola isn't so good—I much prefer Kooky Cola." In such a situation, you would've expected that Fred would recommend his own company, but it turns out that's not the case. Therefore, this constitutes reluctant evidence—that is, when a source presents a point of view or position that would not seem to be in their best interests. Because this is reluctant evidence, we might be inclined to give it more credence. And often, reluctant sources, for both logical and psychological reasons, will carry more weight. If a Democrat tells me that a Democratic President is doing a good job, I will not be particularly impressed. On the other hand, if a Republican tells me the same thing, I am more likely to be impressed, because you wouldn't think that a Republican would endorse a Democratic office-holder.

A couple of other important notes: first, **don't take the word "reluctant" too literally. Reluctant testimony does not necessarily mean that the person is unwilling or hesitant to convey a point of view—it merely means that you wouldn't expect such a statement from such a source.** Now, if you testified in court against some element of "organized crime," it's true that your testimony might be more convincing because most people would normally not want to do that—that would be "reluctant" in the most literal sense. But again, the term is much broader than that—if you have been a lifelong caffeinated coffee drinker, but now you are eager to tell the world that "decaf" is the best drink around, that's reluctant, too, given your background. Second, remember that it is possible to quote a source "out of context" in a way that can be misleading. A good critical thinker ought to wonder at times, "Did this person really say THAT? You wouldn't expect her to." So do be sure that if you claim that a "pro-choice" doctor is actually "pro-life," that you are accurately representing their views. Because reluctant testimony is used quite often and can seem quite convincing, having such a careful mindset is desirable.

SPECIFIC TYPES OF EVIDENCE

Now that we have examined four general categories of evidence, let's look at the specific types of evidence that can be employed in argument. There are four of these as well.

Examples

One of the most common forms of evidentiary support that people provide for their claims are examples, sometimes also called "specific instances." Examples include stories, particular cases, illustrations, and the like. Maybe Bud doesn't like a particular restaurant. We ask, "What's your evidence that it's so bad, Bud?" Bud says, "I had lunch there the other day, and the pasta was cold and the sauce was too spicy." Suddenly we have an example—a specific case of "badness." If you think about it, examples are used a lot in argument:

- Is there waste in the Department of Defense? "Well, here's a wrench that you can buy at any hardware store for $5—the U.S. Navy has been buying them for 50 bucks apiece!"
- Do you think that the Phillies can win the pennant this year? "Well, the other day they lost 18-1 to the Cubs—I don't think so!
- Is nuclear power safe? "Well, there's a nuclear plant just a few miles away that's been in operation since 1968, without a single accident!"

In all of these situations, the claim-maker is depending on a particular incident—an example—to make their case. One thing about examples that's usually the case is that examples have the tendency to be "dramatic" or "emotional." People often choose examples that they know will get people "riled up." As a critical thinker/receiver you might want to keep this tendency in mind.

Although examples have the virtue of being down-to-earth, and although they can affect us emotionally, we must also be aware of the drawbacks to examples as evidence. By definition, an example is just "one" of something, so the key issues involving the use of examples become:

1. Are there a sufficient number of examples?
2. Even if there are a sufficient number, are they representative?

The first test is fairly obvious. If I'm trying to convince you that there is fraud in the welfare system, and I'm using examples as a main form of evidence, I'd better be able to show you quite a few instances of such fraud. But even if I can show you 25 examples, we'd still want to know if they are truly representative, the second test—after all, the welfare system in the U.S. probably serves at least 20 million people, so unless you can show that these 25 cases are representative, we have no way of knowing what to conclude. Put another way, one can almost always find examples of something—even examples of an award-winning teacher who's made a few mistakes. The ultimate issues involve, how *many* mistakes, and were they *representative* of the entirety of this person's performance?

Statistics

Needless to say (but I'll say it anyway), the subject of statistics could be a course and a textbook in itself. There's a lot that one can say about statistics. And it's clearly the case that statistics are used a lot as a form of evidence. When all is said and done, there are two main issues with statistical evidence:

1. **How were the data gathered? How did they arrive at these numbers in the first place?**
2. **How are the data presented or conveyed?**

First, how were the data gathered? OK, someone came up with some numbers. But how did they *arrive* at those numbers? A classic case of this issue takes us way back to 1936, when President Franklin Roosevelt (FDR) was running for re-election against Alf Landon, the Republican candidate. A magazine of that time, the *Literary Digest*, conducted a massive and very ambitious survey. The magazine compiled a list of more than 10 million names, made up from telephone directories, club membership lists, and lists of magazine subscribers, among others. They sent each person a mock ballot to return and wound up with more than 2.4 million responses. Their finding? Landon was going to beat FDR, 57 percent to 43 percent. However, in case you don't know, we've never had a President Landon; in the actual election, Roosevelt carried all but two states in the nation and creamed Landon, 62 percent to 38 percent. The problem? In 1936, a lot of people didn't have telephones, yet this was a survey based in part on telephone directories. Those who did have phones tended to be wealthier. And those who are wealthier often tend to be Republicans. So it should come as no huge surprise that Landon, the Republican, was their projected winner. But in the end, what they had here was a type of "junk data"—that is, statistics that may have been industriously gathered, but in a way that was inaccurate and misleading. In short, they didn't use a random sample—that is, a sample where every American had an absolutely equal chance of being surveyed—so there was no way the results could mirror the voters of the nation as a whole. In the meantime, a fellow by the name of George Gallup—the guy who founded the now-famous Gallup Poll—was doing his own early survey work in 1936, and he predicted, based on samples of only a few thousand Americans, that FDR would indeed win. The lesson? In the world of survey research, a badly chosen big sample is much worse than a well-chosen smaller sample.

It's not just surveys where the issue of information-gathering is relevant. Take crime statistics, for example. If Tinytown has a 100 percent increase in the number of speeding tickets this year, it doesn't necessarily mean that people are driving faster. Maybe last year Tinytown had two officers tracking the streets, but now they have four—meaning it should come as no surprise if the number of speeding tickets doubles. Or, maybe Tinytown has the same number of officers monitoring traffic, but the Tinytown Police Department has decided to enforce speeding laws more strictly. Or maybe Tinytown is so darn small (it's called Tinytown, after all!) that the total number of speeding tickets has increased from a total of one to a total of two, meaning that a 100 percent increase is quite misleading. In any of these ways and more, the numbers could be misleading.

As for presentation of the data, people who make arguments with statistics have some choices to make. One choice is whether to present the statistic as a raw number or a percentage. Another is what time frame the data cover. **In both cases, it would be my observation that people will use whichever figure sounds more impressive for their case.** Take the issue of a raw number or a percentage. If I am a supporter of a state lottery, I'd probably want to use a raw number for how much the state makes—you know, something like $60 million or $100 million in annual receipts sounds pretty impressive. On the other hand, if I am opposed to state-run gambling, I might note that $60 million or $100 million is less than one percent of the state's total income—which, for what it's worth, is usually the case in "real life." In this situation, the lottery supporter may feel that she has "won" the point because her numbers are so large, and the lottery opponent may feel equally victorious because his percentage is so small. Good critical thinkers probably want to know both figures.

As for time frame, arguers can make something look very good or very bad depending on the dates that are used. If I wanted to convince you to invest in the stock market, I'd want to be mindful of what time period I used. Sometimes investment people will go back 80 years and show that over this time, the stock market has always gone up, even if it dips periodically. On the other hand, if stocks have not been doing well in the last year or two, I might look at stock values only in that narrow window of time. Even sports franchises are not immune to this issue. Depending on what time frame I use, I can make the Green Bay Packers seem like an amazing football team, or one that's just OK. And again, the key point here is that people will tend to choose the time frame that best suits their rhetorical purposes, so be on the lookout for misleading information.

For now, we will leave the world of statistics and move to the next type of evidence. But in chapter 4, look for an expanded discussion and analysis of this rather complex form of support.

Testimony

Another main form of support for claims is to quote someone: "According to so-and-so, such-and-such is the case." Arguers quote other people all the time:

- Movie reviewer Chad Celluloid says, "Don't miss this flick! It's brilliant!"
- Geoffrey Culverwell, the noted British historian, believes that "America's involvement in World War II is often exaggerated."
- According to the board of *Consumer Digest*, the Yankaway Eyebrow Plucker is the best on the market.

In each of these cases, someone is using another person or organization for support. In some ways, the key tests for testimonial evidence are not too hard to figure out:

1. **Is the source really an** *expert*?
2. **Is the source** *unbiased*?

First, is this person really an expert? Lots of people are willing to offer opinions, and many even have impressive-sounding titles; however, that does not guarantee expertise. Just because a historian has a Ph.D. does not make this person an expert on all periods of history, for example. Just because someone is a doctor does not mean they are equally knowledgeable on all diseases. Unfortunately, doing a good job of assessing the expertise of a source can be difficult. We often don't know enough about the subject—whether it be electronics, physics, philosophy, or even cooking—to be in a position to evaluate someone's expertise. But try we must.

The second test, is the source unbiased, is also difficult to determine at times. Yet it is also an issue of which many people are only vaguely aware. If, for instance, you are quoting Greenpeace to argue against a new nuclear power plant in your area, even if Greenpeace is a qualified source, it may well be perceived as a biased source. If the coach of the Chicago Bulls says the Bulls are going to have "one heckuva good year," we need to remember that this person may not be dispassionate and unbiased. These are fairly obvious examples; many times the issue of bias is more subtle. But again, try we must.

Objects

Finally, those making an argument will often use a thing—an object—as evidence. This "thing" may be a photograph, or a computer simulation, or a demonstration, or a piece of physical evidence. Sometimes the word "artifact" is also used here; an artifact is not the object itself, but a representation of the object, such as a photo or a scale model. But for our purposes, I think we can call all supports of this nature as "objects."

Suppose I'm selling you a vacuum cleaner. I can quote someone, or I can use a study of vacuum cleaners with some statistics, but it might be more effective for me to dump a load of dirt on your carpet and show you how the amazing Suckaway actually cleans. That's the use of objects as evidence. Of course, the use of objects is not limited to the trivial world of vacuum cleaner sales. When President John F. Kennedy wanted to persuade the American public in 1962 that Russian missiles were being shipped to Cuba and posed a threat to the U.S., he went on TV and showed aerial photos of the missile silos in Cuba. This was probably a better approach than quoting the Secretary of State; it seemed "real" and irrefutable. And, of course, criminal trials are often built around physical evidence in this DNA-obsessed world. So objects can be very convincing. However, there is one key test for this type of evidence that must always be considered:

Has the object been rigged or distorted in any way?

Not everything is what it seems. The world of commercial advertising is full of such situations. That creamy milk in the commercial's bowl of cereal may actually be liquid paste, because it photographs better. The toy car that seems to race around the room at 120 miles per hour due to the camera angle may not be quite so exciting as it crawls across your linoleum floor in the basement. And the proper lighting, along with some computer enhancement, can do wonders to ensure that a cosmetic product looks its best— maybe even "too good to be true." But again, these issues are not limited to advertising. A well-known TV network once aired an alleged "alien autopsy," in which a corpse from another planet was supposedly dissected on film. Was this "real," or not? In 2001, this same network (Fox) aired a show which offered photographic evidence that we have never been to the moon, and all the moon shots were actually an elaborate hoax. Was this photographic evidence convincing? Was it distorted or misleading in any way? We always need to keep in mind that objects can be manipulated. Indeed, my best friend in high school did one of his science projects on UFOs. To prove that UFOs are "real," he displayed a photo of a flying saucer cruising over our campus. Of course, he had a darkroom at home, which made this bogus flight possible. (Today, of course, he would only need a computer!) So, the next time you watch an infomercial, ask yourself, if I had this product at home, would it really perform the way it seems to on the show?

GENERAL TESTS FOR ALL TYPES OF EVIDENCE

Regardless of whether you are using examples, statistics, testimony, or objects as evidence, there are several general tests that you can apply to each. I will propose ten such tests for any type of evidence.

1. Relevance

Relevance goes at the top of the list because it is the most vital and important. If you can't show that your evidence is relevant to the claim in the first place, nothing else really matters; no other test need be applied. For example, if you were trying to convince me to buy a certain car because "research shows that women think it's sexy," I am going to reply, "Even if you're right, this is not a relevant piece of information that will influence my purchasing decision. In fact, if I need a particular car to interest a woman in me, something is terribly wrong!" Relevance is not something that can or should be assumed, even though people can be rather gullible and agree with a claim because there is some sort of evidence to support it. And as discussed in chapter 10, dealing with refutation, saying that an opponent's evidence is "true, but irrelevant" is one of the strongest forms of refutation. In short, just because someone provides you with information does not mean that it's relevant information. You might want to tell me that Biff is intelligent because he owns lots of books, but I might respond by saying that the number of books one has is largely irrelevant to a determination of one's intelligence.

2. Specificity

Evidence must be reasonably specific. It should not be vague. When people say things like "studies show" or "experts believe," your first response should probably be, "Can you name even *one* of those studies or *one* of those experts?" Chances are good that they can't—it's long been my belief that people use phrases like this to sound impressive, but the reality is that they don't know. Perhaps the worst of all: don't let anyone use the phrase "they say" on you (like, "*They say* drinking too much coffee causes kidney stones"). "They say" is the very height of vagueness. As an arguer, you can also enhance your credibility by being specific: for example, rather than referring to your source as "a magazine," or even "an issue of *Newsweek* magazine," it's normally better to say, "an article on U.S. foreign policy in the June 23 issue of *Newsweek* by staff writer Fareed Zakaria." Providing those specifics reassures the audience that you have actually done your research and can be trusted.

3. Objectivity

We've already looked at testimonial evidence with this issue in mind. Evidence which seems to be based on an objective analysis is normally better than evidence that comes from a biased source. If you're going to support the claim that butter is not harmful to your health, you probably don't want to quote the President of the

Butter Institute (if there is such a place!). Better in this case to have a well-known dietitian who has nothing to gain or lose with such an endorsement.

4. Reliability

Reliability addresses the question, "Has this source been consistently correct in the past?" This standard for evidence is sometimes hard to assess if you don't know much about the source—but you should. On many sports-talk radio programs, sports betting firms advertise to entice listeners to wager on pro football games—with their able assistance, of course. Why should you avail yourself of this betting service? Because, they will tell you, in some way or another, "I've beaten the spread on 10 of the last 11 Monday Night Football games"—in other words, I have a track record of reliability. Obviously, those who forecast the weather need a record of reliability in order to be believed. But, so does a historian, or a physician, or a political office holder: the reality is that one's credibility is dynamic, determined by one's audience (not by the source), and often fragile. Therefore, past "mistakes" become a "red flag"—a sign that what the source is advocating may not be correct.

5. Access

Access deals with the issue of whether the source really has "first-hand" knowledge of the subject. We often talk about people who only have "book knowledge"—such people do not score high on this standard. Instead, with this standard, we are looking for people who have been "out there" and "in the trenches"—that is, they have some direct personal experience with the subject at hand. It's one thing to have an understanding of studies done on those who are terminally ill, and quite another to have actually worked with terminally ill patients in, say, a hospice facility. It's one thing to talk about war, and quite another to have actually fought in one. And it's one thing to show portrayals of school on TV, and quite another to actually teach in one! In the end, there is something to be said for direct experience. Of course, like any other standard, access is not "perfect"—simply because someone has first-hand knowledge does not necessarily make them an "expert." In fact, their experience might even limit their view of the issue to only what they have seen, making their view either narrow or distorted.

6. Expertise

Expertise is more like that "book knowledge." A person with expertise has a wide and deep and specific awareness of the subject at hand—a more complete understanding of the issue than your ordinary mortal. Titles such as "Doctor" or "Professor" might indicate expertise, but as always, be a bit of a skeptic—having a title or an advanced degree does not automatically make one an expert in any sense of the word. In fact, with advancing age, I have come to realize how "mortal" any "expert" can be—as we sometimes say, they put on their pants just the same way that you and I do! With the passage of time, I have become less willing to believe something simply because someone has formal training. I do not mean to sound overly cynical or sarcastic, but true expertise, in the deepest sense, is hard to come by in this world. The burden for an arguer, I believe, is to show that their source really has such depth.

7. Recency/timeliness

This standard is a little tricky in some ways. Most textbooks simply say "recency" and leave it at that. And many times, having recent, up-to-date evidence is important. For example, if you were arguing that the disease of AIDS is out of control in the United States, you would not want medical statistics from ten years ago—you'd want the most up-to-date information that you could find. Ditto if you were thinking of whether to invest in a certain stock—you'd want to know how that stock had performed in the last couple of years, not from 1990-2000. So recency is often vital. But two notes of warning: (1) Although the date of your evidence should always be considered, more recent evidence is not therefore *automatically* "better"—recency is one of many standards for evidence, as you are seeing here. For instance, since the human body has not changed too much in the last 20 years, I'd take a well-constructed cancer study from 1995 over a poorly-constructed one from 2005. So, don't "worship" recency. (2) Second, there may actually be times when an "older" source could be better or more appropriate. For example, for more than 40 years now, people are still debating what happened on November 22, 1963, when President John F. Kennedy was assassinated. Chances are some of the best evidence to resolve this issue is still from 1963—although admittedly, "newer" views of that 1963 evidence (such as more sophisticated technological analysis) might make more recent evidence more credible here, too. Overall, I only mean to say that the issue is a little more complicated than saying "later automatically equals better."

8. External consistency

External consistency deals with the question, is the evidence consistent with other available evidence? Put another way, is this evidence in line with what other sources are saying? If so, it doesn't make the source automatically "correct," but it is at least indicative that the source is not "out in left field" somewhere. We are interested in figuring out where the preponderance of evidence resides—where most sources see this issue. The extreme examples of evidence that does not meet this standard are pretty easy to find in your local supermarket. One particular periodical that recently went "belly-up," *Weekly World News*, regularly featured totally ridiculous "news" items. For example, there might be a photo of the current President shaking hands with a space alien visitor, or a story about a 9-foot cyclops from the Chernobyl disaster who wants to play in the NBA, or the discovery that Hitler's nose is still alive—and growing a new moustache! (I wish I were making these up, but they were actual stories in this publication.) So if you read that Elvis is alive and working at a taco stand in Macon, Georgia, and you can only find this story in one place, it ought to serve as a "red flag." But again, to complicate matters, every so often a source "in the minority" can be correct, and every so often the majority can be wrong. Perhaps a good example of the latter involved the period around 2003 when many different sources of information were declaring that "weapons of mass destruction" were being developed in the nation of Iraq, and it turned out—really, by everyone's admission—that this was not to be the case. It's tough to know who to believe, isn't it?

9. Internal consistency

Internal consistency addresses the issue, is the evidence consistent within itself? Is it coherent, or does the source "contradict itself"? For example, if Senator Windbag declares that "we've got to do something about dependence on foreign oil" but drives a gas-guzzling vehicle himself and is opposed to additional gas mileage standards for U.S. cars, one could contend that his stance is internally inconsistent. Of course, like many other things, inconsistency is "in the eye of the beholder," but most people would agree that someone who argues *for* lowering the drinking age to 19 but *against* careful enforcement of DWI laws has taken a position which is internally inconsistent.

10. Cumulativeness

The final test I'll identify deals with the question, does all the evidence "add up" to support the claim or conclusion? Sometimes if you have a lot of "circumstantial" evidence but no direct evidence, you still may draw a definite conclusion. If I see that someone looks tired, and her grades are suffering, and I haven't seen her around very much, and she doesn't crack very many jokes anymore, I might not make much of any *one* of these things—but *together*, they indicate that she may be having personal problems. That's what the standard of cumulativeness is all about—looking across a wide range of information and sensing the "overall pattern," if you will. Like any other standard, we can be fooled by it (just because something looks like a duck and quacks like a duck doesn't *always* mean it's a duck), but it's well worth keeping in mind.

CONCLUSION

Evidence is the foundation for argument in the sense that almost all claims demand some sort of information to support them. There are four general categories of evidence, four specific types of evidence, and ten tests for evidence. Because much is involved in understanding statistics as one type of evidence, chapter 4 takes a deeper and more detailed look at statistics.

REFERENCES

Freeley, Austin J. and David L. Steinberg. *Argumentation and debate: Critical thinking for reasoned decision making.* Belmont, CA: Wadsworth, 2005.

Stossel, John. (1995). "Fact or fiction? Misleading statistics." ABC News, 1994.

www.math.upenn.edu/~deturck/m170/wk4/lecture/case1/html, retrieved September 11, 2007.

Chapter 4

ISSUES IN THE USE OF STATISTICAL EVIDENCE

After reading this chapter, you should understand:

- Whether all concepts can be readily quantified
- Whether precise numbers are necessarily "better" numbers
- What constitutes a representative sample
- Three different ways of expressing a statistical "average"
- Why it is difficult to compare percentages
- The difference between absolute percentages and relative percentages
- The difference between statistical correlation and true causation
- Problems with statistical projections into the future
- Ways that statistical graphs can be misleading
- What it means for a difference to be "statistically significant"

Specialized terms to know:

- validity
- mean
- median
- mode
- outliers

- absolute percentages
- relative percentages
- statistical correlation
- gee-whiz graph
- statistical significance

Like it or not, we live in a world where statistics are used—and probably abused—by arguers on a regular basis. In some fields—the business world and the academic world, for example—statistics are hard to avoid. Indeed, as implied below, in some spheres of argument, numbers have a rather "magical" quality—simply by virtue of having statistics, an argument is presumed to be "stronger" or "better." As Joel Best (2004, 167-168) contends,

> Americans have a widespread, naïve faith in the power of numbers to resolve debates, to provide facts that can overpower opposition. This faith rests on some dubious assumptions. The first is a belief that numbers are by nature factual, that they constitute incontrovertible evidence. This ignores an even more basic truth—that all numbers are products of human efforts. We cannot escape the fact that statistics are social constructions. Recognizing this means that we can't treat numbers as straightforward bits of truth; rather, we must be critical, asking who counted what, and how, and why.

Of course, that doesn't mean statistics have no important place in argument; as Best (2004, 168) points out, "it does not mean that we can't trust any statistics, that we should treat them all as equally worthless. There are better and worse ways of counting, and we can have more confidence in some numbers than in others. All science is not junk science; with a little effort . . . we can distinguish between the two."

So, good critical thinkers need to be more sophisticated in their analysis of statistics as evidence. Therefore, we would be well-served to take a deeper look at numbers, and how they are used in argument.

As noted in chapter 3, two general issues regarding the use of statistics are: (1) how were the data gathered? How were the statistics arrived at in the first place? And (2) how are the data presented? In particular, what time frame is used, and are the numbers in raw form or expressed as percentages? Unfortunately, these two criteria only scratch the surface. So, let's consider some of the following issues:

1. Not all concepts can be readily quantified.

Our culture is obsessed with measurement. We can (or at least, THINK we can) measure your math aptitude, your intelligence, your verbal ability, whether you're an introvert or an extrovert, whether you're happy or sad, and whether you are aggressive, or compulsive, or shy—and, literally hundreds of other things. The issue is, can all those things really BE measured? In social scientific research, this issue is referred to as "validity," a term which unfortunately has different meanings in other contexts, as you'll see in a later chapter. **But within the realm of social science, validity involves, are you measuring what you claim to be measuring?** That question is of critical importance in many research studies, because if you really aren't measuring what you claim to be measuring, your study is in trouble, and in a big way.

Take the concept of intelligence. Many people think that the IQ test is a measure—even THE measure—of intelligence. Yet people who know the history of this test—often called the Stanford-Binet test—also know that the IQ test was never even designed to test intelligence, but merely to determine which French school kids required special education programs. Yet that doesn't stop people these days from reducing people to a two or three-digit number that is supposed to express their level of intelligence. At any rate, the issue of validity is very real here.

Or, within the field of communication studies, one of the best-known measures of "stagefright" is called the PRCA, the "Personal Report of Communication Apprehension." This instrument, a 24-item questionnaire, has been administered to tens of thousands of people to measure what we in communication studies now call "communication apprehension." Now the PRCA may well be helpful in measuring "stagefright," but it's always wise to keep in mind that this is a "personal report" of apprehension—that is, people are doing a "self-assessment" of their attitudes and behavior. And you know what? People often don't have a very clear and objective view of themselves, so the "validity" issue, as usual, rears its ugly head. In the end, there are other ways to measure communication apprehension, including physical measures as well as having trained observers assess people's behavior—they too raise validity issues, of course. The point simply is that just because something is put into a number (for example, a PRCA score of 65, which turns out to be about the national average), doesn't mean it necessarily measures what it claims to be measuring.

Even something as seemingly simple as determining how many people in the U.S. are "unemployed" is a daunting task, statistically. As Jensen (1981, 129) illustrates,

If an arguer is presenting figures on the number of unemployed people in his community, how does he define "unemployed"? Does he include students who are out of school in the summertime? Does he include people who are temporarily laid off for a week or so? Does he include people who are currently training for jobs? Does he include unemployable people, that is, those with serious physical or mental handicaps? Does he include those people who are unwilling to work? Does he include those who are greatly underemployed in terms of their qualifications? Does he include people who have regular jobs but who work no more than 25 hours a week? His figures on the number of unemployed people in his community obviously will reflect how he answers these questions.

The big idea is this: just because someone has put something into numbers does not necessarily mean that the numbers make any sense. Measurement is a very tricky business, and one should not be overly impressed by a number simply because it *is* a number.

2. A more precise number is not necessarily a "better" number.

Let's suppose that I told you that there are 1,223,557 homeless people in the United States. I'll bet you might be impressed. Wow, you say, he's got that total down to the very last digit—not "a million and a quarter," but 1,223,557! My suggestion is not to be immediately or automatically in awe of such a number.

Some things can be quantified with precision. If I say that a particular car has a 198-horsepower engine, there are ways to verify that number and to measure it pretty precisely. On the other hand, consider the homeless: they are difficult to define, difficult to track down, and thus difficult to count. Therefore, any number such as 1,223,557 that purports to be more "accurate" because it's down to the last digit ought to make you wonder. This point is especially important when it comes to projections of the future: any person who tells you that the Chernobyl nuclear accident in 1986 will end up causing 16,984 deaths from thyroid cancer in the next thirty years is really making an estimate—don't let the precise number fool you. Of course, it's not that precise numbers are inherently "bad"—just that you shouldn't be overly impressed by them. And with regard to our homeless statistic, I'd take a carefully-constructed estimate of the number of homeless over someone who simply tried to count individual homeless people near bus depots in several cities.

Another bizarre example: a news article reports on research connected to human life expectancy. In this article, Schmickle (2001, A10) says doctors and other experts are "pessimistic about the United States, projecting that Americans may not reach the 85-year [average life] expectancy until 2182." Imagine that: we "know" that it will be exactly 174 years before the average American lives to 85—not 173, not 175, but 174. Simply put, anyone who is that precise is "blowing smoke," and the "exactitude" of the number does not really enhance its credibility or reliability.

Within the field of communication studies, I have made it a personal crusade to correct a huge misconception about the relative importance of the verbal and the nonverbal message. A fair number of our texts have reported that the overall meaning in communication is "7 percent verbal, 38 percent vocal, and 55 percent facial." Unfortunately, what most people don't know is that those very precise numbers are derived from two studies done way back in 1967, and that the key study involved a sample of only 37 female psychology majors, and one word of language for this sample to react to—the word "maybe" (Lapakko, 1997). Under the circumstances, one would be ill-advised to conclude that any and all communication situations would conform to this nice tidy formula of 7-38-55. But the precision of these numbers is what is seductive—if something is so precise, how can it possibly be wrong? Again, the answer is that precise statistics, in and of themselves, don't mean too much. As Alan Merriam (1990, 338) has observed, "The appeal of numbers as a source of rational order and harmony derives in part from their perceived precision. In contrast to the inevitable ambiguities and abstractions of language, numbers seem to possess exactness and objectivity." The key word in here is "seem"—numbers may seem to possess these qualities if they are very precise, but such precision is often an illusion. In fact, if you really think that only 7 percent of the meaning within communication comes from the words that we use, I am in deep trouble with regard to this textbook, which is totally unable to make use of nonverbal cues!

3. Survey samples must be truly representative.

We all read and hear about a lot of public opinion polls. People such as politicians, marketers, journalists, city planners, TV executives, and educators use polling data in all sorts of ways. Because we live in a democratic republic, what "the people" think is often considered to be critical. Unfortunately, not all polling data is accurate or reliable.

Take, for instance, the polling data you sometimes see on TV. Let's say that viewers can call in and record a "yes" or "no" vote on some subject—let's say, whether casino gambling should be legalized. The results of such a poll, then, will often be reported on the station's newscast—a voice of authority will say something like, "68 percent of those polled favor legalized gambling in this state." What they also often say, however, is that "these results are not to be considered scientific." That's another way of saying that this data may be junk. In any poll or survey, the critical issue is, has everyone had an absolutely equal chance of being selected? If not, then the data are unreliable. In the case of the fictitious legalized gambling survey, only those people who were motivated to call did call—that is, people who had strong feelings one way or the other. That may have skewed the sample, making it unrepresentative of the entire population. Also, it might have been possible for people to call more than once—that too would obviously skew the sample.

Within education, a current controversy involves the sort of polling that you know as "electronic course evaluations." Many colleges and universities are moving toward having students evaluate courses on-line. And many schools make this student participation voluntary—that is, students don't have to submit a course evaluation. So, what might be the problem here? Some believe that only students who have strong feelings one way or the other ("I LOVED this course" or "This course is hell on earth") will be inclined to post an evaluation. And if the response rate for the class is, say 50 percent, one does not know which 50 percent responded, nor what the other 50 percent really felt.

Further, even if I have a very large sample—say, 5000 people— that by no means guarantees that the sample is representative in any way. **There's an old saying in survey research: a large sample does not compensate for an unrepresentative sample.** I could do a national phone survey and get 3 *million* responses, but if those 3 million people were not selected randomly, I'd be better off to have a truly random sample of 1,500 Americans. In fact, most of the well-known polling organizations, such as Gallup, do a national survey with no more than 1,500 people. Many students are surprised that this is the case, but again, the key is representativeness—these 1,500 people are selected very carefully. In a Gallup poll, every American has an equal chance of being chosen—random selection is critical.

Think of it this way: if I have made a huge batch of vegetable stew, I do not have to eat the entire batch to know about its composition. I merely have to make sure that I mix it *very* well and randomly scoop out one serving. If I do, I will have a very good approximation of the whole. (And, I won't get sick or want to "hurl" from eating way too much soup—an added bonus!)

4. There are at least three different ways to define "average."

Nothing drives a statistics person nuts faster than someone who just uses the word "average" to describe the "central tendency" in a group. For a statistician, there are three types of averages. More on that in a moment.

Suppose we were to determine what the "average" income was of members of the Screen Actors Guild of America. Now I must confess that I am speculating here, but I think this analysis is probably about right. Some members of the Screen Actors Guild would be famous actors like Tom Cruise, or Julia Roberts, or Cameron Diaz. But many others—indeed, many, many more—are likely to be semi-employed actors whose main job is, say, waiting tables at a restaurant in Los Angeles, hoping to catch "the big break." So if the big stars make, say, $25 million a year, and a bunch of others make, say, $2000 a year for some work in commercials, what's the most accurate "average" salary?

Well, one way to compute that average is to determine the **mean**. (Statisticians often use the letter "x" with a line over it—"x-bar"—to represent the mean.) In this case, we would add up all the annual salaries of members of the Screen Actors Guild, and we would divide by the number of members. This is often a good way to express central tendency, but notice in this case, we have those famous actors with these astounding salaries included in the mix. These huge salaries are what statisticians call "outliers"—they are not representative values, and they pull the mean out of whack. Take, for instance, the annual income of these five fictitious members of the Guild:

$20,000,000
0
0
0
0
───────────
$20,000,000

In this case, the mean salary of these five people would be $4,000,000 ($20,000,000 divided by 5). But of course, this seems hardly "representative"—after all, only one of the five is making any money at all. That's why another expression of central tendency—the **mode**—is sometimes more appropriate. The mode is the most common value in the numerical list. So, in the example above, the mean would be $4 million, but the mode would be 0. Each number in its own way expresses the "average."

Finally, there is another measure of central tendency that is employed quite often: the **median**. The median is that point in the list of numbers where half of the numbers are above it, and half are below it. To give you a very simple example, here are five numbers:

112
98
85
67
43

In this distribution, the median is 85—two numbers are above it, and two are below. Notice that it really doesn't matter how big or small the numbers are above and below the median. That's why the median is often chosen, because those big "outliers" can't unduly influence it. Indeed, the median might be a much better indication of the "average" salary of members of the Screen Actors Guild, because those big star salaries don't distort what's going on. So far, I have dealt with a hypothetical example, but I can tell you—"for a fact," as they say—that this same dynamic occurs in major league baseball. For many years, *USA Today* has published the salaries of every player on every major league team and then listed the team mean and the team median. In every single case, for every single team, the mean salary was higher than the median, simply because the stars of each team (the "outliers") pulled the mean salary up. So the median might be a better indication of a "typical salary," simply because not all baseball players are paid like Barry Bonds or Alex Rodriguez (two "megabucks" players, in case you don't know).

To summarize: there are three measures of central tendency or the "average." Sometimes all three will end up to be about the same, so it doesn't matter which figure the arguer uses. But consider the following list—let's consider it a group of quiz scores for a class with eleven students:

17
15
15
15
12
11
6
4
2
1
1
——————
99

In this case, the mean would be **9** (99 divided bv the 11 students).

The mode would be **15** (the most frequently occurring value).

The median would be **11** (five scores above 11, and five below).

So which of these "averages" is the "best" in this case? That, my friends, is what people argue about. But be aware of the issues involved with each.

5. Comparing percentages is often misleading and unwarranted.

Is it OK to directly compare percentages? The simple answer is usually no, but you'll want to know why.

Suppose someone argued, "The U.S. doesn't care about education as much as the Chinese do. In the U.S., the federal government spent only 1.4 percent of its total budget on education, compared to a whopping 10.8 percent in China." Wow, you say, that's many times more. But there are a couple of problems here. The first problem is related to this specific subject—it does sort of assume that all funding for education in these two nations comes from their federal governments. In the U.S., the vast majority of education funding is at the state and local level anyway, so such figures are misleading right there. But for a moment let's assume that both nations fund education in identical ways. What we don't know—and definitely need to know—are the base figures on which these percentages are calculated. Because **if the base figures are quite different, then any percentages cannot be sensibly compared.** If, for instance, the U.S. federal budget is $3 trillion, and the Chinese federal budget is $400 billion, the actual dollar figures would be similar. (Get out your calculators: 1.4 percent of $3 trillion is $42 billion; 10.8 percent of $400 billion is $43.2 billion.) I have no clue as to what the actual figures are in this example, but that's not important.

What is important is that you grasp the idea, and I'll give you an even simpler way. You have a choice: you can either have 50 percent of your textbook author's annual salary, or 1 percent of Bill Gates's annual salary. If you chose 50 percent of my pay, you have chosen the wrong door, as we say in the game show world. You'd be far better off to take 1 percent of an immensely larger number. So if I get a 10 percent raise and Bill Gates gets a 3 percent raise, again you'd want to go with the 3 percent—believe me, you'll be money ahead. So, be very careful when you compare percentages—in order to do so, the base figures from which the percentages are derived must be the same.

6. Absolute percentages and relative percentages can be quite different.

I was reading the March 10, 2003 issue of *Newsweek*, which included the following statement: "In 1981, preterm babies accounted for 9.4 percent of all births in this country; by 2001, the rate had jumped to 11.9, a 27 percent increase." The question becomes, is this a big "jump" or not? As usual, it depends on how you look at it.

The *Newsweek* writer wants us to think that this increase in pre-term babies is significant, so they use what's called a **relative percentage**. It is true that relative to 9.4, 11.9 is a number that is 27 percent greater. And 27 percent more of just about anything sounds significant. However, put on your thinking caps and look at these figures another way. In 1981, a little *less* than 10 percent of all babies were preterm (9.4 percent), and by 2001 a little *more* than 10 percent of all babies were preterm (11.9 percent). So, the **absolute** increase is actually only 2.5 percent, which makes the difference seem much less important. So arguers and critical thinkers alike must be mindful of this issue.

Finally, if this will help, let's pretend that the percentage of Americans who own motorized backscratchers increases from 1 percent of the population to 2 percent. Seen as a relative percentage, that's a 100 percent hike. But in absolute terms, it's only an increase of 1 percent. Which figure is better? Again, this will be a potential focal point for argument.

7. Statistical correlation is not the same as causation.

You read a report that says, "There is a .78 correlation between watching TV and exhibiting anti-social behavior." You decide never again to watch the tube, for fear you will assault someone, maybe even in your sleep. Well, it certainly is possible that watching certain shows on TV might provoke anti-social behavior, but the problem is, correlation is not the same as causation. Correlation simply means that two things vary together, in a predictable way: when one goes up, the other goes up (positive correlation). Or, when one goes up, the other goes down (negative correlation). And as some of you may know, correlations range from an absolute positive correlation of +1.0 to an absolute negative correlation of –1.0. A correlation of zero means there is no discernable relationship. In this case, the correlation is +.78, which is relatively high for a social scientific study. But again, remember: that does not necessarily mean that TV is to blame for anti-social behavior. How so, you ask? Well, maybe people who are more anti-social to start with are more likely to watch TV, so it isn't the TV which is causing this behavior, but their own previous conditioning. Or maybe watching more TV is an indication that anti-social people have boring, pointless lives and simply spend more time watching TV as a way to pass the time. Again, the TV did not *cause* their anti-social behavior; rather, it's a *reflection* of their anti-social behavior. If there was a .78 correlation between ice cream consumption and crime, would you blame the ice cream? I don't think so, but you might consider that ice cream sales go up in the summer, and so do opportunities for crime (more open windows, more people out and about). We will re-visit the issue of correlation in chapter 5, simply because this issue relates partly to statistics and partly to the ways in which we reason.

8. Statistical predictions of the future must be based on certain assumptions.

You've probably heard someone say something like, "Who is going to be able to afford a college education for their kids in the future? By the year 2030, four years at a private school is going to cost more than $300,000." (And you thought that college was expensive now!) Well, there are a couple of issues here. The first is not so much an issue of "statistics" as it is something to realize about the subject itself. Yes, costs for everything—including college education—will no doubt increase in the future, but we must remember that wages and salaries will also go up too—maybe not at the same rate, but in a way that makes such a figure less scary. In fact, your textbook author can make his students yearn for the past when he tells them that his first year at a private college was $2400, including room and board. But he also notes that the minimum wage at that time was $1.60 per hour, and that his first high school teaching job paid $7900 for the year! So all of these things are relative.

But the more relevant point here is that any trend is based on that nasty word, assumptions. In order to predict what college tuition will be more than 20 years from now, certain assumptions have to be made—about inflation, the economy, and the financial state of higher education, to name a few factors. Or, consider the example provided earlier in this chapter about a prediction of a life expectancy of 85 by the year 2182. That is at least a century and a half away. In such a situation, it's difficult to have any idea what assumptions to make. Imagine what changes there could be in medicine, genetics, biology, and similar fields even in the next *half* century—such uncertainties make a projection about average life expectancy to the year 2182 seem downright silly.

If the year was 1895, and I told someone living in Los Angeles that L.A.'s population would be more than 10 million in a century, that person would likely say, "The whole town's gonna be covered with horse poop!" (If I have to explain the problem with his or her assumptions, we need to talk.) Anyway, the point is that projections must be based on reasonable, defensible assumptions.

9. How a graph is constructed can be misleading.

A graph tells it like it is—doesn't it? Well, not necessarily.

To this point, I haven't really discussed the visual representation of statistical evidence. However, the graphic portrayal of statistics is an important issue. Perhaps the most common of these issues involves what is sometimes called a "gee-whiz" graph. Of course, it's been given this name because people see it and go, "Gee whiz—isn't that amazing!" The only problem is that depending on how one constructs the graph, the numbers can look very different.

Let's take a hypothetical example. In case you didn't know this, economists in particular are very fond of talking about "widgets." Widgets are simply a fictitious product designed to use for illustrative purposes such as what we are doing right now. Now, currently widgets cost $20, but five years ago, they cost $10. How can we graph this increase? It all depends on how the horizontal "x-axis" and the vertical "y-axis" are calibrated. Here are two ways to display the same data:

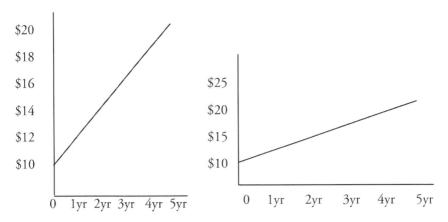

As a child of seven can plainly see, the same information graphed differently gives the reader quite a different view of the price increase in widgets. And as with all of these statistical issues, people are strategic and selective about how they portray the data. If they want you to freak out and feel alarmed about the widget increase, they will show you the graph on the left. On the other hand, if they want to reassure you that every family can still enjoy widgets—even several times a week!—they will show you the graph on the right.

10. A statistically significant difference defies random chance.

I've saved the most technical issue for the last. But hang in there!

In the academic world in particular, researchers will tell you that they have found a difference that is "statistically significant." Say, for example, that they are examining whether one diet plan is more effective than another. What they will do in a research study is randomly divide people into two or more groups. For the sake of simplicity, we shall simply say there are two groups—one using the "Carb-Smashers" diet plan, the other using the "Fat-Melters" diet plan. We will also stipulate that there are 100 dieters in each group (researchers would say, n = 100). After a given period of time—say, six months—the researchers will compare the mean weight loss of the two groups. Let's consider some possible outcomes:

Scenario #1:
Mean weight loss for Carb-Smashers – 11.6 pounds
Mean weight loss for Fat-Melters – 11.5 pounds

The question is, does one diet plan clearly work better than the other? In this case, simply eyeballing the numbers will tell you that there is no apparent difference. To be more technical, there seems to be no statistically significant difference. A difference that is statistically significant is one that defies random chance—that is, the difference is of such a magnitude that it must be due to the experimental treatment—in this case, the diet plan. But with a difference of only 0.1 pounds, it is pretty clear that the difference is not statistically significant—there is no basis for concluding that one diet plan is definitely more effective.

Scenario #2:
Mean weight loss for Carb-Smashers – 37.9 pounds
Mean weight loss for Fat-Melters – 2.6 pounds

Is this difference statistically significant? Well, you don't have to be a rocket scientist to conclude that Carb-Smashers is your more effective diet. All else being equal, and especially if it's equally healthful, Carb-Smashers is for me. With such an outcome, one does not need any technical knowledge of statistics—the answer is sitting right in front of you, plain as day. Because we have a difference here of over 35 pounds, we can reasonably assume that this difference is not due to random variation; instead, it must be due to the particular diet plans involved.

But, it's scenario #3 that is probably more common and certainly more troublesome.

Scenario #3:
Mean weight loss for Carb-Smashers – 18.3 pounds
Mean weight loss for Fat-Melters – 22.1 pounds

Now do we have a statistically significant difference? Frankly, the answer is not obvious. It seems like Fat-Melters might have a slight advantage, but random chance might be able to account for that. If you flip a coin 100 times, it will not come up heads exactly 50 of those times. Sometimes, just due to random chance, 58 of those 100 might be heads, or 43. So too with the diet plans. Even with random samples, the two groups of 100 people are not identical, and so there may be differences due to the people and not the diet plans. Perhaps Group A, just by the luck of the draw, has a few more people with less self-control when it comes to food. So, we need a way to figure out if this difference is truly statistically significant—statisticians to the rescue!

Here things get very technical and complex, but suffice it to say that in most studies where differences in mean scores are compared, three common comparisons are called a t-test, ANOVA (analysis of variance), and X2 (chi-square). What all of these three statistical procedures have in common is a way to provide a standard answer to this problem. They all have formulas—you can find these formulas in statistics texts. These days, you can even go on line and learn more about them.

If you ever read a research study in the original, you will likely see a dazzling array of numbers in many different forms. In comparing our scenario #3 results above, we could use a t-test. And if we did, you would see something in a research article that would look something like this:

$$t = 2.62, df (2,98), p = .04$$

What does this mean, you ask? Well, for our purposes, we're going to ignore the "t" value and that "df" stuff—although, for what it's worth, the "t" is the final result of the t-test formula (of doing the t-test computation), and the "df" stands for "degrees of freedom," which involves basically the size of the samples being compared. But, for our purposes, we only need to concern ourselves with the "p" value. Here, "p" stands for "probability," and it's really the critical number in that line of numbers. Why? Because it tells us *the likelihood of getting a difference of that size by sheer accident.* In this case, that chance is .04—in other words, 4 in 100. Normally, researchers will consider a difference to be *statistically* significant if p is less than .05 (or as they would say, p <.05). So, in scenario #3, even though the difference is modest (3.8 pounds, or 22.1-18.3), it is a difference that appears to be due to the diet plans. Notice that I say "appears," because we can never be totally certain. For example, if on one diet plan, the mean weight loss was 76.9 pounds, and on the other plan, it was 1.3 pounds, the "p" value would probably be something like p < .0001—in other words, the chances are less than 1 in 10,000 that a difference that great could happen by random chance. In other words, the "p" value will NEVER be zero, but sometimes really, really close to that. Anyway, the point is that researchers must invariably compare results between two or more groups, and the "p" value gives us an idea of whether the difference is statistically significant.

Now, it's really important to understand that the term here is *statistical* significance. If a difference is statistically significant, that does not mean it is significant in any other meaningful sense. Take, for instance, our diet plans in scenario #3. If I can lose, on average, 3.8 more pounds over six months using the Fat-Melters diet—but the Fat-Melters diet is three times as expensive as Carb-Busters, and has also been linked to kidney failure (purely hypothetical), then I think Carb-Busters starts to look a lot better, even if I am potentially less likely to lose as much weight. In other words, statistical significance has a narrow and technical meaning, and it should not be misconstrued. In fact, in one final attempt to confuse the heck out of you, it's worth noting that as sample sizes increase, it's easier to detect differences that are, technically, statistically significant. If we had only 10 people trying each of our diet plans, we'd need a pretty big difference in weight loss to conclude that one plan is definitely better. However, let's suppose we did a national study with two sample groups of 100,000 dieters each. In such a case, even if the difference in means between the two groups was rather slight (say, 3 pounds), it might very well work out to be statistically significant. To use the coin flip analogy, if I flipped a coin 10 times, and it came up heads 7 times (70 percent), we'd better be careful about what we conclude, since we only flipped the coin 10 times. On the other hand, if we flipped a coin 100,000 times, and it came up heads 55,000 times (only 55 percent), that would become statistically significant—because over that many flips, you would expect the numbers to be a bit more even (not identical, but more even).

Bottom line: be aware that standard formulas exist for determining statistical significance. Understand what the concept of statistical significance involves. Realize that sometimes, a statistically significant difference is well worth noting and taking seriously. But also realize that this is a statistical concept and may not be "significant" in other more important ways.

CONCLUSION

Studying statistics can easily be a course in itself, but this chapter attempts to highlight some of the key issues connected to the use of statistics in argument. Students of argument need to consider what can and can't be readily quantified; whether a precise number is necessarily better; what constitutes a representative sample; that there are three different types of "averages"; that comparing percentages can be problematic; that there is a difference between absolute and relative percentages; that correlation is not the same as causation; that statistical predictions for the future can be misleading; that graphs can be misleading; and what it means to say that a study has findings that are "statistically significant." Now that we have considered evidence, we can examine how people use evidence to draw conclusions—that's *reasoning*, and it's introduced in chapter 5.

REFERENCES

Best, Joel. *More damned lies and statistics: how numbers confuse public issues.* Berkeley, CA: University of California Press, 2004.

Jensen, J. Vernon. *Argumentation: Reasoning in communication.* New York: D. Von Nostrand, 1981.

Lapakko, David. 1997. Three cheers for language: A closer examination of a widely cited study of nonverbal communication. *Communication Education,* 46: 63-67.

Merriam, Alan. 1990. Words and numbers: Mathematical dimensions of rhetoric. *The Southern Communication Journal,* 55: 337-354.

Schmickle, Sharon. 2001. A life expectancy of 100? Not in our lifetimes. *Star Tribune,* February 19, 2001, pages A1/A10.

Chapter 5

TYPES OF REASONING

After reading this chapter, you should understand:

- The nature of inductive reasoning
- The nature of deductive reasoning
- The three main types of deductive syllogisms
- The difference between "truth" and "validity"
- The nature of reasoning by analogy
- The difference between literal, historical, and figurative analogies
- The nature of sign reasoning
- The nature of causal reasoning

Specialized terms to know:

- inductive reasoning
- deductive reasoning
- syllogism
- validity
- literal analogy
- historical analogy
- figurative analogy
- sign reasoning
- correlation
- causation

Once we get to the topic of reasoning, we are at the heart of the study of argumentation. **Reasoning, after all, is the way that we process information—in Toulmin terms, it's how we move from the data to the claim or conclusion.** Some treatments of the topic might lead you to believe that reasoning is something just to read about and to study—you know, "it's in a book somewhere." But reasoning is really an analysis of how you and I think—it's an examination of how our brains work. Seems to me that's worth studying.

Overall, we shall consider five types of reasoning: inductive, deductive, analogy, sign, and causal.

1. Inductive reasoning

Whether you knew it by this name or not, you have reasoned inductively thousands of times in your lifetime. **Inductive reasoning is reasoning from specific to general**—that is, you take specific bits of information and draw a general conclusion from them. Here are some examples of inductive reasoning:

- I hate broccoli, I hate cauliflower, I hate carrots—hey, I guess I hate vegetables!
- I met a man from Saudi Arabia who was a Muslim. I met a woman from the United Arab Emirates who was a Muslim. There are a lot of Muslims in the Middle East.
- Senator Clanghorne fell asleep during the Senate hearings. Senator Clanghorne believes that 8-year-olds should be allowed to vote. Senator Clanghorne wants bubble gum to be made illegal. Senator Clanghorne is an idiot.

In each case, you'll notice that certain bits of information are used to arrive at a much broader conclusion; that's what makes these trains of thought inductive. Of course, as suggested above, we generalize all the time—even this very sentence is a generalization! Because generalizations are pretty much never based on every case or situation (for example, you probably haven't tasted every vegetable there is, or met every person from the Middle East) inductive reasoning does involve a type of "leap." In that sense, **inductive reasoning has sometimes been likened to arithmetic**—that is, do all of the bits "add up" to justify the broader conclusion?

Moore and Parker (2007, 334) reinforce the idea that a "leap" is always involved with induction, using the example of recurrent flooding on the Gaudalupe River in Texas:

> Because inductive reasoning involves a prediction, the premises of an inductive argument at best *support* a conclusion with a degree of *probability*; they do *not* demonstrate or prove it with certainty. No prediction is 100 percent certain; even if the Guadalupe River had flooded every July in recorded history, it still wouldn't be 100 percent certain that it would flood again this July.

As discussed in chapter 1, some people are uncomfortable with the idea of "probability" as opposed to "certainty." They want to know something "for sure"—heaven forbid that we should deal in mere probabilities! But as I contended in that opening chapter, there are very few things in life that can be considered "absolute truth." However, I would go so far as to say that some inductive generalizations, even if they are not absolutely certain, can come pretty close! I am willing to claim that the sun will rise tomorrow, because it rose yesterday, and the day before that, and several billion consecutive days before that! Therefore, I for one have no problem with inductive generalizations, provided that they keep in mind the two keys to inductive reasoning discussed below.

Another way to view inductive reasoning would be to say that most social science research is largely inductive. Why? Because academic researchers gather a bunch of data—specific pieces of information, such as individual survey responses—and attempt to draw more general conclusions from them. If I survey 1,000 U.S. citizens about their opinions on solar energy, and if I then attempt to generalize about all 300 million Americans from that sample, I am making a leap from these specific instances to the population as a whole. That's the basic nature of inductive thought. Again, there is always the possibility that such a generalization is incorrect or unwarranted (that's why surveys, for example, include "margins of error"), but if they are done with care, inductive generalizations can definitely be both reasonable and convincing.

Since inductive reasoning relies on specific instances or examples as its foundation (see chapter 3), the tests for good inductive reasoning are really the same as for examples as evidence:

Test #1: Are there a sufficient number of examples on which to base the generalization?
Test #2: Are those examples representative?

So, good generalizations are based on a reasonable number of cases, and one can demonstrate that these cases are typical, not unusual.

2. Deductive reasoning

Deductive reasoning is essentially the "opposite" of inductive reasoning. It goes from general to specific. **People who reason**

deductively start from a general premise or idea and then apply that premise or idea to a specific situation. For example:

> Cats are easy to care for. (general premise or idea)
> Max is a cat. (specific situation)
> Therefore, Max will be easy to care for. (conclusion)

Again, it all begins with a general idea—that cats are easy to care for. Then that generalization can be applied to a variety of specific cats, including but not limited to our friend Max.

For whatever reason, logic courses seem to be obsessed with deductive reasoning, and a fair share of such courses involves a close examination of deduction. Logicians are fond of putting deductive lines of thought into a three-statement "proof" called a **syllogism**. The "cat" example above is basically in syllogistic form; only the first statement would be called the **major premise**, the second statement would be called the **minor premise**, and the third statement is called the **conclusion**.

To slightly complicate matters, there are three basic types of syllogisms. The first, called a **categorical** syllogism, is kind of what it sounds like—how things fit into categories or groups. For example:

> Major premise: All full-time students take at least three classes.
> Minor premise: Jeremy is a full-time student.
> Conclusion: Therefore, Jeremy takes at least three classes.

A second type of syllogism is called a **disjunctive** syllogism. This type has a major premise built around an "either/or" premise. For example:

> Major premise: Either you're a jock or a nerd.
> Minor premise: You're not a jock.
> Conclusion: Therefore, you're a nerd.

Later, when we deal with fallacies, I will try to caution you against "either/or" thinking. But suffice it to say that a disjunctive syllogism is built around an either/or premise. Finally, there are **conditional** syllogisms—their premise has an "if/then" form. For instance:

Major premise:	If I study hard, I'll get an A.
Minor premise:	I will study hard.
Conclusion:	Therefore, I will get an A.

Now if you think about it, you might realize that our brains often go back and forth between inductive and deductive trains of thought. For example, take the last illustration. Over a period of time—possibly many years—I may have discovered that I do better on exams when I study hard. I discovered that with a specific social studies exam in 10th grade, a specific math exam in 11th grade, and a specific English exam in 12th. Out of these specific experiences, I may have formed a generalization: that studying hard enables one to get an A. Now, that generalization may become a major premise for deductive reasoning, as the above example illustrates.

But, back to syllogisms. Frankly, this is a subject where one could feel very bogged down. If you examine a logic text—or even some argumentation or critical thinking texts—you will discover that there are a lot of technical rules for the proper construction of syllogisms. (For example, terms such as "affirming the consequent" and "denying the antecedent," and something called "truth tables" will appear in such texts.) Suffice it to say that syllogisms cannot be constructed just any old way—they must be put into proper form. For a categorical syllogism, that form would be:

Major premise:	All As are B.
Minor premise:	All Cs are A.
Conclusion:	Therefore, all Cs are B.

I think that you can sense why this format is correct and makes sense. For instance, we could say:

Major premise:	All amphibians (As) are cold-blooded (Bs).
Minor premise:	Salamanders (C) are amphibians (A).
Conclusion:	Therefore, salamanders (C) are cold-blooded (B).

On the other hand, we could not legitimately say:

Major premise:	Earl (C) is a mammal (B).
Minor premise:	Sheep (A) are mammals (B).
Conclusion:	Therefore, Earl (C) is a sheep (A).

In this example, Earl could be a human being, or some other type of mammal than a sheep. Just because Earl is a mammal, and that sheep are mammals, doesn't necessarily mean that Earl is a sheep. Because this syllogism is not properly constructed, the syllogism is not **valid.** Unfortunately, the term "validity" has multiple meanings—in chapter 4, I discussed another use of this term within social scientific research. However, **in the context of syllogisms, validity has to do with the *form* of the syllogism, whereas truth has to do with the *factual accuracy* of the syllogistic statements.** For example, here's a syllogism that's valid (the form is correct), but is probably untrue (not correct):

Major premise:	All argumentation students have six legs.
Minor premise:	Ashley is an argumentation student.
Conclusion:	Therefore, Ashley has six legs.

Again, you can stick in the As, Bs, and Cs and determine that this syllogism is exactly in correct form. It's valid, but not true. And, the conclusion of a syllogism can be true, but the syllogism itself may not be valid. To use a totally silly illustration:

Major premise:	All sheep are mammals.
Minor premise:	Earl is a sheep.
Conclusion:	Therefore, Sacramento is the capital of California.

Even if Sacramento is the capital, there's no way to arrive at that conclusion from the major and minor premises. So be aware of this distinction between "truth" and "validity."

I likened inductive reasoning to arithmetic. **Deductive reasoning has sometimes been associated with geometry.** Remember those geometric proofs? If you followed them correctly, step by step, you could solve the problem. Well, deductive reasoning is similar in the sense that **IF** the major premise is true, and **IF** the minor premise is true, and **IF** they are connected in a valid way, then the conclusion **HAS** to be correct, just like a geometric proof. So, to use perhaps the most famous syllogism of all time, IF all men are mortal, and IF Socrates is a man, then Socrates MUST be mortal. In inductive reasoning there is almost always that "leap" to the claim; in deductive reasoning, the conclusion is, shall we say, inevitable if the proper steps are followed. However, notice the very critical "ifs" in this paragraph—they become the central issue with deduction. (If I had a million dollars, I could buy a new Lexus, and if I was 7 feet tall, I could play in the NBA—but it's the "if" part that would be in question here! So too with deduction— I've got to be able to show that the "ifs" are really "correct.")

What, then, is the key to good deductive reasoning? Again, a logic text will give you a wide variety of issues to consider that relate to validity. But in real life and actual practice, I believe that the single biggest issue involves the major premise from which one is making inferences. If the major premise isn't sound, then everything that comes from it is also likely to be unsound. To use a computer analogy, a syllogism with a bad major premise is sort of like "garbage in, garbage out." So if your major premise is that "all argumentation students have six legs," you've got to know you're already in deep do-do, so to speak. Therefore, I believe that the key test for deductive reasoning is:

Test: Is the major premise sound?

Many times, people do operate from flawed major premises. Because major premises are simply generalizations, you can imagine a variety of generalizations that may be troublesome, such as:

- All men are emotionally retarded.
- If we have a wet spring, we'll have a wet summer.
- Either you're a friend of mine, or you're my enemy.

Each of these statements could be made into the major premise of a syllogism. But consider what vulnerable generalizations they are to work from. So, as appealing as deduction can be—because, like geometry it offers the promise of a definite answer—doing good deductive reasoning must be done with care.

3. Reasoning by analogy

Sometimes we think from specific to general. Sometimes we think from general to specific. And sometimes we think by comparing two or more things. That's what reasoning by analogy is all about—making comparisons and drawing conclusions based on those comparisons. For our purposes, let's look at three different types of analogies:

1. **Literal** analogies involve comparing things that are obviously in the same class or category. For example:

- Handgun control worked in Pittsburgh; therefore it will work in Buffalo. (comparison of one city to another city)
- State Tech regrets watering down its foreign language requirements, so we at State U should not water down our language requirements. (comparison of one college to another college)
- The Bears couldn't make the playoffs without an established NFL quarterback, so neither can the Lions. (comparing two football teams)

2. **Historical** analogies are a particular type of literal analogy in which two or more time periods are compared. Because historical analogies are used so often, I'm giving them their own category here. Examples of historical analogies:

- This economic period reminds me of what was happening in the late 1920s, just before the big stock market crash of 1929. We'd better be careful!
- This brings back memories of when I was all stressed out in junior high school. To deal with all that stress, I ate myself silly and gained 20 pounds. Now the stress is even worse--I feel another extra wad of fat is about to form!
- We'd better not send U.S. troops to Slobovia, because remember what happened in the 1960s when we started sending troops to Vietnam!

The last example above—"military" in nature—deserves a bit of special attention. For better or worse, our previous military history has been used over and over as a way to either justify or oppose a variety of foreign policy decisions. To this day, some advocates will use Adolph Hitler as an object lesson—the most common argument is that we learned with Hitler that aggression cannot be ignored, and that a dictator cannot be placated. Hence, removing someone like Saddam Hussein from Iraq was warranted and necessary. However, the war in Vietnam has also been used repeatedly in our arguments about foreign policy—most commonly as an argument *against* military involvement in far-flung parts of the world. In the case of Vietnam, the argument goes that such wars are ultimately "un-winnable," and so we should not get bogged down in any similar conflicts. From this perspective, military involvement in Iraq was just another Vietnam, only 35 or so years later. As with any "controversial" issue mentioned in this text, I am not here to adjudicate or "take sides" on these sorts of disputes, but only to point out that historical analogies are very common in arguments surrounding U.S. foreign policy. Of course, it should also be stressed that historical analogies are hardly limited to war-and-peace issues. For example, our nation's experience roughly a century ago with trying to legally ban the sale and consumption of alcohol—the "prohibition" movement—is used to this day as an argument against trying to ban other things, whether those things be guns, cigarettes, or drugs. The basic argument goes, if prohibition of alcohol didn't work, then how could we prohibit other widely-used substances or products?

3. **Figurative** analogies are a distinct type of analogy. When making a figurative analogy, arguers are well aware that they are comparing things from different categories, but either (a) they see some important similarities in the comparison, and/or (b) they are making this comparison because it has some emotional or persuasive impact. Although a logician would probably say that figurative analogies are the weakest form of proof, they often carry a good deal of "rhetorical" or persuasive weight because they can be vivid, and memorable. Examples of figurative analogies:

- The people of the United States are like a flower garden. In a garden, you can't give all the plants the same amount of water, or light, or fertilizer. Each plant has its own unique needs. So too with people: we can't and we shouldn't treat them all exactly the same.
- Your body is like an automobile engine. If you don't give your car fresh oil and plenty of fuel it will cease to operate. If *you* don't get some fresh air and a little protein, *you* will cease to operate.
- Global terrorism is like cancer. If you have cancer, you can't just eat well, take vitamins, and get plenty of sleep—you need to do something decisive. You need to cut the tumor out if you can, or go through chemotherapy—but you need to take strong action. It's the same with terrorism—this cancer will not go away with meditation or peaceful thoughts.

These examples of figurative analogies illustrate their potential appeal, even if from a strict logical standpoint the comparisons probably lack something. That's how it is with figurative analogies—they are appealing but can be misleading. Why? Well, it comes down to the key test for any analogy—literal, historical, or figurative: is what you are comparing actually *comparable*? And so the test for reasoning by analogy becomes:

Test: Are the things in an analogy that are being compared similar in important ways?

If you can't show similarities between the cities or historical periods or whatever you are comparing, your analogical reasoning is in trouble. That's why figurative analogies in particular demand a high burden of proof, if you will—we would need to know, for example, why comparing the U.S. economy to a rattlesnake is really sensible and appropriate. But literal and historical analogies can be no less problematic. For example, with all the discussion these days about "global warming," some have argued that if we could build a nuclear weapon in just a few years (the Manhattan Project in World War II) or put a man on the moon within a span of ten years (the Apollo Program), then we should also be able to stop global warming with a similar dedicated effort. But as Bill McKibben (2007, 35) has argued,

> [The Manhattan Project and the Apollo Program] analogies don't really work. They demanded the intense concentration of money and intelligence on a single rather small niche in our technosphere. Now [with global warming] we need almost the opposite: a commitment to take what we already know how to do and somehow spread it into every corner of our economies, and indeed our most basic activities. It's as if NASA's goal had been to put all of us on the moon.

In other words, McKibben is saying that analogies to these other projects are flawed because these other situations are too dissimilar to the nature of the challenge with global warming.

In the end, with respect to reasoning by analogy, the main thing to remember is that old saying, "You can't compare apples and oranges." If you do, then sometimes the fruits of your intellectual labor will be wasted (sorry for that truly hideous pun).

4. Sign reasoning

Sign reasoning involves reasoning by connecting things that are observable—that is, looking at visible signs, and drawing some sort of "cause-and-effect" connection. We use sign reasoning all the time. For example:

- I ate a barrel of pork rinds, and then I gained a few pounds. I'm startin' to think that those pork rinds are fattening.
- Oh look—a lucky star! I'm going to have a great day tomorrow.
- Jerry always looks kinda jittery. But of course, he's always got that cup of coffee in his hand.

In each of these examples, two things have been linked through observable phenomena. Some such links may be dubious—I'm not sure how seeing a lucky star, for example, ensures good fortune the following day. In fact, most "superstitions" are built around dubious sign reasoning—if I personally walk under a ladder or break a mirror, I do not think they will influence my fortunes, even though some people do. On the other hand, important human discoveries—in science and medicine, for example—began as sign observations. Some doctors began to notice that heavy smokers seemed to have more heart and lung problems than non-smokers—in their minds, there was a connection. Ditto for meteorologists, who noticed that if there was a red sky at night, the weather would be nice the next day ("red sky at night, sailor's delight," as the saying goes). Even in these more credible, scientific examples, **a key point is that sign reasoning cannot and does not explain *why* there is a relationship or connection.** It simply says, in essence, that I see two things happening, and I believe that one may be responsible for the other. As Fearnside (1997, 202) observes,

> Though the ancients did not know what made the tide rise and fall, they took it into account in sailing. Though no one in the Middle Ages could explain how land left fallow could regain some productive power, the three-field system was developed and used. Though the members of the Brit-

ish Parliament did not understand why lime juice helped prevent scurvy, they decided to require that it be served to British seamen.

So, sign reasoning is often a vital precursor to figuring out why "A causes B." But again, because sign reasoning only deals with observable signs or symptoms, and because it can't explain why there might be a connection, it is the less desirable form of causal reasoning. So let's move to what you might call true causal reasoning.

5. Causal reasoning

Causal reasoning is like sign reasoning in the sense that it alleges a connection between two or more things—for example, that automobiles contribute to the "greenhouse effect," that lack of sleep causes more head colds, that juvenile delinquency is mainly due to genetic factors. The difference is that causal reasoning can identify a "causal link"—that is, it can explain the "why" part, unlike sign reasoning. Often, the causal link is something that is not observable. For instance, one might observe that people who eat diets that are high in saturated fats are more likely to suffer heart attacks, but why? It's only when you get inside the body (either surgically, or by x-ray) to see those clogged arteries that you see the real source of the problem. Why is the "red sky at night a sailor's delight"? Again, the answer is not the "red" part, in the sense that if you wanted nice weather the next day, spraying red paint in the sky will not ensure it. Rather, the "real" causes of the weather are those things that meteorologists talk about that we can't even see: the dewpoint, the jetstream, the high pressure ridge, and so on. So, causal reasoning can identify the causal factor. Many academic and scientific studies are geared to doing just that: providing an explanation for why things happen as they do. Still, sign reasoning and causal reasoning really share the same test:

Test for sign and causal reasoning: is the relationship being expressed one of correlation or causation?

You have already been exposed to this idea to some extent in chapter 4, in the discussion of statistical correlations. To cite a silly example, you might consider that there is a definite correlation between professional football and the weather. When the

NFL season begins, the weather is warm pretty much everywhere. But, as the season progresses—especially as we get into November and December—the weather gets progressively colder in many places. This is proof, most definitely, that football causes winter! Of course, we really only have a correlation here: two things that vary in a predictable way in relation to one another. Although you are not likely to be fooled by this football example, there are many other "real world" situations where the correlation/causation issue is really critical. Take, for example, the rather "touchy" issue of pornography and its relation to sexual assault. Once again, I am not here to take sides on this controversy, but merely to point out how the correlation/causation issue comes into play. Many times, convicted sex offenders are found to have a large collection of pornography in their possession. So, it is not surprising that many people take a rather strict "causal" view of this matter—that is, people buy pornography, they consume the images, and they are therefore influenced to sexually assault others. This position may be correct; again, I do not know. But there is another alternative explanation which is built more around correlation. Basically, that argument goes, people who are sex offenders have one "hidden" but very real cause for their behavior: more than any other factor, it is being sexually assaulted as a child that is responsible. Such childhood experiences propel these people into a life of sexual deviance. Now, as a reflection of that pre-existing deviance, they may buy and possess a lot of pornography—but from this perspective, the pornography is merely a symptom of someone who is sexually deviant, not the cause. From this point of view, if, hypothetically, rapists smoke more cigarettes than non-rapists, we should not draw the conclusion that smoking causes rape. And so, the two sides argue this issue back and forth. They seldom call it a debate between causation and correlation, but it really is.

THE "SI JINX": A CASE STUDY

A good "everyday" example of the debate between correlation and causation involves what has come to be known as the "Sports Illustrated Jinx." This jinx, so the story goes, is that if a well-known athlete is featured on the cover of the magazine one week, sometime soon that same athlete—often being celebrated for his or her accomplishments—will lose the big game, get injured, or otherwise have some hardship or disaster befall them. And, for a magazine that goes all the way back to 1954, one can imagine that "bad things" have indeed happened to people featured on the cover. One of the more graphic examples: in 1958, after *SI* put a promising Olympic figure skater on the cover, the entire U.S. figure skating team died in a plane crash. More commonly, of course, the issue involves an athlete or team that seems to "choke" after being featured on the cover of the magazine. In 1970, the Minnesota Vikings were featured, favored to win that year's Super Bowl by two touchdowns. But the following week (as I remember all too well!), the Vikes lost to Kansas City, 23-7. After baseball player Barry Bonds was featured on an *SI* cover in 1993, his batting average went down 40 points in the following two weeks.

Because the *Sports Illustrated* Jinx has become such a well-known belief (or, superstition, depending on your point of view), the magazine itself decided to do an extensive cover story on this phenomenon. *SI's* January 21, 2002 issue included a black cat on the cover, with the question, "Is the SI Jinx for Real?" The cover story, written by Alexander Wolff, was the product of a rather ambitious project. Two *Sports Illustrated* researchers took over six months to analyze all 2,456 covers of the magazine, going all the way back to its first issue in 1954. Then, using some fairly reasonable criteria, they attempted to determine how often someone who was featured on the cover had some sort of "misfortune" soon thereafter. The result? They determined that "of the 2,456 covers *SI* had run, 913 featured a person who, or team that, suffered some verifiable misfortune...a Jinx rate of 37.2%." Further, they noted that the majority of those "misfortunes" were "bad losses or lousy performances by a team, followed by declines in individual performance, bad loss or lousy performance by an individual, postseason failure, injury or death, and blunder or bad play."

So, the question still remains, what are we to make of this finding? If 37 percent of the individuals or teams had something "bad" happen to them after appearing on the *SI* cover, does that mean that the jinx is for real? The answer may be a little more complicated than you might want it to be.

On the one hand, it is very tempting to simply call these unfortunate performances "a coincidence." After all, the performances of individuals and teams will vary, and so we shouldn't be surprised if this results in a "bad" outcome 37 percent of the time. Put another way, teams will lose whether they are on the cover of a magazine or not—just because they were on the cover may well have no causal connection to their performance. I suppose the notion that it's "just a coincidence" is the most intuitively appealing. Also, part of what may be going on here is what statisticians would call "regression to the mean." That's a fancy way of saying this: whether it be football, or bowling, or golf, people who go on a "hot streak" are prone to return to more "normal" performance. (It works the other way, too: if your bowling average is 150 and you roll a 93, chances are good that your next score will be higher than 93.) Often, the reason why athletes wind up on the cover of *SI* is because they have been on one of those "hot streaks"—so much so that it's newsworthy. But even "star" players can only play "over their head" for so long; after a hot streak, they will almost inevitably "fall back" a bit. That falling back should not be interpreted as a "jinx."

On the other hand, it is certainly possible to argue that these events are not merely coincidental—that is, being on the cover of the best-known sports magazine in America may have some causal effect on an athlete's or a team's performance. And if you think about it, that's not such a crazy idea. As the *SI* article itself notes, "Being on the cover changes the way people see themselves, and . . . they're supposed to be superstars now, and if they don't live up to that, they've somehow failed. This changing perception causes many athletes to feel pressure and have a much harder time achieving their ideal performance." In other words, there may be a "psychological" factor entering in here: for some athletes and some teams, being on the cover and getting all that attention might affect their psyche is a way that makes them perform worse. Not only that, but it's possible that once all the opposing teams see that a particular individual or team is being featured as "stellar," they might well want to play a bit harder against them, simply to "put them in their place." So that could be a sort of "causal" factor as well.

In the end, there really is no way to "prove" that one interpretation is absolutely superior to the other. Perhaps if we could construct a time machine and take these people *off* of the *SI* cover and compare the results afterward, we might be able to know—but that, obviously, is not exactly feasible! But again, the point is that people can and will argue about whether two events are causally related, or merely a coincidental "sign" relationship.

Understanding the difference between causation and correlation is a critical skill, and one that every liberal arts college graduate ought to know well. In the end, causality must be demonstrated, not assumed. And, I might close by saying that although arguers make strong cases for causal relationships every day, causality is difficult to "prove." Any one problem or phenomenon could be caused by a wide variety of factors. What causes crime: Genetics? Parenting styles? Our schools? Peer pressure? The media? Cultural forces? Economic factors? The list is pretty much endless. And so when it comes to making a casual statement, it's important to have the kind of evidence, reasoning, and analysis that will enable the receiver to agree with you.

CONCLUSION

Reasoning involves how we think—it describes the mental processes that we use to make particular claims from particular evidence. There are five main types of reasoning: inductive reasoning, deductive reasoning, reasoning by analogy, sign reasoning, and causal reasoning. Now that you have a basic understanding of the various types of reasoning, we must investigate specific ways in which these thought processes can go awry. That's the focus of chapter 6.

REFERENCES

Fearnside, W. Ward. *About thinking*, 2nd ed. Upper Saddle River, NJ: Prentice Hall, 1997.

McKibben, Bill. 2007. Carbon's new math. *National Geographic*, 212: 33-37.

Moore, Brooke Noel and Richard Parker. *Critical thinking*, 8th ed. Boston: McGraw-Hill, 2007.

Wolff, Alan. 2002. Old black magic. *Sports Illustrated*, January 21, 2002, 50-62.

Chapter 6

FALLACIES IN REASONING

After reading this chapter, you should understand:

- What constitutes "fallacious" reasoning
- 25 different fallacies in reasoning

Specialized terms to know:

- hasty generalization
- fallacy of composition
- fallacy of division
- false dilemma
- *post hoc ergo propter hoc*
- *argumentum ad ignorantiam*
- begging the question
- *non sequitur*
- *argumentum ad hominem*
- *argumentum ad populum*
- *argumenum ad verecundiam*
- *argumentum ad misericordiam*
- *argumentum ad baculum*

- *argumentum ad crumenum*
- *argumentum ad lazarum*
- *reductio ad absurdum*
- "straw man" argument
- equivocation
- the line-drawing fallacy
- slippery slope argument
- two wrongs make a right
- perfect solution fallacy
- historian's fallacy
- gambler's fallacy
- red herring

Anyone who graduates from a college or university without an awareness and understanding of fallacies in reasoning has been educationally shortchanged. The world of fallacies is interesting and useful, and you should see its connection to everyday situations you yourself encounter.

Many of these fallacies have Latin names. I suppose the best I can say here is that when you use the Latin, you will impress people—telling your parents that their view exemplifies the fallacy of *post hoc ergo propter hoc* might at least lead them to believe that their tuition money is having *some* results! For certain fallacies, there is a Latin name, but it is not commonly used—so I am only using the Latin when I think it's necessary and appropriate. (For example, one fallacy, begging the question, also goes by the Latin name *petitio principii*—but I don't think ANYONE really uses that term!) Finally, do not be overwhelmed by the Latin—learning these terms is manageable; you really do have the brainpower to learn them. Indeed, many sound like what they are, such as the *ad populum* fallacy we'll examine later.

But, I'm getting ahead of myself. The first question ought to be, what exactly is a fallacy, anyway? If you were to consult a dictionary, you'd find that the word is derived from the Latin *fallere*, meaning "to deceive." So one way to think about fallacies is that they are deceptive—they deceive the receiver into thinking something that they should not. Some people would equate fallacies with "mistakes" or "errors" in reasoning. That's not an inappropriate view either, although I might qualify it a little. Fallacies reflect a poor thought *process*—a way of thinking and reaching a conclusion that is vulnerable, and based on weak premises or assumptions. Of course, if you employ a poor thought process, you are usually going to wind up with a bad product or answer. Still, every once in a while, people can think in this manner and by sheer luck wind up with the correct answer. Take, for instance, the first fallacy in this chapter, the hasty generalization. Normally, we do not want to generalize on the basis of just a few examples—that's what the fallacy is all about. Nonetheless, there are times when we have all generalized on the basis of just a couple of examples, and it turns out that our generalization seems to be correct. So, are fallacies "errors," plain and simple? I'd be inclined to say that they represent ways of thinking that are more likely to *lead* to errors. It's just that every once in a while, people can think in these ways and still come up with the right answer—sort of like in your math class, when you happened to get the right answer, but in a totally incorrect way! But, just so I'm clear about this, fallacious reasoning is normally not to be encouraged. If I can make it real simple, let me say, FALLACIES: BAD.

With this as a backdrop, we can now begin to look at specific fallacies. I want to make it clear that in the literature on argument, and on logic, there is no absolute uniformity in the way these fallacies are labeled, defined, or treated. As Wilson (1999, 202) contends, "there is nothing especially systematic about any list of named fallacies. However they are organized, such lists are little more than casseroles made up of folk wisdom that has accumulated over the centuries." Although this statement may go a bit too far (mere "casseroles"? just a collection of "folk wisdom"?), it is the case that every source treats fallacies a little differently. You may indeed be motivated to look in other sources to see what types of different treatment there are.

FALLACIES IN INDUCTIVE REASONING

Hasty generalization

This fallacy does have a technical name that's used sometime: the fallacy of converse accident. As noted above, a hasty generalization is an inductive generalization made on the basis of too few cases. For example:

- *"The other day, I saw Leo jogging in the park—that guy must be a real fitness freak!"*
- *"When we got to Phoenix, it was pouring rain! Why would I ever want to live in a place with a climate like* **that***?"*
- *"Your Aunt Maude gave me a piece of cake—what a nice person she is!"*

The reality is that unless we see Leo a lot, we have no idea how typical this jogging behavior is. It's too soon to generalize. Leo might spend most of his time as one of those fabled Couch Potatoes. And just because it was raining in Phoenix on the night you arrived, it does not mean they have a lot of monsoons in Arizona! And Aunt Maude could be a really annoying person—don't let that one piece of cake fool you. The hasty generalization is one of the easiest fallacies to understand and also one of the most common. When you base a very broad conclusion on a very small sample you are providing weak support for that conclusion.

Fallacy of composition

This fallacy involves how we move from specific to general. In this way of thinking, we falsely assume that what is true of each part is true of the whole, when the parts are put together. That ain't necessarily so. For example:

- *Every part of a Honda Accord is made out of a new lightweight metal alloy—therefore, I should be able to lift my Honda out of a snowbank."*

- *"Since human beings are mortal, that means the human race must someday come to an end." (Just because each* **individual** *will die doesn't mean that the race as a* **whole** *must die.)*

With both of these statements, the person is assuming that what's true of each part is also true of the whole. Another more "practical" example from communication studies: in small group communication courses, you will often learn about something called the "assembly effect." It simply means that groups do not necessarily function as each individual does. Jane may be nice; Tim may be nice; Sasha may be nice; and Herb may be nice; but that doesn't necessarily mean they will be a nice *group*—what's true of the parts may not be true of the whole.

One final example of a fallacy of composition relates to education, and some of your instructors are not going to like me for mentioning this! One of the trendy concepts in education these days is the idea of having *rubrics*—that is, a set of categories used to evaluate student work. For example, if someone gives a classroom speech, the rubric might include: up to 5 points for the introduction, up to 5 for organization, up to 10 for delivery, up to 10 for evidence, and so on. Then, the thinking is that if we add the points in each of these categories, we can arrive at a total score that accurately reflects the speech as a whole. Well, maybe—but maybe not! Again, the whole is not *necessarily* the sum of its parts—if, for example, your introduction was so offensive to the audience that the rest of the speech was a "lost cause," then the "introduction" category has been seriously undervalued. So, I would contend that most educational rubrics—although certainly widely-used and defensible in many ways—do potentially raise the issue of the relationship of the parts to the whole.

FALLACIES IN DEDUCTIVE REASONING

Fallacy of division

A fallacy of division is essentially the opposite of a fallacy of composition—in this case, falsely assuming what's true of the whole is true of each individual part. For example:

- *"The Johnsons are always fighting—I'd hate to meet someone from* **that** *family in a dark alley!"*
- *"What a huge hotel! The rooms must be enormous."*

- *"The French are so cultured—I bet Pierre goes to the opera at least once a month!"*

In each case, what is true of the whole may not be true of the individual parts. The Johnsons may quarrel as a group, but that doesn't necessarily mean that each member of the Johnson family is belligerent. Just because the entire hotel building is large does not mean that each individual room is large. France may be a very "cultured" nation in general, but that won't apply to every single person in Paris. Or, a quick "food" example: sometimes a packaged food product can, as a whole, taste "pure and natural"—but sometimes you'll be surprised to read the not-so-all-natural individual ingredients on the side panel!

False dilemma

Remember disjunctive syllogisms from chapter 5? Those are the kind whose major premise is of the "either/or" variety. A false dilemma involves presenting two possible alternatives (an either/or situation) in a way that is inappropriate or misleading—in other words, a false dilemma is a flawed disjunctive syllogism.

As suggested in chapter 5, "either/or" thinking can be troublesome. It's not always fallacious by any means, but there are often more than two alternatives. The following are examples of false dilemmas:

- *"You are either part of the problem, or you are part of the solution."* (Can't you possibly be some of both?)
- *"America—love it or leave it."* (A popular bumper sticker from the old days—either love everything in America—or move to Russia!)
- *"Get a college education and become a success, or stay out of school and become a complete failure."* (If only it were that simple!)
- *"Either we legalize drugs, or we keep building more new prisons and keep filling them with all kinds of drug offenders."* (Can you think of other options?)

Not too long ago, I saw a poster advertising a discussion event on the truthfulness of the Bible—the heading said, "Word of God—or mountains of gibberish?" Clearly, it seems to me, there are some other alternatives here—that is, even if the Bible is not considered the literal "word of God" in every sense, the only other alternative is not to consider it as "mountains of gibberish." That's a false dilemma. In general, be careful when you are presented with only two alternatives.

FALLACY IN CAUSAL REASONING

Post hoc ergo propter hoc (literally, "after this, therefore because of this")

The *post hoc* fallacy is one of the most common, and one of the most important. Fortunately, it's easy to understand, too. With this fallacy, one falsely assumes that if B follows A, then B was caused by A. So, I go to the dentist to get a root canal, and then a couple of hours later I get a massive headache. Did the first cause the second? Maybe—but maybe not. The big problem is assuming that the first caused the second. For example:

- *"Shortly after Gertrude started dating Chad, she developed an ulcer—that man is going to be the death of her yet!"*
- *"Mildred got her car washed, and then the thunderstorm hit— doesn't she know any better than that?"*
- *"The Milwaukee Brewers moved into a new stadium, and then they started to win lots of games. Why didn't they build that stadium sooner?"* (Just because more wins came after moving into the new stadium does not necessarily mean that the stadium is responsible.)

In politics, this fallacy seems especially common. Teneesha Williams is elected mayor of Smallville, and then the crime rate goes up in the next year. What a horrible job she's doing! Well, there are a number of possible reasons why crime may have increased, many of which have nothing to do with the mayor. So again, it's unwise to assume that the first event caused the second. The key here, as you learned in chapter 5, is to be able to provide the "causal link"—in this case, something specific that Mayor Williams did or didn't do that might have contributed to the crime rate.

FALLACIES INVOLVING THE BURDEN OF PROOF

Argumentum ad ignorantiam

As implied in chapter 1, when people make arguments, they face a burden of proof. They must provide sufficient evidence to lead us to agree. In the case of *argumentum ad ignorantiam*, this burden is ignored in one of two ways:

(a) assuming something is **true** because it has not been proven **false**, or
(b) assuming something is **false** because it has not been proven **true**

> **Examples of (a) would be something like:**
> - *"No one can disprove that raspberries cause cancer, so they must."*
> - *"You can't disprove that there's a God, so that means there is."*
>
> **Examples of (b) would be:**
> - *"Jack absolutely did not commit that burglary, because the jury found him innocent."*
> - *"Herbal remedies can never work, because a recent study didn't show that they could."*

In each case, someone is drawing a conclusion that is based on a rather "extreme" assumption of what can or can't be demonstrated, especially in form (a) of this fallacy, which would enable me to say something like, "Those strange lights in the sky were an alien craft, since no one's been able to prove otherwise." And the second form, (b), would lead us to a premature conclusion such as, "There isn't any intelligent life on other planets because no one has clearly demonstrated that there is."

So how should we deal with a situation where the evidence is limited? As Bassham et al. (2008, 149) note, "When we lack evidence for or against a claim, it is usually best to suspend judgment—to admit that we just don't know. When an arguer treats a lack of evidence as reason to think that a claim is true or false, he or she commits the fallacy of appeal to ignorance." Again, if you think about it, ignorance is an odd and questionable premise for a claim.

Begging the question

This is another very important fallacy, but one that's a little harder to grasp for some. At the heart of begging the question is "proving" an assertion by simply repeating or rephrasing it. Kahane and Cavender (2006, 60) define this fallacy as "A. Therefore, A." For example:

- *"American products are superior to Japanese products because they are comparatively better."* (If you think about it, that statement really says nothing—something is "superior" because it's "better"?)
- *"Skydiving is dangerous because it's unsafe."* (This **sounds** like a reason, but it really isn't.)
- *"Billy is right because he's never wrong."* (Again, don't be fooled by a statement like this, even if it's said with confidence.)

Another form involves a "circular" type of reasoning, in which the person assumes as a premise the very conclusion they intend to prove, sometimes called "arguing in a circle." For example:

- *"We know we can trust* National Tattler *magazine, because it says on the cover that it's 'the most reliable magazine in America.'"*

Still another form of this fallacy is when people use premises that are more asserted than proven. For instance:

- "When are we going to stop wasting money in our bloated foreign aid budget?" *(In this case, it has neither been demonstrated to this point that money is being "wasted" or that the budget is "bloated"—simply* **saying** *it does not make it so, and that begs the question.)*

So, begging the question takes many forms, and it may take you a while to detect them and fully grasp this fallacy—but in time you will! As Ruggiero (2004, 118) aptly notes, begging the question can have a subtlety to it that is connected to how we use language. As he observes,

> If someone says, "Divorce is on the rise today because more marriages are breaking up," few people would fail

to see the circularity. But consider the same sentence in expanded form: "The rate of divorce is appreciably higher in the present generation than it was in previous generations. Before a reason can be adduced for this trend, a number of factors must be considered, including the difference in the average age at which a couple marries. However, most experts tend to believe that the cause is the increased number of failed marriages." Same circular argument but more difficult to detect. The point is not that writers deliberately construct circular arguments but that such arguments can develop without our being aware of them.

Finally, just so you know, the term begging the question is often used on TV and in newspapers these days—unfortunately, when they use it, 99 percent of the time they are not using it "correctly," at least in the way logicians use it. A sportscaster will say something like, "Their star quarterback is injured, which begs the question, will they be able to win without him on Sunday?" Used in this manner, "begs the question" merely means "*leads* to the question," a totally different meaning, and not what's being discussed here.

OTHER FALLACIES

There are a wide array of other fallacies that are identified in the literature, and here we shall highlight some of the best-known and most important.

Non sequitur

To make your life a little more difficult, it could be argued that virtually every fallacy discussed in this chapter is a form of *non sequitur*. After all, literally *non sequitur* means "does not follow." Therefore, anytime one thing does not follow from another, in a certain sense it is a *non sequitur*. So, one could contend that any of the fallacies discussed to this point involve situations where one thing does not follow from another. However, in common usage, the *non sequitur* label is usually reserved for situations where the data and the claim just don't seem to connect. For example:

- *"The public schools just aren't doing their job anymore—no wonder our kids are all strung out on drugs."*

In this case, what the first half of the sentence has to do with the second is, shall we say, difficult to determine. When people say things that seem "off the wall," the concept is also probably relevant. For instance:

- *"Identity theft crimes are revolting, which just goes to show you why Abraham Lincoln should never have been elected President in the first place."* (I dare you to make a connection between those two ideas!)

Argumentum ad hominem

Sometimes personal attacks take the place of substantive argument. If they do, then the *ad hominem* fallacy may be relevant. With *ad hominem* ("to the person") you hope to discredit a person's idea by throwing rhetorical mud at them. For example:

- *"Don't put any stock in her views on deficit spending—she spent seven yearsvisiting a psychiatrist!"* or
- *"Don't support his stand on family issues because he's a male chauvanist pig."*

In each case, one is really running down the person more than their ideas. It is worth noting, however, that people will argue about whether this fallacy is even relevant or applicable in the first place. As Bierman & Assali (1996, 173) explain,

> In some cases, a person's characteristics, motives or circumstances are relevant to the acceptability of her claims. For example, being a psychotic or a compulsive liar are surely relevant to the credibility of a person's statements. Thus, lawyers who impeach the testimony of witnesses by questioning their character or motives are not always committing fallacies.

In a similar vein, Rottenberg (1988, 195) contends:

> Accusations against the person do not constitute a fallacy if the characteristics under attack are relevant to the argument. If the politician is irresponsible and dishonest in the conduct of his or her personal life, we may be justified

in thinking that the person will also behave irresponsibly and dishonestly in public office.

Nonetheless, we are in yet another "grey area" with respect to what constitutes a fallacy. For example, when President Clinton was implicated for having an affair with Monica Lewinsky, some shouted, "*Ad hominem!*" In short, they were saying, "The President's personal life is none of your business—it has nothing to do with public policy." On the other hand, some people said, "No—you don't get it. The President's personal life is relevant here—he represents this nation and its moral values, and so this type of behavior IS relevant, especially if he is being deceptive." Again, I am not here to adjudicate this dispute—merely to say that some people see fallacies in some situations while others don't.

Argumentum ad populum

Did your mother ever say to you, "If everyone ELSE jumped off the Golden Gate bridge, would you do it too?" Well, the next time she does, you can say, "Mom, you're bringing up the *ad populum* fallacy." What she's trying to tell you is that just because the majority believes or does something, that does not automatically make it "right" or "true." (Literally, *ad populum* means "to the people.") So, for instance:

- *"Polls show that more than 80 percent of the American people want certain books banned in the schools—we need censorship now!"*

Again, just because the majority supports something does not necessarily make it right. However, it's worth noting that in a democratic society, we often attach a lot of weight to public opinion—"public support" for an idea is a very common argument, often a very persuasive one, and frequently worth considering. And if, for example, if you wanted to convince me that "reality shows" on TV attract a lot of interest, then public opinion polls would be quite appropriate as evidence. But, in many situations, don't just assume that the more who believe something, the more correct they necessarily are. That assumption would lead us to absurd statements such as:

- *"There are more adherents of Religion X in the world than Religion Y, so Religion X must be the **true** religion."*

Argumentum ad verecundiam

This fallacy has been discussed in two different ways: (a) inappropriate appeal to *tradition,* or (b) inappropriate appeal to *authority.* Inappropriate appeal to tradition would be something like:

- *"It is better to wash dishes by hand than by washing them in a dishwasher because we have been washing dishes by hand for centuries."*

Just because something has been done for a long time doesn't automatically make it "true" or "correct." Using that standard, all manner of despicable human behavior could be condoned because "it's always been that way." So, in and of itself, "tradition" is not necessarily considered a strong rationale. As for (b), inappropriate appeal to authority, just about any TV commercial featuring a celebrity would be relevant here. For instance:

- *Whitney Houston says that Dell Computers are the best on the market—why, I'm going to ask my folks to buy me one of those!"*

As much as we might like Whitney Houston (or Ben Affleck or Jennifer Aniston or Denzel Washington), most celebrities have no specialized knowledge of computers that makes them more credible than the famous imaginary character, Joe Schmoe. But this fallacy is not limited to movie stars. If, for instance, your state's governor sounds off about the impact of day care on kids, but has no background in child development matters, the same fallacy would apply. Or, if one of your communication professors contends that solar power is seriously flawed, you'd want to know more about their background—simply having, say, a Ph.D. in one field does not make someone an expert in others.

Argumentum ad misericordiam

If I can get you to feel pity for me, is that sufficient reason to agree with me? According to *argumentum ad misericordiam,* the answer is no. This fallacy involves an inappropriate appeal to pity. For example:

- *"Gee, Professor Einstein—I had the flu for two weeks, and I broke up with my boyfriend last month. Don't you think you could give me a little higher grade in this course?"*
- *"We should vote for Smith because his wife died just a few weeks ago and so he needs to know that we care."*

However, this is not to say that appeals to pity cannot "work," in the persuasive sense. Many times people will respond to the pitiful situation of others and grant them favors or special considerations as a result. But from a strictly logical standpoint, appeals to pity are in some ways both irrelevant and insufficient as grounding points for a logically-satisfying argument.

To make matters more complicated, however, not all appeals to pity may be regarded as fallacious. In fact, Douglas Walton (1997) has written an entire book on this one fallacy! His conclusion? Walton believes that "There are some cases, like charitable appeals—for example, requests for funding for medical research to aid or relieve the distress of afflicted children—where the *ad misericordiam* type of argument is used in a reasonable, or at least nonfallacious way" (xiii).

Watson believes that there are some types of appeals, such as charity drives, where appeals to pity may be condoned, while in other cases (he specifically mentions students who seek a higher grade in a course because otherwise they will suffer financially or academically) an appeal to pity is largely inappropriate. Does all of this mean that the Jerry Lewis Labor Day Telethon is ethically defensible, but that a "save the baby seals" campaign with gory photos of seals being clubbed to death is not? Unfortunately, there is no "absolute right or wrong answer" here, and so arguers must make their case either way and hope it's convincing. In other words, some pity appeals may be defensible, while others may not be.

Argumentum ad baculum

If pity isn't acceptable as argument, then neither is force. *Argumentum ad baculum* involves inappropriate appeals to force or the threat of force to cause acceptance of a conclusion. As such, they are a type of fear appeal. For example:

- *"You'd better not vote for pro-abortion laws, because we'll be out in front of your house with pickets every night for the next year!"*
- *"You'd better be a good boy this year or Santa won't bring you any Christmas gifts!"*

In argumentation, the goal is to make an argument that is so sound and compelling that people want to believe it or agree with it, as opposed to feeling threatened or pressured. Arguments that are built around threats are considered inappropriate.

Argumentum ad crumenum

With this fallacy, the arguer falsely assumes that there is a direct relationship between "cost" and "quality." If something costs more, it's assumed that it is of higher quality. For example:

- *"My son went to Stuffy University, and Stuffy's tuition is twice that of State U—therefore, Stuffy's education is better. In fact, it's twice as good!"*
- *"Please don't give me one of those 'domestic' bottled waters—I deserve the one in the silver-plated bottle from the French country-side."*

This fallacy also can relate to people—the idea that if a person is wealthy or highly paid, they must be better, wiser, or more "correct." But in case you didn't know this, rich people can be dead wrong!

Argumentum ad lazarum

However, just to complicate matters, there is a fallacy that is essentially the reverse of *argumentum ad crumenum*. With *ad lazarum*, the fallacy is assuming that something is necessarily a better value because it costs less, or that someone of little means is "wiser" or "more intelligent." For example:

- *"That Yugo is quite a car! For only $5000, you are getting a real value in transportation."* (In case you don't know, the Yugo is a fabled example of a foreign import that was cheap, but really wasn't a great value for most people over time!)
- *"Old Jed has been farmin' that little plot of land for more than 40 years, and although he's not rich, he's close to the earth and knows*

more about life than any fancy city slicker!" (In other words, he's not one of those "pointy-headed college professors" who lacks common sense!)

As with *ad crumenum,* the big idea is that you should assess a claim or an argument on its substantive merits—not on the characteristics of the source, or something as superficial as the price.

Reductio ad absurdum

The main problem with the use of *reductio ad absurdum* is that it involves taking an opponent's idea to an extreme, to an absurd level, in a way that is inappropriate and misleading. For example:

- *"Well, if you oppose the 19-year-old drinking age because young people cause accidents, why not raise the drinking age to 65? Then we'd **really** cut down on highway deaths!"*

What's "wrong" here, of course, is that this statement takes the opposing idea and twists it to make it seem silly. Another example would be:

- *"If we're not going to have gun control, we might as well just give everyone a gun."*

In this case as well, by reducing the opposing argument to the absurd, the opposing argument is twisted in such a way as to be misleading. However, to (once again) make things a little more complicated, there are occasions when arguers might **purposely** use *reductio ad absurdum* as a *refutation* tactic. How so? Well, suppose that Angie says that we are spending too much on education. I might respond by saying, "Well, if the level of funding for education really isn't important, then why don't we *reduce* the amount of money that we give the schools, or maybe not give them any money *at all!*" In such an instance, I am not really serious about that suggestion. I am purposely taking Angie's idea to the extreme in order to make a point—in this case, that at some level, the amount we spend on education really *does* matter; if you don't think so, try giving our schools less, or nothing! If the "twisting" is done in such a manner, it may help reveal the underlying problem with the opponent's position. Of course, it is still "twisting," but it is designed with refutation in mind, not as a literal and necessarily fallacious interpretation of the opponent's position. Nonetheless, our friend Angie might still accuse me of using *reductio ad absurdum* in a misleading and fallacious way, and I would have to defend my response as being relevant and appropriate. But, *reductio ad absurdum* can, in the right situation, be used as a refutation tactic.

"Straw man" argument

Another form of "twisting," related in some ways to *reductio ad absurdum*, is the so-called "straw man" fallacy. (We could use "inclusive language" and say "straw person," but that just sounds a little odd to me.) With this fallacy, an arguer misrepresents an opponent's position to make it easier to attack. Govier (1992, 157) offers a nice definition when she writes: "The straw man fallacy is committed when a person misrepresents an argument, theory, or claim, and then, on the basis of that misrepresentation, claims to have refuted the position that he has misrepresented." Often, this misrepresentation involves oversimplifying the opposing view. For example:

- *"Since all those liberals want to do is spend as much of your money as they can, you know how I'm going to vote in November!"* (Yes, liberalism is associated with bigger government, but do liberals really want to just "take all your money"? That's an exaggeration and an oversimplification.)

Another form of straw man involves focusing on a minor weakness—something that may be hard to deny—but is really not terribly important. Poor Senator Dan Quayle—as the elder George Bush's running mate in 1992, we learned, through a school visit he made one day, that he thought the word "potato" was spelled with an "e"—"potatoe." Now he could not deny that he had made this gaffe, and I suppose it's nothing to be proud of—but is it the sort of issue that should determine how one votes? Seems to me this is seizing on a small point, not representative of the man's overall intellect, and therefore a straw man—light and easy to knock down. As Carey (2000, 144) explains, the straw man fallacy "derives its name from the similarity of a distorted version of a position to a scarecrow. Neither bears much more than a passing resemblance to that which it represents." So, if you feel that someone is distorting an opponent's argument in order to make it easier to defeat, the straw man fallacy may well be relevant.

Equivocation

Equivocation is a fallacy involving the use of language. Essentially, it involves using the same word or term in two different ways so as to mislead. It's when a term or expression is used in one sense in one place and a different sense in another. For instance:

- *"Doctors say you should avoid stimulants, so you'd better avoid that argumentation course, which some people say is very stimulating!"*

In this case, the word "stimulant" is being used in two different ways: physicians are no doubt referring to physical stimulation of the central nervous system, while the second half of the sentence is referring to *intellectual* stimulation, which is something quite different.

One can imagine lots of "silly" examples of equivocation; for example, "You must be very bright, because that's a very bright shirt that you have on." But in the real world, the important examples of this fallacy involve playing with words for a strategic advantage. For instance, take the word "murder." If we disapprove of murder, shouldn't we also disapprove of the murder of thousands of tons of carrots and broccoli in people's meals? Clearly in this case the term "murder" is being used not only to describe the intentional destruction of a human being, but also the preparation of common non-meat food items. Is that the same kind of "murder"? Seems like an equivocal and sneaky use of language to me—and I'm a vegetarian!

A final example: I've seen a persuasive message which has a box of facial tissue at the top, with the caption, "Excuse me America, this is tissue." Down below is a drawing of a baby in the womb, with the admonition that "An unborn baby shouldn't be thrown away like a piece of tissue." Although they may have a point here, it's a little misleading to equate facial "tissue" with the "tissue" of a fetus, if only because we are predisposed to devalue facial tissue by absent-mindedly throwing it in the trash—but I don't believe that even "pro-choice" advocates would ever regard abortion in such a casual light. Simply put, these two situations involve a different sense of "tissue."

The line-drawing fallacy (sometimes called "argument of the beard")

This fallacy involves the notion that if it's difficult to draw a line between two things, then one simply shouldn't even draw a line. The fallacy is in thinking that "one more doesn't matter" in a situation where a line has to be drawn on a continuum. For example:

- *"The scores on the last 10-point quiz were 10, 9, 8, 7, 6, 5, 4, 3, and 2—looks like I'll have to give everyone an A!"*

Yes, it's difficult to draw a line between two grades, but at some point you must, even if it's a little "arbitrary." Not so sure about that? Consider this illustration:

- *"The speed limit is 55 miles per hour. So, it's really OK to go 56, because that's only one mile per hour more. And if 56 is OK, then 57 ought to be, too. And 58 miles per hour is only one more than that. So, you can never really draw a line."*

One could continue this train of thought indefinitely. One could say, "Well, 86 miles per hour is only one more than 85, and 87 is only one more than 86." No—at some point, one must say, this number (whatever it is) constitutes "speeding" and will be prosecuted, even if it's only one mile per hour more than a "legal" speed.

One particularly important and noteworthy situation in which this fallacy may have been relevant is in what has become known as the "Rodney King case." In 1991, Mr. King was hit about 55 times by four Los Angeles police officers in the process of being arrested; he suffered some broken bones in the process. Well, in 1992, the four police officers were tried for using excessive force in the arrest, but all four were acquitted. According to Moore and Parker (2007, 181-182), one of the jurors in the trial of the police indicated that an argument like the following finally convinced her and at least one other juror to vote "not guilty":

Everybody agrees that the first time one of the officers struck King with a nightstick it did not constitute excessive force. Therefore, if we are to conclude that excessive force was indeed used, then sometime during the course of the beating . . . there must have been a moment—a particular blow—at which the force became excessive. Since there is no point at which we can determine that the use of force changed from warranted to excessive, we are forced to conclude that it did not become excessive at any time during the beating; and so the officers did not use excessive force.

In other words, because a line between "necessary" and "excessive" force is a difficult line to draw, two jurors decided that no such line was possible. Since no such line is absolutely obvious, their feeling became, why try to draw a line at all? That is the very essence of a fallacious mindset when it comes to setting limits.

Slippery slope argument

You will see this term fairly often in newspapers and magazines; it's gotten a lot of attention in recent years. Sometimes "one thing does lead to another"—that is, A does cause B and that in turn leads to C. But this fallacy falsely assumes that once we go in a particular direction in a "small" way that we will inevitably go much further down the "wrong path"—that is, A will lead to B, and to C, and to D, and all the way to Z, if you will. Chaffee (1997, 531) defines it this way: "The fallacy of slippery slope thinking suggests that one undesirable action will inevitably lead to a worse action, which will necessarily lead to a worse one still, all the way down the 'slippery slope' to some unavoidable terrible disaster at the bottom." For example:

- *"If we were to censor this one book from the public library, then sometime in the future there will be another book, and another— and pretty soon, they'll be burning piles of forbidden books in front of the building, including the Holy Bible!"*

The fallacy is in assuming that things would really result in such a disastrous outcome based on the censorship of this one book. Those who think this way would say that even though it's just one book, it will inevitably lead us down the "slippery slope"—but they need to show that this is really likely. Otherwise, it's a fallacy. Slippery slope thinking is frequently rather "dramatic"—for example, the argument that if homosexuals are legally allowed to marry, then pretty soon there will be group marriage, or people will be able to marry animals. In the end, the issue involves whether such a final step is really possible, or just an unrealistic kind of "scare tactic."

Two wrongs make a right (*"tu quoque"*—Latin for "you, also")

With this fallacy, someone defends a "wrong" by pointing out that others, or their opponents, have acted in the same (equally bad) manner. For example:

- *"Why pick on me, officer? Nobody these days drives the speed limit."*
- *"Why are you coming down on me for using marijuana, dad? Didn't you smoke it too when you were in college?"*

If, for instance, the current President was accused of some sort of wrongdoing, he or she could say, "But President Clinton was almost impeached, and so was President Nixon." This type of defense is really an attempt to divert attention and to avoid owning up to the problem. So just because your big sister got into trouble in her sophomore year in college doesn't give you the right! Again, persuasively, such an approach might sometimes actually work, but that doesn't make it a logically compelling argument.

Perfect solution fallacy

This is a fallacy that occurs when an argument assumes that a perfect solution exists and/or that a solution should be rejected because some part of the problem would still exist after it was implemented. Essentially, the fallacy is in thinking that any problem can be totally eradicated, and that if it can't be, there's no reason to try. For example:

- *"This 'terrorist safety net' is a bad idea. Terrorists will still be able to get through!"*
- *"These anti-drunk driving campaigns are not going to work. People are still going to drink and drive no matter what."*

Again, in each case, while some terrorists may still get through, and some drunk drivers will still take the wheel, it would be fallacious not to do anything simply because we can't get them all. The "perfect solution" fallacy *is* a fallacy because in the real world, there's no such thing as perfection.

Historian's fallacy

You've heard the saying, "Hindsight is 20-20"? This fallacy occurs when it is assumed that decision makers in the past could see things from the same perspective and with the same information when later discussing the decision. For instance:

- *"They shouldn't have fought World War I, because it accomplished nothing and only led to World War II."* (Who knew?)
- *"If the Federal Aviation Administration had implemented a ban on box cutters on airplanes many years ago, the 9/11 tragedy would never have occurred."* (In case you don't know, box cutters were apparently used as a weapon by some of the 9/11 airplane hijackers.)
- *"Billy should've known better than to drive that car home from work the other night—there are a lot more accidents after dark, and he got rear-ended.."* (What are we supposed to do? Stop driving after sunset?)

Does this mean that people or institutions can't be faulted for "dumb decisions" that have been made in the past? Of course not—but it does mean that a look backward at those decisions has to be based on what we knew at the time, not on what we now know.

Gambler's fallacy

There are many people who do not have a firm grasp of the laws of probability. If they flip a coin five times and it comes up "heads" every time, they might "bet the farm" on the sixth flip being "tails." But the hard truth is, if the coin is being flipped in a random manner, the odds of "heads" on that sixth flip are still exactly 50-50. Ditto for the Powerball lottery—if the number 17 has been selected as one of the Powerball numbers for the last four drawings in a row, the odds of 17 coming up the next time are exactly the same as they always have been: one out of however many Powerball numbers there are. So if you are ever in a place where casino gambling, for example, is legal, you will want to keep this principle in mind. The laws of probability are hard and cold, and the people who own and operate, say, slot machines have a better sense of that than most of their patrons.

Red herring

A red herring involves bringing in a clearly irrelevant point to distract people from the "real" issue, just as a red herring was dragged on the ground to distract the hounds from the scent of the fox (that's one story used to explain the derivation of this term). For example, in a discussion about the impact of TV violence on children, someone brings in the issue of too many sleazy commercials on cartoon shows—in this context, that's a red herring because it has nothing to do with the issue at hand, TV violence. In other words, with this fallacy, Topic A is under discussion, but Topic B is introduced as if it is relevant to topic A, but it's not. Unfortunately, sometimes this diversionary tactic enables an opponent to derail the discussion away from Topic A, which, either consciously or unconsciously, is often their goal!

Another "grey area alert"

Remember that in chapter 1, I issued a "grey area alert" about factual, value, and policy claims, making the point that sometimes it's hard to distinguish between the three. In some ways, the same holds true for fallacies. The examples presented in this chapter are fairly "transparent" and straightforward, but "real life" will often throw you some curveballs. There will be situations where more than one fallacy might be relevant, or aspects of two different fallacies might apply. My concern, once again, is that sometimes people are looking for the definitive "right" answer, as if this were mathematics. Good news: it's not. (That *is* good news, isn't it?)

For example, if Fred says that ever since he and the rest of his family started eating more tomatoes, their health has improved "because we all feel better," what should we call this? Begging the question? A hasty generalization? A *post hoc ergo propter hoc* fallacy? A *non sequitur*? The answer is not self-evident and one's analysis would need to be explained and defended. So, be prepared to use fallacies as an analytical framework, but feel free to use them with a degree of creativity. If I say that I am going to give my students grades because "we've always had grades," and "without grades, student motivation would plummet and they'd learn close to nothing," there's a little *argumentum ad verecundiam* in there as well as a little slippery slope.

CONCLUSION

Well, that's a tour of some of the most well-known fallacies. In general, fallacies are thought processes that should be avoided because they are usually misleading and illogical. Even though 25 fallacies are discussed here, there are others as well! If you are so inclined, do a little poking around and you will surely locate more. Most textbooks on logic or argumentation will discuss many different fallacies, and the electronic encyclopedia Wikipedia (a source often maligned by professor-types, just so you know) has an interesting treatment of the topic under the heading "logical fallacies" (www.wikipedia.com).

In the meantime, if you are interested in testing your understanding of fallacies, see **Table 6.1**—all 25 of the fallacies in this chapter are included (one example of each). This "fallacy quiz" should give you a pretty good indication of how well you have been tracking on things. Good luck!

TABLE 6.1 – FALLACY QUIZ

Here's a fun party game: give your guests this list of statements and see if they can identify which fallacies they represent! Or, see if you can! You will find the answers on page 255.

1. Homosexuals cannot be religious leaders because religious leaders throughout the ages have always been heterosexuals.
2. Marcie is intelligent because she is exceptionally smart.
3. White collar crime is on the rise, which just goes to show you why that Clinton fellow was never in favor of lower taxes for the poor.
4. I know you're a liberal because you put a liberal dose of mayo on all your sandwiches.
5. Don't support the Vice President's stand on family issues because he's a male chauvinist pig.
6. The Steelers are the best team in pro football, so surely they have the best defensive line.
7. A macrobiotic diet and life in a mud hut has given the Maharishi his divine wisdom.
8. If you start smoking cigarettes, pretty soon you'll try marijuana, and then you're certainly going to end up being a crackhead.
9. I saw Biff in the library on Saturday--he must be a really excellent student!
10. The majority of people are against the war in Iraq; therefore the war is wrong.
11. So you think prostitution should be legalized? Why don't we just open up whore houses next to churches?
12. I've had five lousy poker hands in a row—I'm sure the next one will be the charm!
13. We should hire Jimmy because he's really been down on his luck of late.
14. Nobody can show that avocados don't prevent heart disease; therefore they must.
15. Our professor had better give us good grades or we will give her poor evaluations.
16. Having express lanes on the freeway for carpools just won't work—some people will just buy mannequins to make it look like they have another rider!
17. You say that Maria is the best actress on campus. But are you forgetting that Maria always complains about what parts she gets in the plays? Obviously you are mistaken.
18. The U.S. may have imprisoned suspected terrorists without due process of law, but that's nothing compared to what happens to people in a Communist country.
19. The Governor said either you are a Republican or you're no friend of mine.
20. Since water, malt, and barley are good for you, that means beer is good for you.
21. I've already had six candy bars, so what's the problem with having just one or two more?
22. Senator Windbag mispronounced the name of Iran's President. So how can his Middle East policies make any sense?
23. I never had any grey hair--until I met you!
24. Lord knows why the Petersons were so stupid: they actually re-modeled their house just a few weeks before that nasty tornado ripped through the town.
25. This argumentation text by Lapakko costs less than most of my other texts; clearly my other texts must be better.

REFERENCES

Bassham, Gregory, William Irwin, Henry Nardone, and James M. Wallace. *Critical thinking: A student's introduction,* 3rd ed. Boston: McGraw-Hill, 2008.

Bierman, Arthur K. and Robin N. Assali. *The critical thinking handbook.* Upper Saddle River, NJ: Prentice-Hall, 1996.

Carey, Stephen S. *The uses and abuses of argument.* Mountain View, CA: Mayfield Publishing, 2000.

Chaffee, John. *Thinking critically,* 5th ed. Boston: Houghton Mifflin, 1997.

Govier, Trudy. *A practical study of argument,* 3rd ed. Belmont, CA: Wadsworth, 1992.

Kahane, Howard and Nancy Cavender. *Logic and contemporary rhetoric: The use of reason in everyday life,* 10th ed. Belmont, CA: Wadsworth, 2006.

Moore, Noel Brooke and Richard Parker. *Critical thinking,* 8th ed. Boston: McGraw-Hill, 2007.

Rottenberg, Annette T. *Elements of argument: A text and reader,* 2nd ed. New York: St. Martin's Press, 1988.

Ruggiero, Vincent. *Beyond feelings: A guide to critical thinking,* 7th ed. Boston: McGraw-Hill, 2004.

Walton, Douglas. *Appeal to pity: Argumentum ad misericordiam.* Albany, NY: State University of New York Press, 1997.

Wilson, David C. *A guide to good reasoning.* Boston: McGraw-Hill, 1999.

Chapter 7

THE USE OF LANGUAGE IN ARGUMENT

After reading this chapter, you should understand:

- What it means to say that language is "symbolic"
- Different ways to define a word
- The difference between the denotative and connotative meanings of words
- Why arguers are sometimes clear with their use of words, and sometimes not clear
- Why arguers sometimes want to arouse our emotions with their words
- Why arguers sometimes want to calm us down with their words
- Different types of language that are misleading or "loaded"
- How concrete language differs from abstract language
- What metaphors are and how they influence our understanding of an issue

Specialized terms to know:

- defining by negation
- defining by etymology
- operational definitions
- denotative meaning
- connotative meaning
- euphemisms
- dysphemisms
- hyperbole
- weasel words
- god and devil terms
- persuasive definitions
- relative terms
- abstract words
- concrete words
- metaphors

Yes, a good argument will be based on sound evidence and sound reasoning. But all of that evidence and reasoning must be put into a code that we commonly call language. An examination of argument simply cannot ignore language, because virtually all arguments are constructed with words. And as you might expect, there are many different issues associated with the use of language in argument. In these pages, I would like to identify what I believe are some of the most important things that one ought to know:

1. Words have no intrinsic meaning. They only mean what people think they mean. That makes communication more difficult.

Semanticists—people who study words—have made the point in many different ways that in the end, words are merely collections of phonemes (individual sounds) and morphemes (groups of sounds) designed to represent "reality." But the critical point is that they are NOT "reality." If I have a writing implement in my hand, I may call it a "pen." But if I'm from Mexico City, I might say "pluma." Either way, it's still a pen, if you get my drift—the pen itself doesn't change, only the label we give it. In communication studies, we often say, "Meanings are *not* in words—meanings are in *people*." That saying is meant to convey a similar idea. Even if in your view, the meaning of a word is totally clear, you simply cannot assume that it will be interpreted in the same way by your receivers. If I say that the President is "conservative," what does that mean? That the President is a Republican? Tight-fisted with money? Opposed to abortion and the legalization of marijuana? Quiet and reserved, as opposed to "wild and crazy"? Unfortunately, the word "conservative" has a number of potential meanings. And, unfortunately, this is the case with all words—so, from a communication studies perspective, accurately sending and receiving a message is quite difficult due to the very nature of language. Indeed, most of us in communication studies would contend that communication is a constant battle against confusion, and that communication fails as often as it succeeds—in part because language itself is inherently ambiguous.

Even when words are carefully chosen, people can and will argue at length as to their exact meaning. Take, for example, these two statements:

1. **Congress shall make no law respecting an establishment of religion, or prohibiting the free exercise thereof;**

or abridging the freedom of speech, or of the press; or the right of the people peaceably to assemble, and to petition the government for a redress of grievances.

2. A well regulated militia, being necessary to the security of a free state, the right of the people to keep and bear arms, shall not be infringed.

In case you don't know what you were just reading, those are the first two amendments to the U.S. Constitution, often called "The Bill of Rights." On the face of it, they seem like fairly clear and straightforward ideas: Congress shall make no law respecting or prohibiting religion; Congress shall make no law to abridge freedom of speech or freedom of the press; and the people's right to bear arms shall not be infringed upon. But as you should know, the exact meaning of those two statements has been debated now for over two centuries:

• Does the first statement mean that we can't even have "Christmas parties" in the office? Does it mean that Muslim supermarket cashiers have a constitutional right not to scan a customer's bacon because of the Muslim prohibition against pork? Does it mean that I can or can't use nasty four-letter words on my own cable access show? Does it mean that I can legally call for the violent overthrow of the government?

• Does the second statement mean that a convicted felon just released from prison has a right to carry a handgun? Is the statement advocating a personal, individual right to bear arms, or is it concerned with the establishment of state militias? If I'm mentally ill, do I have a right to own a handgun? And what does a "well regulated" militia even mean? What does a "poorly regulated" militia even look like? And, what constitutes a "militia" in the first place?

With both statements, the point is that no matter how hard you may try to be clear with language, you discover that words can create as many questions as they answer. Words are often the best communication tools that we have, but they are, by nature, ambiguous. That's why it's dangerous to have a mindset which says, "I put this idea into my own words, and I did so as clearly as I possibly could, so therefore I'm sure that the meaning is clear."

2. There's more than one way to define a word, and the "dictionary definition" is not always the best way.

Since words can have multiple meanings and inherent ambiguity, arguers often try to define important words that are connected to their claims. If I say I want to "legalize drugs," those two words are both ambiguous and need definition. The question is, how? What constitutes a "drug," and how exactly would you "legalize" them? Many students turn to "the dictionary" (as if there is one and only one dictionary in the world) and provide the denotative definition. If you are going to use a dictionary, you should probably at least specify which one. Even more important, sometimes students use a standard dictionary to define a technical term; in such cases, a more specialized reference book would be a better source. For example, if you were arguing about crime and were trying to define "probable cause" for an arrest, a book like *Black's Law Dictionary* would be a better source than Webster's. Similarly, if you were looking for an authoritative definition of Crohn's Disease, a medical dictionary would usually be better than a general dictionary. However, there are other ways to define words that are sometimes more helpful. Your other options include:

- defining by **negation**—what the word is not (by "drugs," I do not mean those substances people take by prescription under a doctor's care)
- defining by **authority** (according to the Surgeon General of the U.S., a "drug" is...)
- defining by **example** (an example of a "drug" under this plan would be marijuana)
- defining by **function** (a "drug" is any substance that has an effect on the central nervous system)
- defining by **etymology**—the derivation of the word ("euthanasia" is derived from the Greek, meaning "easy death")
- defining by **comparison and contrast** ("decriminalizing" drugs is more permissive than making them "illegal," but less permissive than fully "legalizing" them)
- providing an **operational definition** – for purposes of this presentation, "drugs" will be defined as marijuana and cocaine, and "legalize" will mean available for sale by the government for any person age 21 or older. (An operational definition

specifies how something will be defined in the context of a particular discussion—in specific, measurable, concrete terms. For example, an operational definition of "short" men is any man under 5 feet, 5 inches in height. An operational definition of "intellectually prepared for college" might be having a composite score on the ACT exam of at least 25.)

In any controversy, you will need to consider what words require some type of formal, explicit definition. For example, if I were giving a speech on "mental illness," I would want to be very clear about what I meant by this term, to make my case understandable. The same holds true for just about any topic: "the Middle East," "defense spending," "entitlement programs," "secondary education," and so on—in each case, I'd want to define my terms before I went any further. Just be aware that there is more than one way to do this, and also be aware that arguments about some current events issues become arguments about words: the people involved end up arguing about whether the definition for a key term in the controversy is both fair and accurate before anyone ever gets to the real "substance" of the issue. Therefore, having clear and reasonable definitions is helpful so that people do not get bogged down simply trying to determine and to agree upon the meanings of words.

3. Language is not static—the meanings of words change over time.

Arguers must realize that language changes over time. (If you don't believe me, just pull out any play by William Shakespeare and start reading!) Sometimes words add new denotative meanings; for example, "gay" not only denotes "happiness," but now, also, "homosexual." Other words change in their connotative sense. When I was in college, many political candidates proudly proclaimed that they were "liberal"—the word had honorific overtones. But now, when politicians want to discredit someone, they often use the so-called "L word," as "liberal" has become sort of a "*dirty* word." And some words that didn't really exist a few decades ago are now standard ways of looking at things—for example, the idea of "sustainable" agriculture or "sustainable" energy programs simply didn't exist when I was a boy; we now have a word that didn't exist at one point in time. Similarly, we now talk about "green" products; we seem to assume that "green is good," although the term is new and is applied to a variety of products that make a rather wide variety of claims. The exact meaning of "green" is rather elusive, but "environmentally conscious" people like to use it because it seems favorable. At any rate, good arguers and good critics of argument are sensitive to the ways that words can morph into something new or appear out of nowhere.

Table 7.1 indicates how our language has changed due to the world of computers—a world that, believe it or not, didn't exist all that long ago.

4. Sometimes arguers will try to be clear with their use of words; but sometimes they will be *intentionally* vague or unclear.

In general, clarity is a good thing. And of course, people who make arguments will often strive to be very clear with the words they use. Indeed, I would argue that on ethical grounds alone, a *clear* argument is one characteristic of a *good* argument. But as a critical listener, and as a potential "opponent" to someone else's argument, remember that people choose their words strategically—and often, one strategy is to intentionally use words that are unclear.

Why, you ask, would someone want to be purposely vague? The general answer is, because the "truth" sometimes hurts, and vague language is one means of avoiding the truth. So if I call my new tax on gasoline a "user fee," one must think for a moment: what is a "user fee"? Hmm—it couldn't be a tax, could it? At least it's not called a tax, and so maybe it's not as bad. Or, if I tell you that the military is providing "air support," I am using a term that has a number of possible meanings, one of which is "to drop bombs." But "air support" sounds better than "bombing," right? And so to avoid too much negativity, I use a more ambiguous term. Charles Larson (2007, 122) explains that

> Persuaders use several methods to create strategic ambi-
> guity. One is to choose words that can be interpreted in
> many (often contradictory) ways. A politician may sup-
> port "responsibility in taxation and the cost of educating
> our youngsters." Those who think teachers are underpaid
> might hear this as a call for increasing funding for educa-

TABLE 7.1: HOW LANGUAGE CHANGES OVER TIME

Remember when ...

A computer was something on TV
from a science fiction show of note
a window was something you hated to clean...
And ram was the cousin of a goat....

Meg was the name of my girlfriend
and gig was a job for the nights
now they all mean different things
and that really mega bytes

An application was for employment
a program was a TV show
a cursor used profanity
a keyboard was a piano

Memory was something that you lost with age
a cd was a bank account
and if you had a 3 *" floppy
you hoped nobody found out

Compress was something you did to the garbage
not something you did to a file
and if you unzipped anything in public
you'd be in jail for a while

Log on was adding wood to the fire
Hard drive was a long trip on the road
A mouse pad was where a mouse lived
And a backup happened in your commode

Cut you did with a pocket knife
paste you did with glue
a web was a spider's home
and a virus was the flu

I guess some will stick to their pad and paper
and the memory in their head
I hear nobody's been killed in a computer crash
but when it happens it'll be something to dread

Anonymous
Retrieved from: http://library.thinkquest.org/5585/funwithwords.htm on 8/25/07

tion. Those who hold the opposite view could as easily interpret the statement as meaning that education spending needs to be cut. The key word that increases ambiguity is "responsibility." The speaker or writer does not say what cause he or she favors.

Of course, Larson is talking about the world of persuasion, which, as I noted in chapter 1, tends to use more "one-way" communication, creating situations where ambiguity can be used with more ease. One would hope in the world of argumentation, where "two-way" communication is more common, that critical listeners and sharp opponents will be able to see through intentionally ambiguous language and confront it directly. But the "bottom line" is that sometimes people are not inclined to "tell it like it is."

5. Sometimes arguers use words that are designed to get us emotionally *worked up*; but sometimes they will use words to get us to *calm down*.

You probably know by now that words have a denotative and connotative meaning. The **denotative** meaning is essentially the "dictionary" meaning—so the word "knife" denotes a sharp tool used to cut various types of objects and foods. On the other hand, the **connotative** meaning involves the feelings associated with the words. For example, "house" and "home" are words that both denote the same place, but the connotative meaning is different. A "home" is a warmer, friendlier, more active, more "homey" place (sorry, I couldn't resist that). Therefore, arguers pay attention to the connotative senses of a word. Take the abortion issue, for example. Many people who are opposed to abortion will probably talk in terms of "killing a baby." Such a phrase has some emotional bite to it, and since anti-abortion advocates want us to be emotionally alarmed, they will be more inclined to use such words. At the same time, those who favor abortion rights are more likely to refer to an abortion in terms of "terminating a pregnancy," or "aborting a fetus." They do not want us to feel the reality of abortion too strongly, and so they tend to choose words that will calm us down a bit. I am not advocating for either side here; I merely mean to say that people who make arguments pay attention to the emotional tone of language.

Usually, people recognize very quickly that language can be used to arouse strong emotions, but sometimes, they haven't considered the use of language to get us to calm down. One could argue that a lot of "bureaucratic" rhetoric—from institutions and governments—is designed to get us to worry a little less. And that can be done by toning down the language. For example, if I don't want you to be too concerned about "industrial pesticides," I can refer to them as "runoff," and if I want to fail your son in school, I will say that he is being "held back." If I want you to be a little less emotionally concerned about crime, I am more likely to talk about the "homicide rate" than the "murder rate"; the latter term simply sounds "worse." And if you want us to feel that there will always be plenty of gasoline available, you don't alarm us with terms like "emergency supplies"; rather, we feel a bit more calm knowing that we have a "strategic reserve" of oil stored away.

6. There are a variety of types of language that can be regarded as misleading or "loaded."

Those who employ words have many ways to be potentially misleading. Among those linguistic devices would be:

• **euphemisms**. Euphemisms are polite ways to take the "sting" out of a word. We usually don't say, "I'm going to urinate"—instead, we say, "I'm going to visit the restroom." This type of euphemism is fairly innocent—even welcome!—but when used in "argumentative" contexts, euphemisms are designed to mislead in more important ways. So that if we say that our troops were killed by "friendly fire," that's a euphemism for "we killed our own people by accident." If, in a war, there is "collateral damage," that means innocent people were killed in the attack. And, as noted above, if we offer "air support," that's a euphemism for "bombing." Finally, in the community where I live, some 50 deer had overpopulated a nature center, and the deer were struggling to find enough to eat and to avoid being hit by cars on nearby streets. The nature center decided to inaugurate a "trap and dispatch" program, which, unfortunately, really means luring the deer into cages and shooting them in the head. But in order to "sell" the argument that the program was necessary, "trap and dispatch" has a better ring to it than some more "vivid" labels.

• **dysphemisms**. Dysphemisms are essentially the opposite of euphemisms. As Moore and Parker (2007, 119) explain, "Dysphemisms are used to produce a negative effect on a listener's or reader's attitude toward something or to tone down the positive associations it may have. Whereas 'freedom fighter' is a euphemism for 'guerilla' or 'rebel,' 'terrorist' is a dysphemism." Other examples:

- my "religion" becomes your "cult"
- my "clinical depression" becomes your "insanity"
- my nation sends out "information"; your nation distributes "propaganda"
- my candidate is "outgoing"; your candidate is "overbearing"
- I am "chemically dependent"; you are a "drug abuser"

• **hyperbole**. Hyperbole (pronounced high-*per*-boh-lee) is extreme exaggeration. If someone says, "This vacuum cleaner is the best consumer product ever made," they are engaging in hyperbole. So too a political candidate who says, "My opponent is the biggest scoundrel in history." Reasonable claim-makers use reasonable language. Some arguers mistakenly believe that the "stronger" their language is, the more convincing their case will be. However, if you engage in extreme exaggeration with your words, it may well backfire—whatever merit there may have been to your argument is tainted by the "linguistic overkill." (By the way, the word "hyperbole" is like the word "dishonesty"—it doesn't have a plural. Don't say someone used "hyperboles," any more than you would refer to their "dishonesties.")

• **weasel words**. Weasel words are words that appear to say something significant, but actually don't. If I say that this car is "virtually" maintenance-free, the "virtually" is a weasel word—obviously a car needs some maintenance and repairs over time, so you can't say it's really "maintenance-free," only "virtually" so. Other weasel words include "up to" (you can make *up to* $500 a week stuffing envelopes at home), ""helps" (This new program *helps* fight crime), "possibly" (This is *possibly* the greatest breakthrough in energy policy), and "potentially" (The Rangers are *potentially* the best team in baseball). A weasel word is kind of a "fudging" word. Can you think of others?

• **God and devil terms**. This terminology, coined by a fellow named Richard Weaver in 1953, refers to our use of words that have highly positive or highly negative connotations. Weaver used these labels because he felt that God and devil terms are so "unchallenged," shall we say, that people bow down and worship them without a lot of reflective thinking. Because these are not scientific categories, there is no "measure" for a God or devil term. But with respect to God terms, I would argue that one word which is clearly a God term in contemporary American society is "freedom." Anyone who claims to promote "freedom" is almost assumed to be promoting something that is good—it almost doesn't even matter what it is. To a lesser extent, perhaps, other words in our culture seem to be unchallenged as being "good," including "scientific studies," "progress," "fact," "family values," and, freedom's cousin, "independence." On the other hand, some popular devil terms over the years include "Communist" (a great way to discredit anything—just call it "Communist inspired"), "terrorist" (there are no "good terrorists" in the world), and "cancer" (White collar crime is a *cancer* in our society). The main problem with God and devil terms is that they evoke such strong emotional responses that reasoned discourse takes a back seat; such words can make it difficult to carefully analyze any issue or problem.

• **persuasive definitions and labels.** Sometimes people making arguments need or want to define their terms, and often the language they use will be "loaded." If someone defines a "politician" as "someone who wants to take as much of your tax money as possible," that is obviously not a neutral definition. But other persuasive definitions can be more subtle. If I define a "single payer" health care system as "a socialistic system in which the government controls health care," I am already predisposing many of you to think negatively about it. (With God terms in mind, better that I say, "In a single payer system, you will have the FREEDOM to seek medical treatment whenever you need it!")

When it comes to "labels," it is worth noting that some people use the term "estate tax" to describe the taxes on their possessions when they die, while opponents of estate taxes often call them "the death tax," which sounds much more horrible. And it should also be noted that in recent years, two government programs have been given linguistic labels that are so "favorably slanted" that it would seem almost impossible to disagree with them. One is "The Patriot Act"—who could be against patriotism? The other is "No

Child Left Behind"—can you picture that little girl standing on the curb, "left behind" by a callous and indifferent school system?

- relative terms. Some terms are absolute—for example, "all" or "none." But many terms are relative—they only have meaning in relation to something else—and can therefore be misleading. To say that "Americans are self-centered" may be a point that can be supported, but "self-centered" is a relative term. All people everywhere care about themselves to some degree—the issue is whether that trait is more characteristic of people in the U.S. You could say that your best friend is "intelligent," but that's a relative word, too—maybe this person is bright, but no Einstein. And to say that a new welfare program would be "expensive" also brings in a relative term—"expensive" in comparison to what? So, when arguers use relative terms, you must at least challenge them to explain the context in which they are making the claim—if a new law would make driving "safer," the question still remains, safer to what extent, and in what sense?

7. Language can be more concrete or more abstract; arguers and critical thinkers must be mindful of the difference.

Some words can refer to very specific things. Other words can refer to a wide variety of things. In simple terms, this is the difference between concrete and abstract language, and it's an important difference when considering how arguments are constructed.

Perhaps the best-known theorist dealing with this issue was the late S.I. Hayakawa, once a U.S. Senator from the state of California, once a university president, but also a professor who studied language. In a well-known book titled *Thought and Language in Human Action*, Hayakawa (1964, 179) identified what he called a "ladder of abstraction." Without actually putting these words on a cute little ladder, as Hayakawa, did, I will simply list the words in his most noted example:

Wealth
Assets
Farm Assets
Livestock
Cow
Bessie
_____
the "molecular cow"

Notice that a word such as "wealth," at the top of the ladder, can refer to a lot of different things, including—but certainly not limited to—the other things on the list. Indeed, one cannot picture a "wealth" in one's mind; it lacks a specific, concrete "connection." In order to picture "wealth," one must mentally imagine stacks of $100 bills, or a large home, or a stretch limo. Therefore, the word "wealth" is highly abstract—it can stand for a lot of different possibilities. Words such as "assets" and "farm assets" move down the ladder of abstraction just a bit—they are somewhat more concrete, but still mostly abstract. After all, "farm assets" can refer to land, seed, tractors, barns, baling equipment, machinery for irrigation, or many other things. As we start talking about "livestock" and "cows," we can begin to picture such things in our mind—they have what would be called a "concrete referent"; that is, they refer to something that is specific, visible, and tangible. And then, at the bottom of the ladder, we have Bessie herself—the most concrete word on the list because it denotes a particular cow who (if we knew all of our cows!) would be a very clear and "down-to-earth" reference. It's also worth noting that Hayakawa put the term "molecular cow" beneath a dotted line on this list. Why? Because he wanted to remind us that all words, no matter how abstract or how concrete, are still not the "real things"—they are symbols. As noted at the beginning of this chapter, words have no automatic or intrinsic meaning—they try to represent what's in the world, but there are in the end only representations. "Bessie" is a combination of six letters that is meant to represent a real, living, breathing, milk-producing animal: what Hayakawa refers to as the molecular cow.

Well, Lapakko, that was a nice little lecture about the difference between concrete and abstract words, but what difference does it make in terms of argument? Glad you asked. I'm here to provide a somewhat complicated answer. It's complicated because so much depends on the situation (as we are told about many things in life!). And it's complicated because concrete words have "strengths" and "weaknesses," as do abstract words. It's also complicated because the ladder of abstraction can be used and respected—or misused and abused—by people making arguments.

Concrete words have the virtue of being "clear," for lack of a better word. When you talk about bombs, or football stadiums, or buttered pasta, or aluminum cans, we usually know what you're talking about—they are concrete. So, from the standpoint of sending and receiving, concrete words "communicate" pretty well. On the other hand, if you think about it, concrete words have a built-in limitation. Because they are "narrow" in their orientation—very specific—they do not enable one to communicate the "bigger picture," if you will.

Abstract words, on the other hand, have the opposite kind of dynamic. In one sense, they are very unclear: what do "freedom," or "justice," or "equality," or "compassion" really mean? We are left to figure that out. Yet at the same time, abstractions serve a very important purpose: they can in fact bring a lot of concrete things into a meaningful perspective. For example, if I merely say that someone I know believes only the U.S. has good radio stations, and that someone else I know thinks American-made shoes are the best in the world, and that yet another person believes the U.S. makes the best pizza on the planet, I still only have three concrete examples. What I need is an abstract word to put them all together. In this case, "ethnocentrism" might be a good choice, since people who are ethnocentric tend to judge things only from their own cultural perspective; they tend to automatically judge things from their culture as "better" simply because it's "what they are used to." Although "ethnocentrism" is an abstraction, it's a useful one here to bring together a variety of concrete examples. The word reflects an overall theme that transcends the particular concrete examples.

So, should you as an arguer use more concrete language or more abstract language? In general, I think the best answer is that you use a judicious blend of the two, providing concrete words for clarity and abstract words to provide that sense of perspective. However, as noted earlier in this chapter, arguers are often "strategic" in their word choices, no less in this regard than others. If I want you to adopt even stronger laws against drunk driving, you can bet that I will use some very graphic language (e.g., concrete details of DWI-related car crashes—"blood and gore," if you will) rather than only relying on abstract words such as "irresponsible behavior" or "deterring motor vehicle operators who are impaired." Again, arguers will use words that get the sort of response they are looking for. If I want you to be very alarmed about hunger in America, I will likely be somewhat concrete. Perhaps I will profile a particular family where all that's available for dinner is one (very concrete) box of "mac and cheese." Conversely, if I want to downplay the hunger problem, I might use a more abstract term such as "nutritional deficiencies," which is not incorrect, but is less "alarming." Bottom line: concrete words have their function and place; abstract words have their function and place; and you as an arguer and as a critic of argument need to consider what level of linguistic abstraction is both effective and acceptable.

8. Metaphors raise some of the most interesting issues, and they affect the way we think.

When people write about language, they usually include all the "poetic" uses of words, including alliteration, assonance, parallel structure, personification, and so on. And while I have nothing against the use of pretty words and various linguistic devices, the one that seems to get little attention—but should—is the metaphor. Why? Because metaphors are more than linguistic "window dressing"—they affect how we think and feel about issues. And equally important, we use metaphors naturally, all the time, without usually realizing what we are doing—they are not something that we need to consciously invent, as we might with some other literary devices. Therefore, we need to pay attention to metaphors and how they operate.

First, a distinction should be made between similes and metaphors. A simile is a *direct* comparison, using "like" or "as." For instance, "Her skin is as white as snow," or "He defeats his opponents like a knife cutting through butter." Because they use "like" or "as," similes are rather "up front"—they say flat-out that a comparison is being made.

Metaphors, however, are *implied* comparisons. They do not use "like" or "as." As such, they are a little "sneaky." If I say that our military is engaged in "surgical air strikes" or "surgical bombing," I am comparing bombing to surgery, and that is what's sneaky. Because, if you think about it, surgery must be done with great precision and care—even being "off" by a few millimeters could be catastrophic for a patient. However, can dropping bombs from 5,000 feet ever be as precise as, say, a triple-bypass procedure? Of course not—but the surgical metaphor is some-how reassuring, if in a way misleading. The point is that meta-phors influence how we perceive a given issue. Take, for instance, the idea that we need a "safety net" of social programs to help the poor. What kind of metaphor is this? Well, it's a circus or a tra-peze metaphor. There is not a literal, real "net" that will catch the poor as they fall—the net is metaphorical, and as such, not real. People do fall and crash, so to speak—a "safety net" will not stop all "economic deaths." But, because it is a net, and it does catch trapeze artists, one is tempted to think that it can do the same for any homeless person. That, of course, is baloney. Finally, one example of a very powerful metaphor from our military history involves the Vietnam War, which killed over 50,000 U.S. soldiers. One of the most popular arguments in favor of that war involved the metaphor of the "domino effect"—that is, if South Vietnam fell to the Communists, then so would Cambodia, and Laos, and Thailand, and so on—to the point where all of southeast Asia would become Communist. The implied comparison to domi-noes was persuasive to some, because we all know how easy it is to knock over a pile of dominoes! I know this sounds silly, but at a psychological level, such a metaphor does influence our thinking—if dominoes can fall over that easily, so, apparently, can entire nations. Therefore, for that and other reasons, we "stayed the course" in Vietnam and ultimately paid a rather sizeable price for it.

An important and well-known book on metaphors—*Metaphors We Live By*, by George Lakoff and Mark Johnson—makes the point that "our ordinary conceptual system is metaphorical in nature," and that metaphors "structure how we perceive, how we think, and what we do" (Lakoff and Johnson, 4). The authors even point out how metaphors influence how we think about argument itself. If, for instance, we think of "argument as war," then Lakoff and John-son note some common war metaphors used to talk about argu-ment:

- He attacked every weak point in my argument.
- His criticisms were right on target.
- I demolished his argument.
- He shot down all of my arguments.

Of course, we don't have to use "war" metaphors to describe arguments. We could, for instance, use, say, weather metaphors:

- She really snowed him with that argument!
- That point was certainly a bolt out of the blue!
- He has not been able to survive the storm of controversy.
- The planning commission has had a drought of ideas.

Or, for that matter, we could use *music* metaphors:

- Bob's plan struck a responsive chord with the group.
- His proposal just seemed a little off-key.
- new policy for education will promote harmony in our community.
- That suggestion was music to our ears.

Again, these examples are simply within the realm of talking about argumentation itself. But perhaps more important, when people argue about specific issues, they may use a wide variety of metaphors that will influence our understanding of the issue. To cite just a few:

MEDICAL METAPHORS
- "We must cure the ills of society."
- "We must deal with the cancer of crime."

LIGHT-DARK METAPHORS
- "It is the dawning of a new day."
- "We've come out of the dark era of institutionalized racism."

SPORTS METAPHORS
- "We've got to hold the line against inflation."
- "That proposal should be a slam-dunk."

SEA METAPHORS
- "We are drifting through troubled waters."
- "There's a tide of opposition to such an idea."

CONSTRUCTION METAPHORS
- "The foundations of society are crumbling."
- "We must build a bridge to the 21st Century."

MACHINERY METAPHORS
- "This program needs to be overhauled."
- "We need to tune up the welfare system."

GARDENING METAPHORS
- "The defense budget needs pruning."
- "Education will plant the seeds of change."

FOOD METAPHORS
- "That is really a half-baked idea."
- "We only want to cut the fat out of the budget, not cut it to the bone."

MILITARY METAPHORS
- "He shot down all my arguments."
- "The health care bill will be won or lost in the trenches."

So, I hope I have convinced you that metaphors play an important role in how we talk about issues, and how we react and feel when other people use them.

CONCLUSION

Overall, the "big idea" in this chapter is that words are much more than labels for things and ideas. In argument, words are in part a means to simply communicate, but more importantly, words are used *strategically* to influence us in particular ways. Effective arguers choose their language with care, knowing that how an argument is worded can and will make a difference. By the same token, effective readers and listeners pay attention to these word choices, knowing that left to their own devices, advocates will often use words that are favorable to their position but also potentially misleading.

REFERENCES

Hayakawa, S. I. *Language in thought and action*. New York: Harcourt, Brace & World, 1964.

Lakoff, George and Mark Johnson. *Metaphors we live by*. Chicago: University of Chicago Press, 1979.

Larson, Charles U. *Persuasion: Reception and responsibility*, 11th ed. Belmont, CA: Thomson-Wadsworth, 2007.

Moore, Brooke Noel and Richard Parker. *Critical thinking*, 8th ed. New York: McGraw-Hill, 2007.

Weaver, Rrichard. *The ethics of rhetoric*. Chicago: Regnery, 1953.

Chapter 8

A DRAMATISTIC PERSPECTIVE ON ARGUMENT

After reading this chapter, you should understand:

- What a dramatistic approach to argument involves
- Burke's pentad as a dramatistic perspective on argument
- Bormann's symbolic convergence theory and its connection to argument
- Jensen's heuristic and its implications for argument

Specialized terms to know:

- scene
- agent
- act
- agency
- purpose
- fantasy theme
- fantasy type
- rhetorical vision
- personal and impersonal villains
- remote or precipitating problems
- problems of commission or omission
- problems of attitude or deed
- problems that are present or impending
- problems of affluence or scarcity
- procedural vs. substantive solutions
- solutions of expansion vs. contraction
- solutions of survival vs. enrichment
- "forward to utopia" vs. "back to eden solutions"

In this chapter, we shall come close to crossing the lines between "argumentation" and "persuasion" as well as "reason" and "emotion." Traditionally, argumentation texts and courses have focused on what Aristotle would call "logos"; in that sense, argumentation courses are often considered a sort of inquiry into "applied logic" or "informal logic." And it should be stressed that reasoned discourse is still perhaps the "heart and soul" of the study of argument.

Having said all that, the field of communication studies has broadened considerably in the last several decades. What began as a discipline that basically taught public speaking skills and simple rules of logic and presentation has mushroomed into a field that has examined all sorts of communication: both verbal and nonverbal, public and private, logical and non-logical. Students can now take courses in the discipline in such diverse subjects as interpersonal communication, intercultural communication, small group communication, organizational communication, nonverbal communication, rhetorical criticism, feminist rhetoric, health communication, media studies, broadcast production, public relations, and many more.

As part of this overall "broadening" trend, one perspective on communication has emerged that has captured the imagination of many. Although it can be described with various labels, I shall refer to it here as the "dramatistic" perspective on argument. Initially, the word itself may confuse you. After all, anything that's "dramatistic" sounds like something from a play—and what would theatre have to do with communication in general and argument in particular?

Dramatism in a nutshell

The answer to this question is more straightforward and commonsensical than you might have thought. The big idea is this: when people think about ideas, subjects, and issues, and when they express themselves about them, they will invariably use approaches that are connected to *drama*. From a dramatistic perspective, things don't simply "exist"—they *mean* something in a dramatic sense. And because people make meaning out of things in a dramatic manner, arguments that resonate with the audience, dramatistically, are more likely to be effective and well-received.

To use an example that has defined the early 21st century for many in the United States, the 9/11 attack on parts of New York City and Washington, D.C. involves more than simply planes crashing into buildings. That may be the objective reality, but people have "symbolized" about this reality in ways that are definitely dramatistic. How so? Well, first, like any good play, a popular version of the 9/11 story has a particular **villain**. In one popular dramatization, the specific villain is a fellow named Osama bin Laden, who is a fundamentally evil person who wants to destroy

America. Also, another villain is not a person, but an organization: Al-Qaida, which is believed to have orchestrated the 9/11 attacks. But, any good play also has **heroes** as well. The heroes in the "mainstream U.S." version of this drama are the people who came to help after the devastation: New York City firefighters, the mayor of New York, even President Bush, who came afterward to share his grief at the scene. However, besides villains and heroes, there are also **victims** in any drama. In this case, the most obvious victims were those 3,000 people who perished unexpectedly on that day. Indeed, the "unexpected" nature of their deaths made them seem more victimized—it was not as though these people had been sitting in a cancer ward knowing they were about to die. In a broader sense, most every American felt like a victim—some of us for the first time in this way, since attacks of this nature on our soil were largely unprecedented. Finally, any play takes place on a stage—what dramatistic theorists usually call the **scene**. In the case of 9/11, the scene is also vital to the dramatic quality of the action: these attacks took place at venues that symbolized the economic and political role of the United States in the world. The Twin Towers in New York City symbolized our economic power, and the Pentagon obviously is a symbol of our military might. As such, they were far from "accidental" targets, chosen randomly—in a dramatistic sense, the scene has meaning, too.

But you may still be wondering, what does this have to do with argumentation? The answer is that arguments are often *framed* dramatistically; they tap in to our *sense* of the dramatic; and we *respond* to them differently as a result. If argumentation is a process of trying to influence people with our words and ideas, then dramatism offers one window on how that process occurs.

With this perspective on argument, it is also important to realize that what argumentation becomes is an effort to dramatize about an issue in a way that resonates and makes sense for a particular audience. Although the dramatization about 9/11 discussed above is a popular and well-known dramatization, there are other "competing" dramatizations as well. For example, in another conceptualization about 9/11, the "villain" is actually the United States—that is, U.S. political and military "meddling" around the world is responsible for this attack. The "victims" have been people in the Middle East who have been killed and repressed by the imperialistic foreign policy of the U.S. The "heroes" become those people who are willing to stand up to the U.S. and all it represents—even if it means giving up their life in the process. And the "scene"—especially the scene in the U.S.—is of a country that's decadent, materialistic, lacking in values, and devoted to imposing its will on the rest of the world. Frankly, for some in the U.S., it is very unsettling to realize that Osama bin Laden is indeed a "hero" in some of these dramatizations, fighting the battle of the "underdog" against a mighty superpower. But such a dramatic portrayal functions argumentatively as a way to conceive of the terrorism issue very differently; because such dramatizations are powerful, we need to be aware of this process and be able to come to terms with it.

BURKE'S PENTAD

If there is a "founder" for the dramatistic perspective, it would be Kenneth Burke. Burke, sort of a combination philosopher, literary critic, and rhetorical theorist, passed on in 1993, living well into his 90s. During a long and distinguished career, he published a wide variety of books that explained his views on how people symbolize ideas. One of his best-known works is *A Grammar of Motives*, which outlines what has come to be known as "Burke's pentad." A pentadic view of communication contends that there are five elements present in any drama:

• **The scene.** Where does the action take place? What does the "stage" look like? For example, if people argue that our need for more mass transit is critical by showing photos of rush-hour gridlock in many major cities, they are focusing on the scene— where the action takes place. If I'm running for a seat on my local school board, and my campaign brochures show pictures of dilapidated school buildings and overcrowded classrooms, that also is a scenic emphasis. With respect to illegal immigration, an argument that focuses on the "porous borders of the United States along the Arizona desert" gives the issue a scenic orientation.

• **The agent.** Who is on stage? Who are the relevant "players"? In the case of something like global warming, who are the most important "characters"? Automobile drivers? The President? Lawmakers? Different dramatizations of this issue will feature different actors. Political campaigns often put a lot of stress on the agent—that is, the person who is running for office claims to have certain qualities that we want in a leader. Again, many dramatizations of the 9/11 attacks focus on Osama bin Laden—they have a strong emphasis on the agent.

- **The act.** What is the key act in the scenario of events? Again, with the issue of terrorism in mind, in the dramatic scenarios of many, the key moment in time is September 11—this despite the fact that other acts of violence had occurred prior to 9/11. Or, if I am running for political office, and my key goal is to "reduce taxes for the beleaguered middle class," I am focusing on the act—what I will try to *do* in office.

- **The agency.** How did the actors do what they did? By what means did they accomplish what they set out to do? Part of the 9/11 drama is that the airborne terrorists sort of "snuck aboard" the planes, with only box cutters as weapons—that was how they did what they did. As a result, most "solutions" to 9/11 in the airline industry have paid close attention to what people have in their luggage. Consider how different our "solutions" might be if the agency were different—for example, if the hijackers had overcome security personnel at the gate with machine guns.

- **The purpose.** Why did the actors do what they did? Were their motives "good" or "bad"? For example, do people immigrate to the U.S. illegally in order to take advantage of the U.S. welfare system, or to provide support for their families? Are they looking for "an easy way out," or are they "hard-working and dedicated"? Any discussion of the immigration issue will deal with some of these less "rational and objective" matters. Similarly, any discussion about regulating business involves motives and purpose. Are large corporations simply trying to make as much money as possible at the expense of consumers, or do they really want to serve the community in as many ways as they can? Clearly the answer to such questions reveals how an arguer is dramatizing with respect to purpose.

So, Burke's pentad is simply a way to consider the various parts of the drama—the way in which people symbolize about events, dramatistically. Used in an appropriate and sophisticated way, the pentad can help us understand this important dimension of argument. However, those for whom the pentad is "new" will either use it in a superficial way or really misunderstand how it can best be used. Take, for instance, Burke's notion of "scene." Suppose the President gives a speech on U.S. energy policy from the White House. Someone who treats the pentad too superficially and too literally is likely to say, "The scene is the White House." Well, that's not really "wrong," but it's not a dramatistic perspective or analysis. A dramatistic analysis must have a dramatistic *flavor*— simply "listing" things tells us nothing. In this case, one could begin by noting that the White House is a symbol of Presidential power, and that's why the speech is being given from the White House. But, frankly, a more interesting and meaningful pentadic analysis will examine how the President **constructs** the scene *in the speech itself*. For example, if the issue is energy policy, how is the scene portrayed? Is the U.S. portrayed as a place that is "fragile and depleted" with respect to energy resources, or is the scenic portrayal that of a nation with vast untapped energy sources that are simply waiting to be processed? Which dramatization is perceived as more plausible has lots to do with what you think our energy policy ought to involve. With respect to the scene, how is our nation depicted? Is the U.S. a place that is polluted and overrun with pipelines, oil platforms, and strip mines—or is it a relatively "pastoral" place with lots of room for both the elk and the petroleum companies? As always, I am not here to take sides on this issue—only to show the how the scene is dramatized has a lot to do with how we view the issue.

A "scenic" view of the 2008 Presidential election is also illuminating. Republican Vice Presidential candidate Sarah Palin was from Alaska. What kind of place *is* Alaska? In one dramatization, Alaska is a "desirable" location that is far from the corrupt, very "political" city of Washington, D.C.—it's from a place like Alaska that a candidate can emerge who is "untainted" by the "sleazy politics" of the nation's capital. (And, from Alaska, one can see Russia!) But another dramatization makes Sarah Palin the former mayor of a little town that's way too far from the "real world." And Alaska itself is a remote, unimportant part of the United States— too remote to be in touch with the problems facing the nation. In any event, Alaska is still the same place—it's a matter of how it is symbolized or portrayed. And again, Washington, D.C. can either be portrayed as the hallowed "cradle of democracy" in America, or as a political cesspool that gives members of Congress a warped, insulated view of the world. (Either way, or portrayed in some other way, it's still our capital!)

BORMANN'S SYMBOLIC CONVERGENCE THEORY

Another theorist who has examined the way in which people symbolize about issues and events is the late Ernest Bormann from the University of Minnesota. Early in his career, Bormann began to realize that students in small task-oriented groups would engage in a lot of conversation that was not directly connected to the task at hand. Rather, it was focused on the past or on the future, and it usually involved dramatic portrayals of things that reflected the feelings and the mind-set of the group. For example, if one group member—say, "Ted"—had once again missed a group meeting, the other members of the group would tell dramatic stories about Ted. Maybe they would liken Ted to a soldier who had gone AWOL (absent without leave), and then make jokes about how this absent soldier would lose the next war for them, and that he would likely be missing from his own funeral. Or, on another topic, maybe members of the group would start to talk about college life in general, comparing their school to a giant factory, stamping out people who are all identical, manufacturing them to fit in to society, and without any sort of warranty or recall program in place for "defective merchandise." Such stories, often embellished with great detail, were initially referred to by Bormann as "fantasy themes" created by the group. That term has nothing to do with "sexual fantasies" or "crazy falsehoods," but it has everything to do with how people symbolize about their world and share those symbolizations. Fantasy themes are stories with a dramatic element that people identify with, share, and "chime into."

So, how does all of this relate to argument? Well, eventually Bormann began to realize that this type of dramatizing occurred not only in small groups, but in the society at-large. These dramatizations involved "good guys" and "bad guys"; there was an agreed-upon plot line; there was a stage on which the players acted. And, each dramatization, if it is shared by groups of people, gathers a type of argumentative momentum—that is, commonly-shared dramatizations can convince people of many things. Eventually, Bormann developed a more comprehensive term for this phenomenon; what started as "fantasy theme analysis"—a tool to help understand how two or more people share meaning—became "symbolic convergence theory," a broader sense of how and why people share these meanings. Viewed through the lens of symbolic convergence theory, almost all arguments have a dramatistic component—that is, they offer a belief about the world and symbolize that belief in dramatic terms. As Bormann (1980, 188-189) explains it,

> The central focus of the symbolic convergence perspective is upon the common communicative processes by which human beings converge their individual fantasies, dreams, and meanings into shared symbol systems. . . . The convergence viewpoint provides an assumptive system for the analysis of messages in order to discover the manifest content of fantasy themes and evidence that groups of people have shared the symbolic interpretations implied by them. The shared fantasies may begin to cluster around common scripts or types, and when members of the community allude to such shared scripts they provide further evidence that the symbol systems are shared.

Consider, for example, those who believe in "conceal and carry" laws—that is, they argue for the right of most citizens to be able to carry a handgun, presumably for personal protection. Such an argument is likely tied to a number of specific fantasy themes, such as:

Joe Sixpack bought a gun ten years ago to keep in his house so he could protect his family. Joe has always been a law-abiding citizen and in the past ten years has never used that gun, but he and his family sleep well at night knowing that it's there. **OR**

Nicole never even used to go out at night after 6 p.m., but now that she has a legally-obtained firearm, she walks through the toughest parts of town without blinking an eye.

A fantasy **theme** is a specific dramatization—for example, individual stories about responsible, law-abiding gun owners are "good citizens" who help protect their loved ones and deter criminals. But Bormann believed that different fantasy themes dealing with different issues can have common thematic elements that make them a **fantasy type**. In this case, for instance, one could propose a fantasy type that I will call "the power of the individual." Law-abiding individuals who own guns are one example of this fantasy type. But so is the person who patrols the streets of a crime-ridden neighborhood at night and watches out for illegal activity. And so is the person who single-handedly raises money for the Cancer Society by biking across the entire state of North Dakota. And so too is the housewife who sends little gifts to all of our troops stationed overseas. In each case, the fantasy is that an individual who stands up for "what's right" can and will make a difference. In other words, a fantasy type looks across a set of particular fantasy themes and tries to see what they have in common. And again, to keep argument in mind, if I can convince you, dramatistically, that individual people can make a difference, then I might be able to convince you to donate your time or your money to some worthy cause; the critical issue becomes whether you are willing to "buy into" the dramatization.

For those who favor the right to carry handguns, some of those fantasy types would probably be:

- **The world as a crazy, chaotic, unpredictable place.** One "scenic" dimension of this argument might be that you never know what will happen. Just watch the news—the world can be a pretty dangerous place! Most every day can be "normal," but you never know when some "kook" or "bad guy" might come into your life out of the blue. Crime is out of control, and so are criminals themselves. Therefore, you need to be prepared.

- **Police as overburdened and unavailable.** In a crisis, you can't just call the cops. Police would not really be the "villains" here, but there could be a sense that when you're in a crisis, calling 911 just won't do the trick—before anyone shows up you might be dead. Hard as they may try, the police will not always be there to help you. The world often demands that *you* take action when there is a crisis.

- **The United States as a bastion of "freedom."** The story of our nation, some would say, is that we broke away from British rule in order to become free and independent. With that freedom, we must have the right to defend ourselves and our loved ones. Indeed, the 2nd amendment to the Constitution was written by those noble "founding fathers" to protect the very right to bear arms. And in a more "extreme" version of this fantasy, we need to be armed to protect ourselves against our very government, because government could someday be even more of a "villain" than it already is. An armed citizenry keeps the government honest.

- **Carrying handguns thwarts criminals.** By their nature, criminals are sneaky opportunists who will take advantage of innocent, law-abiding people—but if they think that ordinary people are "packing heat," they will think twice before trying to mug, rob, and murder someone. Handguns themselves become a sort of "agent of peace," and their presence can, ironically, make things more safe.

- **The ordinary person is responsible and can make a difference.** Quite possibly another fantasy connected to this argument is the idea that we can all be "heroic" and do our part in the world. People who own guns are competent and conscientious people who care about using guns responsibly, who take the necessary training to use them, and who teach their kids about gun safety. Gun owners are quite different people than criminals; they use guns rarely, and then, only "properly."

Without going into great detail, the dramatizations of those who are *opposed* to conceal and carry laws are constructed much differently. Recall that in the "pro-gun" dramatization, the "scene" is populated by criminals who can take advantage of you. For handgun opponents, the "scenic" dimension puts more stress on the guns themselves—they are everywhere, and they become the inanimate villains. In this alternative dramatization, one of the main problems is that there are so many guns out there that they are simply too available to anyone who wants one, thus inviting problems. And the dramatic portrayals of gun *owners* in this scenario tend to differ. Rather than being "protectors of order" and "true-blue Americans," gun enthusiasts are viewed as people who are a little too militaristic and paranoid, not to mention foolish. They (gun owners) don't realize that most guns are used in fits of drunkenness or rage, and that the main people who can get hurt or killed with a gun are either you the gun owner or people you know. Finally, rather than being a villain in this drama, the government stands as perhaps the only institution that can bring some order to the situation; the alternative, in this dramatic scenario, is a world that is even more dangerous when even more and more handguns are legally permissible. Indeed, in a typical handgun control argument, one of the biggest villains of all is the National Rifle Association—the NRA—which in this view has thwarted our attempts to adopt sane gun control laws for decades. In this dramatization, far from being patriotic, the NRA is the biggest enemy that we have to effective control of violent crime.

But now, to take it a step further, Bormann believed that various fantasy types can have things in common which can be considered a **rhetorical vision**. A rhetorical vision is a broad, overarching dramatization that explains any number of specific fantasy themes and fantasy types. I would contend, for example, that for some time in the United States, there has been what I will call a **"conservative rhetorical vision"** and a **"liberal rhetorical vision."** What does this mean? I shall try to illustrate.

Consider some of our common social problems—for example, poverty, crime, illiteracy, obesity, and so on. I would contend that the conservative rhetorical vision and the liberal rhetorical vision of these problems tend to be quite different and quite predictable. In the conservative rhetorical vision, why are people in poverty? Why do they commit crimes? Why are they overweight? The common answer is that they as individuals are to blame. The problem is *their* problem, and if these people could only work harder, or be better Christians, or spend more time on homework, or push themselves away from the dinner table sooner, they would be able to take care of these problems. In short, people are responsible for the problems they create, and the answer lies within the individual. **I would even suggest, just playing around with these ideas, that there are at least three different types of conservative rhetorical visions:**

- **The "Christian right" type**

Specific fantasy themes: stories about the Christian orientation/tradition of the culture and the "Founding Fathers," stories about the "godlessness" and "secularism" that are creeping into our society, stories about abortion and stem-cell research as illustrative of this godlessness, stories about prayer being suppressed in schools and other public places, the secularization of holidays, the lack of sexual morality and prevalence of drugs

- The "big government is bad" type

Specific fantasy themes: stories about excessive regulation of businesses, stories about people who have been "taxed to death," stories about people who have been harassed by government agencies, stories about unnecessary layers of bureaucracy, stories about increases in federal budgets, stories about "corrupt politicians," stories about how the government is plotting to become like "Big Brother" to take over every aspect of our lives

- The "stand up for yourself" type

Specific fantasy themes: stories about people becoming too dependent on welfare, stories about individuals who have "made it" by the sweat of their brow, stories about people who have learned to protect themselves with a personal handgun, stories about people who have overcome obstacles with determination and without government "handouts"

On the other hand, the liberal rhetorical vision tends to dramatize about these problems with a different emphasis and flavor (although you should keep in mind that throughout this discussion I am drastically oversimplifying things to make them initially easier to grasp—the real world is a little more complicated!). In the liberal rhetorical vision, if you're a criminal, it's more often because life has given you some bad breaks; if you're overweight, it's connected to genetics; if you're poor, it's because the capitalist system oppresses you. If people are gay, it's not that they choose to be gay; rather, they are predisposed to homosexuality—it's an "orientation," not a "lifestyle." (In the "Christian right" fantasy type, gay people, if they try hard enough, can actually learn to become straight!) And when there are problems, the government is there to help—to support and to nurture those in need, to assist them. But in the conservative rhetorical vision, as Ronald Reagan argued as he assumed the Presidency in 1981, government is not the solution—government is the problem. And therefore, Mr. Reagan spent eight years trying to get government "off the backs of the American people." Indeed, one of the fundamental differences between the conservative and the liberal rhetorical vision involves the role of government. In many conservative fantasy themes, government—whether the issue is taxes, or education, or religion, or business—tends to rob people of their freedoms. But in many liberal fantasy themes, government involvement is critical—whether it be to help those in poverty, to end discrimination, to keep businesses in line, to protect the environment, and so on.

Again, simply "playing around" with these ideas (which is part of the fun in using symbolic convergence theory in its qualitative form) **I might propose three different fantasy types within the overall liberal rhetorical vision:**

• **The "secular humanist" type**

Specific fantasy themes: stories about evangelical Christians who want to impose a Christian morality on the rest of the world, stories about conservatives who are out of touch with advances in science (such as evolution), stories that celebrate "modern" research such as stem-cell research, stories of abortion doctors and gay people being harassed and murdered, stories about how women are unfairly regarded as subservient to men, stories about the general narrow-mindedness and lack of cultural sensitivity of conservatives

• **The "Marxist critique of society" type**

Specific fantasy themes: stories about the oppressive power of the wealthy; stories about tax breaks and special privileges for the rich; stories about people who are oppressed because of their gender, or skin color, or sexual orientation; stories about how corporations now run the world; stories about how "special interest groups" control the nation's capital; stories about illegal immigrants whose contributions to the U.S. are ignored, stories about the "myth" that the U.S. is a "melting pot" that provides equal opportunities for all, stories about the need for government to be involved in addressing these issues, including the need for taxing the wealthy more aggressively

- The "pacifist" type

Specific fantasy themes: stories about the belligerent nature of the United States, stories about misguided military interventions in Vietnam and Iraq, stories about "animal rights" and the abuse of animals in "factory farms," stories about the virtues of vegetarianism and organic farming, stories about the inhumanity of corporal punishment and capital punishment, stories about homophobia, stories about the value of meditation and other forms of "Eastern wisdom," stories that praise the value of individual and group therapy and the self-realization that it promotes

Well, perhaps you get the idea. Many arguments are more than "data" or "information"; they have a "flavor" to them that is dramatistic in nature. And in Bormann's view, the dramatistic themes—the symbolic reality portrayed—become an inescapable and essential component of most any issue. So, whether you are making an argument, reading or hearing an argument, refuting an argument, or simply analyzing an argument, it's helpful to be tuned in to the dramatistic elements within a message.

JENSEN'S HEURISTIC

Finally, a less well-known but very thorough and perceptive analysis of problems, solutions, and the arguments about them was developed by Professor J. Vernon Jensen, author of *Argumentation: Reasoning and Communication*. In this 1980s argumentation text, now out of print, Jensen develops a "heuristic"—that is, a set of systematic questions—that a student of argument can use to analyze how a particular issue is conceived of and discussed. And, like Burke and Bormann, Jensen's approach has a decidedly dramatistic flavor. In part, Jensen's perspective is to look at problems in terms of **villains, victims,** and **allies.**

Take, for example, the **"villain"** in any particular problem. Jensen would have us consider, among other questions:

- **Is the villain personal or impersonal?** Some people argue that a particular problem is due to some person or persons. Maybe the President is to blame; maybe it's a particular criminal; maybe it's the guy next door. On the other hand, sometimes the villain is not a person at all: "capitalism" is to blame, or "the internal combustion engine," or "the system." Clearly this is an important distinction, because how we analyze a problem reflects in turn what would be the most appropriate and effective solution. If we see "television" as the villain with respect to lower educational performance by our K-12 students, that's quite a bit different from blaming "parents" or "teachers" for the problem. With respect to drug abuse, some people see the drugs themselves as the villain, while others would argue that those who sell and use drugs are to blame.

• **Is the villain remote or precipitating?** Jensen would have us consider whether the source of the problem is immediately visible (precipitating), or whether the real source of the problem goes back in time and is thus more remote. For example, the problem of crime in America could be identified as the immediate actions of particular criminals, or it could be viewed as something that has been created by a whole series of legal, social, political, and economic factors over the last fifty years. If there is a violent incident in one of our schools, do we see the villain as the person who committed the violence (the precipitating cause), or do we blame a culture that has failed to "properly" raise our kids and give them good moral values (a more remote cause)? As with all of these categories, the idea is not necessarily to pick one of the two as "right" and the other as "wrong," but to see that many problems potentially have both dimensions and that we must be aware of both of them.

• **What motivates the villains?** With the issue of "terrorism" in mind, the question of motivation becomes critical. Some would argue that what motivates terrorism is a belief about the role of the United States in the world; others would say that it is a religious and cultural belief. Some believe that a very simple story line is evolving here: terrorists are people who just hate the United States and the "western world" and simply want to kill as many people as possible. Others would contend that "terrorists" are people who are poor and alienated; they seek justice and are so desperate to achieve this end that they will resort to violence. To the extent that Islam as a religion has become part of this debate, some are asking, what kind of religion *is* Islam? Does it motivate people to violence? Or, are its foundations built around many of the same motivational principles as Christianity?

Another example: to the extent that "politicians" are seen as villains with respect to some issues, some arguers only tend to give them negative motivations—for example, "those politicians only want to protect the rich and to line their own pockets." Other people see political office holders as "public servants" who do a lot of hard work, conscientiously, on behalf of their country and their constituents. Which dramatization appeals to you more might say a lot about whether you support term limits for members of Congress!

With respect to the "**victim**," the Jensen approach invites questions such as these:

• **What are the qualities of the victim?** Clearly, in argument, *who* is being victimized matters. Generally speaking, if the "victims" have desirable traits, then it's going to be easier to argue that something is wrong. On the other hand, if the "victims" are perceived as less desirable, then even if my case is good in principle, I may have difficulty. If I'm defending the mother of two toddlers in a civil lawsuit, it's very different than if I'm defending a child pornographer—even if the two were equally "wronged" in some way. On a geopolitical note, one of the reasons we fought what is now called the "First Gulf War" in the early 1990s was because many believed that poor little Kuwait, a tiny nation next to Iraq, was being victimized by Saddam Hussein—and therefore, the U.S. needed to step in and rescue this little innocent nation. As with all of these matters, whether that was "true" or not is not really the issue here: from a dramatistic perspective, how people perceive a situation—their "subjective reality"—is what matters.

• **Are the victims personal or impersonal?** As with "villains," the victims of any social problem may not be people. The victims may be people--the homeless, or the poor, or people of color--but the victims can also be things like "the economy," "the environment," or "the health care system." In the ongoing debate over global warming, it makes a difference as to whether you see the victim as being beachfront property, people living in certain regions of the world, or particular species of birds and animals.

In addition to villains and victims, Jensen adds another layer to the drama of argument: **allies**. In his view, different people and ideas may function as allies for an arguer, which raises questions such as:

• **Are the allies current or past?** Sometimes arguers rely on contemporary experts to make their point—for example, that "the latest research" shows the value of regular exercise. Other times, arguers use allies from the past—for example, the ancient Greeks believed in the value of "sound mind and sound body," pointing out the longstanding belief in the importance of exercise. Some who defend the right of Americans to own handguns use "the founding fathers" as their allies, believing that those who founded this nation believed in such a right. Others, however, say that a "modern" understanding of the 2nd amendment to the Constitution, which deals with handguns, provides no such right.

• **Are the allies experts or lay people?** Some arguments use people who are considered experts to make their case—for example, that almost all scientists agree that the worldwide supply of fossil fuels in dwindling. On the other hand, sometimes an argument will be based on what "common people" believe—for after all, common people have common sense! So, some say we should not try to keep our teenagers away from alcohol because "everyone knows they will just find a way to get booze whether it's legal or not."

Now, besides these more "dramatistic" categories, the Jensen heuristic also includes other analytical distinctions that are worth considering as we examine problems and solutions.

With respect to **problems**, Jensen also asks us to consider:

• **Is it a problem of commission or omission?** For example, one could criticize the television industry for "showing too much sex and violence" (a problem of commission), or, for having too few shows that deeply investigate important social problems (a problem of omission). In other words, sometimes the current system might be indicted for something harmful that it *is* doing, while other times the concern is about something good and important that it is *not* doing. If you believe that your weight problem is due to eating three sweet rolls for breakfast every morning, that's a sin of commission; if you believe the problem is that you don't get enough exercise, that's a sin of omission. Some people looking at our military involvement in the Middle East will argue that "sitting by and doing nothing" would be a sin of omission, while others argue that intervening in the affairs of another nation, militarily, is a tangible error of commission. Again, it can't be stressed enough that there is probably not one "right" answer in these types of situations—only differing ways of conceiving of the problem that must be considered.

• **Is it a problem of attitude or deed?** Your local basketball team is not doing well. Is it a problem of deed? Do the guards have poor mechanics when it comes to the jump shot? Or is it a problem of attitude—in this case, that no one really *cares* to improve? For many years in this nation, racial discrimination had characteristics of both—some believed that "deeds" such as separate drinking fountains for African-Americans and discriminatory voter registration laws were the reasons for injustice, while others cited the main problem as being one of attitude. The "attitude" point of view says that no matter what the laws may be, the key issue is to have a feeling of respect for one another, and that no law can really change that. Even at your job, your manager might be quite angry if she knew that you broke the laptop on your desk (a deed), but if she felt that your attitude was positive, she might be willing to forgive you. From the perspective of Burke's pentad, a strong emphasis on "deed" is really a dramatistic focus on the "act," and a strong emphasis on "attitude" is more related to the issue of "purpose." If the President withholds certain information from the American public, we might well conclude that it's not a commendable "act," but if we realized that he was doing so out of a concern for national security, we might see it as a legitimate "purpose." The issue becomes, should we focus on what the person *did* or with what *mindset* they did it?

• **Is the problem local or distant?** This "spatial" dimension of the problem is also important. Do we view the problem as a local problem, a state problem, a national problem, or even an international problem? Depending on how you answer that question will have a lot to do with what makes for the best "solution." And again, like all of these other categories, there is no automatic "right" answer—often, a good case can be made for different points of view. If we have problems in the Gotham City Schools, is that because Gotham City High has lousy teachers? Poor administrators? Parents who don't know how to help their kids? Or is the problem that state aid for local school districts is insufficient? Or, is the problem that the federal government has not provided sufficient attention to the problem? Sometimes the key issue in the argument involves how "close" or how "far" the real source of the problem is. Of course, this is not necessarily an "either/or" issue. For example, one well-known slogan in the environmental movement these days is "Act locally and think globally." What this implies to me is that one needs to consider their own personal acts (do you "reduce, reuse, and recycle"?) but also have an awareness of the "big picture" around the world. That means that if you try to recycle the old computer in your house by taking it to the local recycling center, you may also have to consider that this computer may wind up being disassembled in some small, less industrialized nation by people working in a rather polluted environment. At any rate, the analytical issue involves whether to focus more on what's happening on your block, or what's happening in Tokyo; both are potentially relevant.

• **Is the problem long-standing or recent?** Has the problem existed for a long time, or is it a fairly recent development? Once again, how you answer that question has a lot to do with possible solutions. For example, if all civilizations throughout all times have had problems with "substance abuse," then issues involving alcohol and drugs need to be seen differently than if you think drug abuse is a fairly recent phenomenon that's really only been around in a significant way for the last thirty or forty years. If there has always been "juvenile delinquency" in some form, that's different than saying teenagers have only been behaving anti-socially in the last few decades.

• **Is the problem present or impending?** Is the problem happening right now—today—or is it something that's going to happen if we keep moving in this direction? The issue of global warming readily comes to mind here—some people say the environmental damage is already with us, while others argue that we are several decades away from significant problems. The issue of Social Security also is relevant: some believe that the Social Security system is already in deep trouble right now, while others contend that it is and will be solvent for some time into the future. Obviously, it makes a real difference which way we view this "temporal" dimension of the problem.

• **Is it a problem of affluence or scarcity?** Is it that we have too *much* of something, or not *enough*? It could be argued that many "industrialized" countries are dealing with too much—too many cars, too much air pollution, too many electronic gizmos, too many things to do, etc. etc. But, our problems could also be viewed as a matter of scarcity: the scarcity of "family time," the scarcity of "common sense," the scarcity of health care personnel, and so on.

Finally, Jensen also looks at the **solutions** people propose. What characteristics are relevant here?

• **Is the solution procedural or substantive?** Sometimes people call for solutions that are really procedural—for example, they want to set up a committee to study the problem. Or, maybe they like the current law in place—whether it be a criminal law, an environmental law, or a law regulating business—but they want the law to be enforced more consistently. That, too, is largely a procedural change. On the other hand, a substantive change involves a solution that is "definite" and "different." For example, if I said that we should legalize marijuana across the United States for medicinal purposes, that would be a substantive change in the law. So too would be a call for a new pro football stadium in our community. People will often argue about whether a change needs to be procedural or substantive.

• **Is the solution voluntary or mandatory?** This is obviously an important question, and one that people argue about quite a bit. There was a time in our nation when wearing a seat belt when driving was entirely voluntary; many people thought it was their "right" to *not* wear a seatbelt, just as some have thought that "big brother" (that is, the government) should not require us to wear a helmet if we ride on a motorcycle. Others, however, regard mandatory seat belt and helmet laws as essential to everyone's health and welfare, and that government is not acting like an "evil dictator," but rather, sort of a "benevolent uncle" who wants to protect us from ourselves.

Whether a solution should be voluntary or mandatory is one of the biggest issues within arguments on a wide variety of issues.

• **Do we repair, or do we replace?** This is essentially what is described in chapter 2 as the issue of "blame/inherency." Can we fix/repair what we have now, or does the solution need to be something entirely new? At what point do you fix the computer, or dishwasher, or vacuum cleaner that you have now, and when do you simply need to buy one that's entirely new and different? This is the question that arguers and policy makers face on innumerable issues as well. As all this relates to "fantasy themes," sometimes people will say that trying to fix what we are doing now is "just putting a band-aid on the problem," or that "it's like trying to fix a 1973 Buick with 200,000 miles on it." In other words, the prevailing fantasy is that the policy is like a wound or an old car.

• **Is the solution one of expansion or contraction?** You've just opened a new pizza parlor, and business is great. In order to better serve your customers, not to mention maybe make more money, should you open up a second pizza parlor? That would be a solution that involves expansion. If we decide to put mental health care coverage under a health care plan that previously only paid for "physical" illnesses, that too is a solution involving "expansion." In other words, sometimes people believe that "more" is the answer. Other times, it's contraction: we're having problems at Acme Widget Company, and so we have to cut all departmental budgets 10 percent, across the board. Even Major League Baseball, a few years ago, thought about contraction as a way to address some of its problems: one such proposal was to make pro baseball "leaner and meaner" by simply eliminating the franchises of the Montreal Expos and the Minnesota Twins. But, the Expos moved to Washington, and your textbook author is happy to say that the Twins still play in his home state! At any rate, it's important, once again, to remind you that this set of criteria doesn't necessarily mean that one of the two options is automatically "right" or "better." Maybe the Acme Widget Company would be better off in the long run with an "expansion"—rather than cut their budgets and "contract," maybe they should develop and market some new product line that would restore them to their old glory ("expand"). But, these are the things that people think about and argue about.

• **Is the solution one of survival or enrichment?** There are some solutions that would be "nice" to enact ("enrichment") and others where our health and welfare absolutely demand a solution ("survival"). As with all of these categories, people will argue about what type of solution is being offered. For some, a new major league baseball stadium in town might be regarded as nice (who doesn't like a new state-of-the-art ballpark?), but for others, a new stadium is considered crucial to the economic health of the community ("survival"). Similarly, some regard the U.S. space program merely as an interesting adventure that should be funded when money is available, whereas others see it as essential to our long-term survival, providing valuable and essential benefits to humanity.

• **Is the solution "forward to Utopia" or "back to Eden"?** Some solutions have a sort of dramatic appeal because they represent a new, modern "Utopian" approach. These days, many of the forward-to-Utopia solutions involve the computer—for example, let's computerize the parking services for our firm and do all business about parking permits on-line, or better yet, find our Soul Mate on-line through some sort of computer dating service. Or, stem-cell research fits here: the use of new biotechnology using highly sophisticated procedures to cure certain nasty diseases has a "futuristic" feel to it. On the other hand, sometimes advocates are really calling for a return to "old" values and simpler solutions— metaphorically, to the golden age before Adam and Eve ruined the Garden of Eden. For example, rather than touting our ability to do even less invasive and more sophisticated heart bypass surgery, a back to Eden solution would be, good ol' common sense—eat right and exercise more. If you do, you can throw all of that medical equipment away. In a similar vein, a back to Eden solution for the schools would involve "getting back to the basics" rather than relying on technology—what we really need, from this perspective, are teachers and kids who care and are willing to put in some good old-fashioned effort. There is dramatic appeal in that idea as well.

CONCLUSION

Seen in its totality, a dramatistic perspective on argument is a rich and potentially insightful way to understand how arguments function as they do. If you can learn to think dramatistically, you will also come to realize some important lessons in how arguments are made, defended, refuted, and analyzed.

REFERENCES

Bormann, Ernest. *Communication theory*. New York: Holt, Rinehart, and Winston, 1980.

Burke, Kenneth. *A grammar of motives*. Berkeley, CA: University of California Press, 1969.

Jensen, J. Vernon. *Argumentation: Reasoning in communication*. New York: D. Van Nostrand, 1981.

Chapter 9

CONSTRUCTING A CASE FOR CHANGE

After reading this chapter, you should understand:

- The advantages of advocating change
- The advantages to opposing change
- How policy issues usually involve a debate between "realism" and "idealism"
- What a "should/would" argument involves
- Different organizational formats: topical, problem-solution, causal, comparative advantage, method of residue, criteria-based, and the motivated sequence
- Why and how arguers should structure a solution
- Why the organization of a case needs to be explicit

Specialized terms to know:

- power of fiat
- topical organization
- problem-solution organization
- causal organization
- comparative advantage organization
- method of residue organization
- criteria organization
- attention step
- need step

- satisfaction step
- visualization step
- action step
- preview
- oral signposts
- agency
- mandates
- enforcement
- funding and staffing

So, you know all the theoretical underpinnings of argument. You understand all about claims, evidence, reasoning, and the use of language. But now you have to take all that and put it into a meaningful package. That's what this chapter is all about.

Advantages of advocating change

Before examining the various organizational structures that one might employ, it's first worth considering the general advantages and disadvantages of trying to propose a change. If you are arguing that we should change a policy, one factor that is often in your favor is that there are indeed lots of perceived problems in the world. For example, we all know that there is hunger, and air pollution, and overpopulation, and homelessness, and crime, and so we know that people are trying to find ways to deal with these problems. Put another way, we normally don't debate issues when people think that everything is just great; the very fact that they are being debated is an indication of some "restlessness" in the world. Sometimes the perception of a problem can predispose people to yearn for *some* sort of solution, and that obviously helps anyone calling for change. On a related note, the other advantage change agents tend to have is that they may well be perceived as trying to "make the world a better place." People who propose solutions to problems can seem like the "good guys," because they want to actually "do something," if you will. Change agents can seem committed, concerned, and sometimes, even optimistic and idealistic.

Advantages of opposing change

On the other hand, those who oppose change have some common advantages as well. For one thing, those who defend the current system—the status quo—have the advantage of presumption. As discussed in chapter 2, presumption is a natural tendency to want to stay with what we have until someone can show a clearly better alternative. Opponents of change have presumption in their favor. Second, there is often a good set of reasons why we are doing what we currently do. Yes, sometimes on the face of it, the status quo seems downright silly—why, we ask, should there be such a crazy policy? (For example, the Electoral College can seem like a strange, outmoded way to elect a President—that is, until one examines how and why it operates as it does.) Well, those who oppose change would be well-advised to carefully investigate why we are doing what we are currently doing; there is often a "method to our madness" that can be the basis for opposing a change from what we have now. Finally, I would contend that in general, it's easier to demonstrate that there are "problems" than it is to demonstrate that there are workable and desirable "solutions" to those problems. We all know there are problems; the "trick" is finding a way to *deal* with them. In that sense, if you are advocating change, it's critical that you can show a workable and desirable solution. If you are opposing change, chances are some of your strongest counterarguments will involve whether the proposed plan of action will really work, and if, on balance, it would be an improvement.

Realism vs. idealism

Another common pattern that I have seen in many contested issues involves a clash between "realism" and "idealism." Take, for example, the question of whether we should provide, at taxpayers' expense, food and lodging for all homeless people in the United States. In an ideal world, no one in this nation should go hungry, and everyone should have a roof over their head. So, from an idealistic standpoint, such a plan is very appealing. Who could be opposed to trying to help people out? On the other hand, a more "realistic" view of this issue raises other considerations. Realistically, how could we finance such a plan? Who would pay for all of this? And would it simply encourage more people who are "down on their luck" to give up the quest for employment and self-sufficiency? Similarly, we might like to mandate that all U.S. high school graduates should have to pass some sort of "minimum competency test" in order to get their diploma, but in "real world" terms, is this feasible? Would such a test be culturally biased? Would it be detrimental to otherwise capable students who are not especially good at standardized tests? And would schools sort of "lower their standards" and make sure that no matter what happened, students were appropriately "coached" to pass such an exam at the expense of "deeper" learning? Again, the "real" and the "ideal" might be very different.

If indeed most any issue has a more "idealistic" side and a more "realistic" side, it would be important to be mindful about which side you happen to be on. If your position seems hopelessly idealistic, you will need to convince others that such a proposal really can work and is not "pie in the sky." Conversely, if inherent to your position is a sort of hard-nosed reality about "the way things are," you may need to demonstrate that you are not simply a cynical, "contrary" person, but want a better world as well—it's just that your vision of that world has to always take into account certain pragmatic realities. In any event, I see this dynamic in many debates about controversial issues, and you need to be aware of its potential relevance to how you construct your case.

The issue of "should" versus "would"

One final matter needs to be examined before looking at the various options for structuring a case. In academic debate, the team advocating change—usually called the "affirmative" team—has what is called the "power of fiat." Fiat (Latin for "let it be done") is a theoretical construct which focuses on whether a proposal is **desirable**, rather than whether it is likely to be **enacted** in the "real world." What that means is this: if I say we should ban all pornography, but you say that would be unconstitutional because it violates the 1st amendment to the Constitution—so therefore we can't do it—I am entitled to say, "I don't care what *is* the case—I am advocating what *should be* the case. So, if it takes an amendment to the Constitution to ban all pornography, then that's what we should do. In any event, I do not have to prove that my pornography ban *will* happen, or is even *likely* to happen, only that it *should* happen." So, in contest debate, people do not have to argue about whether something actually would happen, only whether it should. Saying that there is currently a law against what the affirmative is advocating is not usually considered a relevant argument.

However, in the "real world," the "should/would" issue gets a bit trickier. On the one hand, those advocating change may well want to argue that if a change is worthwhile, it's also worth changing whatever other laws need to be changed in order to make it happen. Therefore, if we have to repeal or modify a particular city ordinance in order to build a new community center, then so be it! On the other hand, because we are not in the more narrow and "theoretical" arena of academic debate, the hard reality is that some proposals for change might be so problematic in a practical sense that they would not be worth doing. Political resistance could be so strong, or the legal "ripple effects" of a change might be so disastrous (such as repealing the 1st amendment) that there is no virtue in considering such a change. Suffice it to say that in academic debate, advocates for change don't have to demonstrate that their proposal will or can be adopted, but advocates in the larger society probably need to be more sensitive to this issue. Merely saying, "Well, we *should* require all people to go to college, even if it's not legal, likely, or feasible" might seem too unrealistic to consider. In the end, outside of the academic debate world, advocates must be able to show that a plan of action *is* realistic in the sense that it could readily be implemented and wouldn't become a legal and political nightmare.

Organizational formats

When making a case for change, it's helpful to have a way to organize it. The most obvious reason to do so is for clarity—explicitly organized information is usually easier to grasp, and is also easier to remember. But another important reason to be concerned about organization is really strategic, because how you organize and structure a case can have an impact of how persuasive or convincing it is. As Zarefsky (2005, 195) argues,

> Organization is a major strategic resource that greatly affects the outcome of a speech. You need to bring critical thinking and reflection to such organizational decisions as the number and order of ideas, how you group them, what you call them, and how you relate them to the audience.

Therefore, let's see what options you have in this regard.

Most any composition text or most any public speaking text will explain ways to organize a message. Some of these organizational formats are more appropriate and more workable for informative messages than argumentative or persuasive messages. The two formats that are less applicable for argument, but more applicable for simply sharing information, would be:

- chronological organization – first I'll discuss the U.S. economy in the 18th century, then the 19th century, and then the 20th century.
- spatial organization – first I'll discuss the U.S. economy in the Northeast, then the U.S. economy in the South, then the Midwest, and finally the West.

It's certainly not impossible to organize an argumentative case in either of these ways, but they tend to be more common and more useful for "packaging information" than "packaging arguments." So, let us consider some other more viable options for an argumentative message:

TOPICAL ORGANIZATION

Sometimes also called "categorical" organization, you simply try to provide a list of your best reasons for supporting the thesis—the central idea—of your case. In an oral message, you would commonly have 2-5 such reasons, and you would want to make sure that they do not "overlap" and are clear. For example:

The U.S. educational system should be changed to a year-round school calendar.
1. Such a change would enhance student learning.
2. Such a change (4 shorter vacations per year) would improve student motivation and morale.
3. Such a change would make more efficient use of school facilities.

Or, if you were making the case that we should ban capital punishment in the United States, your organizational structure might be:
1. Capital punishment discriminates on the basis of race.
2. Capital punishment has resulted in the execution of innocent people.
3. Capital punishment does not deter violent crime.
4. Capital punishment is inhumane.

For many issues, a topical organizational scheme flows naturally from your research and your thinking. The main thing is to have discrete, separate, identifiable reasons, and that's what a topical approach is designed to do.

PROBLEM-SOLUTION ORGANIZATION

In contest debate, this approach is often called a "need" case, in that it tries to identify a need—a problem--and then provide a solution to it. Essentially, the case is comprised of two main parts (problem and solution) which may in turn be subdivided into separate aspects of each. In chapter 2, you may remember the concept of stock issues—in a problem-solution format, you are basically dealing with each of them: (a) to show a significant problem in the status quo, (b) to show that this problem is inherent to the status quo, (c) to provide a workable solution, and (d) show the desirability of the solution—in particular, that its benefits outweigh any possible disadvantages. A problem-solution approach seems clear and logical, and it's a very common way that cases are made in our culture. An example would be:

States should ban the use of cell phones by automobile drivers.
1. Driving while talking on a cell phone has led to many fatalities (significance).
2. As long as state laws do not prohibit cell phone use by drivers, these fatalities will continue (inherency).
3. A cell phone ban is feasible and has worked in many jurisdictions (solvency).
4. The advantages of banning cell phones far outweigh any possible drawbacks (desirability).

CAUSAL (OR CAUSE-EFFECT) ORGANIZATION

This case development approach involves a sequence of major points that build on one another—the first is the cause of the second, the second is the cause of the third, and so on. For example:

1. Poor academic skills are a significant problem in the public schools.
2. Those who lack sufficient academic skill are more likely to become unemployed.
3. Unemployment is a major factor in increases in the crime rate.
4. Increases in crime hurt innocent people and put undue stress on our prison system.
5. Therefore, we need better academic programs in the public schools.

Or, if you were making a case to mandate more energy-efficient vehicles in the United States, your causal case could look like this:

1. Currently, people can drive any type of car that they want, including many that are not energy-efficient.
2. Such a situation creates greater consumption of petroleum products.
3. Greater demand for petroleum increases our economic dependence on other nations.

4. This dependence forces the U.S. to cater to other nations and make foreign policy decisions that are not in our best interests.
5. Therefore, the federal government should mandate that all passenger vehicles sold in the U.S. after the year 2015 must get at least 30 miles per gallon of gasoline.

If you can get the receivers to think in the "logical" way that you are proceeding, the conclusion—your proposal—may seem almost inevitable. But of course, if one or more of the points leading to your proposal is called into question, then life becomes a little more difficult. But this approach has merit in the right situation.

COMPARATIVE ADVANTAGE ORGANIZATION

An examination of the comparative advantage case format is helpful and important; unfortunately, it's also involves a more elaborate explanation.

To this point in the text, it has been more or less assumed or implied that a case for change needs to be built around "problems." After all, that's what the problem-solution format is all about, and that is how stock issues have been discussed so far. And, frankly, many people instinctively want to know if there are problems, because, as I have mentioned previously, some will say, "If it ain't broke, why fix it?" Well, a comparative advantage case operates from a different premise, and with a different rhetorical emphasis.

Suppose you wanted to convince me to buy a new car. You could tell me about how ugly and unsafe my current vehicle is. You could tell me that it pollutes the air and is costing me way too much in gasoline. All of those claims would be indictments of the status quo—that is, my current car. However, let's suppose that my car is less than a year old, only has 8,000 miles on the odometer, and gets pretty decent gas mileage. *Now* how are you going to sell me a new, different vehicle? Initially, it might seem hopeless—and it probably is more difficult. But, a comparative advantage approach is designed to deal with obstacles of this sort.

Rather than harping on deficiencies or problems within the current system, a comparative advantage case puts its emphasis on future benefits of adopting the proposal, and in a very intentional way. In a sense, a comparative advantage case makes no effort to "attack" the status quo—often because the status quo is doing all right. (Remember that almost-new car I'm driving—I'm reason-ably content with it.) So, I must be able to identify future benefits. Suppose you concede that my current car is a pretty decent ride—you can even admit that. But. If you were to buy this other car, there are advantages to the purchase that you simply can't get with what you have now. For example (hypothetically):

1. This new car gets 4 miles per gallon better mileage—you'll save $500 in gas per year.
2. This new car has 12 cup holders, not just 6—it's more con-venient for you and your family.
3. This new car has 8 speakers instead of just 4—your CDs will sound amazingly better.
4. With standard *side* air bags, this new car is safer than what you have now.

There—you've just given me four comparative advantages to purchasing a new car. Now it is worth noting that each advantage is, in a sense, an implied criticism of the status quo. To say that the new vehicle will get 4 miles per gallon better mileage is also to say that my car is deficient to some extent. And if 12 cup holders is more than I have now, the alleged advantage is a type of veiled "problem" with the status quo. However, in a true comparative advantage case, the advocate for change doesn't want to get into a battle over the status quo. After all, if my current car already gets 25 mpg, it's hard to put it in the same league as a real "gas-guzzler"—the reality is that it gets adequate mileage. So, from a comparative advantage perspective, I'm better off, in this case, put-ting the stress on the "improvement" that will come with a differ-ent vehicle. Therefore, comparative advantage cases are especially useful when there aren't a lot of enormous problems in the sta-tus quo—in other words, you can't show people being murdered, bridges crumbling, rampant disease, or the like. But what you can show is something that is comparatively better.

Now all we need to do is make the transition from cars to pol-icy systems. Selling a new policy (for example, free state-funded tuition for all community colleges in the U.S.) involves the same sort of benefit-listing as in the car example. Why should we have state-funded tuition for all community colleges? Here are some (again hypothetical) comparative advantages:

1. Under such a plan, more high school graduates would attend college.
2. With such a plan, the U.S. would have a more highly-skilled workforce.
3. With this plan, crime in the U.S. would decrease because more young people would be making productive use of their time.

Notice again that in each case, the focus is on future benefits—not deficiencies in the current system. As Inch, Warnick, and Endres (2006, 262) explain this idea,

> Sometimes, the present system is already attempting to cure the ill, and there is no obvious deficiency in the way the system is dealing with a problem. In such cases, an advocate may want to argue for a new system that is superior to the present system. . . The comparative-advantages argument develops the position that in comparison with the current system, the proposed system has more benefits. Instead of isolating a problem and offering a cure (as with the needs case) the focus of a comparative-advantages argument is to argue that the advocate's proposal is comparatively stronger or more beneficial than the current system.

The final important issue here is to examine how the stock issues relate to a comparative advantage case. Initially, they might seem to be irrelevant, because such a case does not claim a significant, inherent problem. Instead, the first two stock issues become:

• **Can I present a *significant* advantage?** If I am claiming an advantage, a commonsensical question would be, is it significant? Anyone arguing comparative advantages will want to make them compelling.
• **Can I show an *inherent* advantage?** In this case, inherency means, can I show that the benefits are unique to my proposal? If the status quo could potentially achieve these benefits, then my advantages would not be inherent to my proposal. From a stock issues perspective, I need to be able to show that these benefits flow only from doing what I want to be done—otherwise, why adopt the proposal?

The last two stock issues—solvency and desirability—remain the same. I must be able to show that my proposal would actually do what it claims to do (solvency), and that on balance, the advantages outweigh any potential disadvantages (desirability).

Again, a comparative advantage approach is especially helpful when you cannot demonstrate terrible problems in the present but can show potential benefits of a change in the future.

METHOD OF RESIDUE ORGANIZATION

This approach also has a special place. It's particularly useful when no option is "perfect," including yours! This organizational schema essentially goes through the various alternatives, one by one, and shows that each alternative policy has its flaws, thus making yours more attractive, or at least, less unattractive. For example, I think we can agree that nuclear power is not without its critics. Yet, we all want our TVs and refrigerators to run, and because we do, we need to consider the various energy alternatives:

1. Coal is very abundant—but it leads to air pollution, worsens the Greenhouse Effect, and contributes to global warming.
2. Solar is very clean—but rather expensive and not very dependable.
3. Geothermal is efficient—but not available in many places.
4. Wind power is everywhere—but wind farms are visual eyesores and cannot produce enough electricity.

And so on. Basically, you list each of the other options and "knock them down" one by one. Now, suddenly, you hope, nuclear power doesn't look quite so bad. And so you introduce it, itemize its virtues, deal with its drawbacks, and then hope to show that on balance, in an imperfect world, nuclear power is the way to go. Again, this approach is especially helpful when you are advocating for the "least worst" option.

CRITERIA-BASED ORGANIZATION

A criteria case can be very "seductive." If you can get people to agree to the criteria you provide, you're halfway there.

A criteria case first sets out certain standards or criteria by which we might evaluate an issue, a candidate, a policy system, whatever. Then, once these standards are set out, the arguer proceeds to compare the various alternatives along these criteria. Sometimes you will see this essential approach in a magazine ad—for example, what characteristics would we like in a cold remedy? Well, it should deal with fever, it should treat body aches, it should take care of your runny nose, it should not prevent you from driving heavy machinery, and so on. Then, you'll see a chart or grid of some sort comparing the various cold remedies against these criteria. And guess what? Your brand—Cough No More—has little Xs in all of the columns, because it does all of these things, whereas the other brands only deal with some and not others. That, my friends, is a criteria case.

Now, considering a more serious issue—let's say, mass transit—we can do the same sort of thing. What criteria would we like to see in any mass transit system? For one thing, it should be convenient to use. It also ought to be reliable and predictable. The cost to ride it should be affordable. It shouldn't disrupt our current streets and traffic. And, it should be friendly to the environment. Once we have established these criteria, then we can compare the alternatives—e.g., buses, light rail, subways, and so on—hoping in the end to show that our preferred alternative stacks up better, given these criteria.

One strategic advantage of a criteria case is that if you can convince the receivers that these criteria are reasonable, then you are halfway there—all you need to do then is show that your preferred option is better. On the other hand, if you are critically analyzing a criteria case, be sure that all the relevant criteria are being examined—very often, people will be selective in the criteria they employ, because their preference doesn't do so well in certain ways. That cold remedy I mentioned earlier might be the most expensive, or worse, linked to physical addiction or a rare form of cancer! If any of these were the case, you can bet that the company will not include "affordability" or "side effects" in their little magazine chart.

Finally, it's worth noting that sometimes a criteria case is called a "goals" case. They are really the same type of thing—it's just that the criteria are called "goals" instead. So, for instance, with the issue of mass transit above, each of the criteria would simply be labeled as "goals" for a desirable mass transit system. But the basic logic behind this organizational approach is fundamentally the same.

THE "MOTIVATED SEQUENCE"

Finally, it is worth including one approach to structuring a case for change that has been around since 1938. Developed by Alan Monroe at Purdue University, it goes by the name of the "motivated sequence," and it appears regularly in many communication studies textbooks of various sorts. This approach to organizing a case goes in five steps, and these steps would be especially appropriate in a "real world" argumentative situation where getting the audience to actually *do* something is important. These are the steps:

1. **attention step** – I must first say or do something that will get your attention—maybe a scary statistic, or a dramatic story, or a novel, memorable use of language.
2. **need step** – Then I need to show you that there is indeed a problem which needs to be addressed—here's where I point out all of the ills in the status quo.
3. **satisfaction step** – As in a problem-solution case, this is where I present the proposal that will address the problem(s) from the need step.
4. **visualization** step – Here I would try to lay out a picture of how the world would be a better place with this proposal—essentially, I am dealing with the stock issues of solvency and desirability. How will things be better if we enact this plan?
5. **action step** – OK, now that I've gotten you concerned about the problem and excited about the solution, what do I want the audience to do? How, in some meaningful way, can they help address this problem? In this section, it's important to have actions that are clear and definite and seem to "empower" people in some way.

THE NEED TO STRUCTURE THE SOLUTION

To this point, it has been assumed that if you are making a case for a change in policy, that you would clearly articulate what that policy would involve. After all, a case for change makes little sense if you cannot explain what the change would involve, and if you cannot do so in a fairly methodical manner. As Freeley and Steinberg (2005, 208) point out, a solution should normally include these elements:

1. **Agency**. In this part of the solution, you would specify who is responsible for administering it. Is this a federal plan? A state plan? A plan that would be enacted by local school districts? In short, whose plan is it?

2. **Mandates**. What exactly is being required, banned, or regulated—and how? If you are "banning smoking in all public places," what is a "public place"? Will it be a complete ban, or a ban within so many feet of building entrances? Will it apply to people in casinos operated by Indian tribes, which are often subject to a different set of laws? Will private businesses be regarded as "public" spaces?

3. **Enforcement**. Will there be a penalty for non-compliance? What will it be? How will you ensure that this policy can actually work? Are there fines, prison terms, or economic incentives involved?

4. **Funding and staffing.** Who will pay for this proposal? Who will manage and staff the program? Will the program require tax increases, or diversion of funds from other sources, or something like "user fees"?

5. **Other details.** Are there any other provisions to this solution that are necessary to make it work? Will more police need to be hired? Will state laws have to be changed? Will additional money for related problems be necessary?

In the end, the main idea is that your plan of action should seem well thought out and reasonably clear and definite. Simply saying something like "I propose to regulate what kids watch on TV" is so indefinite as a plan of action that it is virtually not a plan at all.

THE NEED TO BE EXPLICIT

Whatever organizational framework you use to build a case, it is essential to remember that if this case is in the oral mode, you simply must share this organizational structure with the audience. With a written argument, there is still a need to be orderly and explicit, but people can potentially go back and re-read your essay to discern the structure. However, with a speech, the audience is highly dependent on you the speaker to put things in an organizational framework for them. Therefore, it is common and helpful to do three basic things:

1. At some point early in the speech—typically, after an attention-getting introduction—provide the audience with an explicit organizational **preview** or **overview**. Where will you be going? Give them a clear and definite sense of the structure. Orally numbering each main point is a tried-and-true way to separate one major argument from another, but it is not exactly an absolute requirement.

2. In the body of the speech itself, provide **"oral signposts."** Oral signposts are simply words that tell the listener you are moving from one major point to the next. For example, you might say, "Now that I have developed my first main argument, let me turn to my second point, which is.....". Again, you must remember that the audience often cannot see the notes in front of you, so you must help people grasp the pattern.

3. Finally, as you conclude, do not feel that it is unnecessary or redundant to briefly **summarize** your main points. Even taking 10-15 seconds to do so will bring in some people who might have been "drifting off" a bit in the middle of the speech.

All of this can be summarized in a manner you may have heard before: tell 'em what you're going to tell 'em--tell 'em--and then tell 'em what you told 'em. This is still good advice, and if done creatively can still be interesting. Finally, with the widespread use of technology such as PowerPoint, the need to be as explicit about your organization may be reduced somewhat—since the audience can probably see your basic outline—but the most effective communication will reinforce these main points on both a visual and an oral channel. Put another way, don't expect the audience to magically "read and comprehend" your structure by having them stare at visual aids. Even with PowerPoint, oral repetition will be helpful and appreciated.

CONCLUSION

There are many ways to build a case. Those who advocate change have certain advantages, and those who oppose change have certain advantages. Cases can be organized by topical organization, problem-solution organization, causal organization, comparative advantage organization, method of residue organization, criteria-based organization, and by means of the "motivated sequence." Whatever case structure you employ, you need to make that structure clear and explicit for your audience. If there are ways to construct a case, there are many ways to weaken an opposing case as well, which is the focus of chapter 10.

REFERENCES

Freeley, Austin J. and David L. Steinberg. *Argumentation and debate: Critical thinking for reasoned decision making*, 11th ed. Belmont, CA: Thomson-Wadsworth, 2005.

Inch, Edward S., Barbara Warnick, and Danielle Endres. *Critical thinking and communication: The use of reason in argument*, 5th ed. Boston: Pearson, 2006.

Zarefsky, David. *Public speaking: Strategies for success*, 4th ed. Boston: Pearson, 2005.

Chapter 10

REFUTATION

After reading this chapter, you should understand:

- What refutation is, and the difference between refutation and rebuttal
- The four basic steps in refutation
- The four main refutational responses
- Twelve specific ways to refute an opposing claim or case
- Five judging paradigms that are used to evaluate debates

Specialized terms to know:

- refutation
- rebuttal
- turning the tables
- even-if response
- pre-empting an argument
- minor repairs
- counterplan
- tabula rasa perspective
- skills perspective
- stock issues perspective
- legislative perspective
- hypothesis-testing perspective

Now that you've learned something about *developing* a case in chapter 9, the natural and related question becomes, how do you *oppose* or *refute* someone's case? That's the focus of this chapter.

Before going any further, it's also worth making a distinction between two words that are sometimes used interchangeably: **refutation** and **rebuttal**. For our purposes, we would want to make a distinction between these two activities. As noted below, refutation involves trying to **weaken** an opposing argument or case—it is, if you will, trying to "make holes" in the opposing position. On the other hand, rebuttal involves trying to **rebuild** one's case in light of opposing refutation—"fixing the holes," if you will. As McBurney and Mills (1964, 294) point out:

Refutation and rebuttal are not synonyms in our view; the former denotes the presentation of evidence and reasoning designed to weaken the case of an opponent, while the latter may denote both the attack upon an opponent's case and the defense of one's own against the refutation attempted by an opponent. In other words, refutation means attack, while rebuttal means both attack and defense (rebuilding).

To summarize: if you are trying to weaken an opposing case for the first time, you are engaging in refutation; if you are trying to rebuild your own case in light of what your opponent has said, that's rebuttal.

Unless you're a contest debater, you probably haven't gotten much training or experience in refutation, yet refutation is an important and worthwhile skill. After all, aren't there times when you want to "prove someone wrong," as we say? That's what refutation is all about. Ziegelmueller, Kay, and Dause (1990, 201) use a sports analogy to stress the importance of refutation:

Football history is filled with teams that had outstanding offensive units but failed to become champions for lack of an adequate defense. In argument, refutation is the defensive half of the game. If you are skilled only in forwarding your own analyses, then you are only half prepared. You must also be able to examine the analysis of your opponents and understand its weaknesses, and you must be skilled in the methods of refutation. Many football games are lost for lack of an adequate defense, and many arguments are lost because an advocate was not skilled at refutation.

However, the sports analogy has its limitations—in particular, the idea that the "wins" and "losses" in argumentation are like those in football, where the other side can be clearly "defeated." In my view, refutation is best defined as an attempt to *weaken* an opposing argument. I use the word "weaken" intentionally, rather than "disprove" or "defeat," simply because "disproving" a case is usually unrealistic. Besides, as I indicated in chapter 1, we should be wary of the word "prove" and its finality; if so, the same holds for the word "disprove." In short, "I'm absolutely right and you're absolutely wrong" will not be something you can say very often in refutation. If your opposition has done any sort of a decent job of assembling their case, you're not going to be able to flat-out "disprove" it anyway. What you should be able to do is cast doubt upon it, identify key problems or weaknesses in it, or find reasons to question its wisdom. But the reality of real-world issues is that there are usually two or more viable positions to take on them, so black and white thinking is seldom appropriate in refutation.

If refutation is trying to weaken an opposing case, it should also be stressed that refutation is not an exercise in personal animosity, or belittling the opponent. Put another way, the focus should be on the content of the case, not on the person presenting it. Because some people see refutation as a combative, competitive activity—which, admittedly, it often is to some degree—they also go into the "war mode" when they try to refute their opponent. However, being obnoxious or unpleasant is neither logical, ethical, nor effective. It's not logical because it has nothing to do with the actual case. It's not ethical because it attempts to prevail by the force of one's personality rather than one's ideas. And finally, and maybe most important, being unpleasant is usually not effective—if anything, being a jerk will backfire. If someone agrees with your view, they will do so *despite* your unpleasant demeanor rather than *because* of it. So, in the process of doing refutation, you want to still seem likeable and credible, and you can help do that by controlling your more "nasty" impulses. Showing friendliness and respect to those who oppose you can and will score you a lot of points with anyone who is listening; to use a cliché, in refutation, you're trying to win both the audience's mind *and* heart. In short, you want them to agree with you, and they are more inclined to do that if they like you.

Another important point about refutation is that, like most other things in life, it can be done more easily and more effectively with sufficient preparation. Sometimes people marvel at how well contest debaters can "think on their feet," as we often say—that is, they seem to have a ready response for just about anything that comes their way from the opposition. Although it is true that debaters probably do learn better than most people how to respond spontaneously to a competing argument, the reality is that refutation usually begins with careful advance preparation. As Verlinden (2005, 200) suggests,

> When you have a chance to prepare for an argument, while you do research, look for arguments your opponent might use, take notes on them, and look for evidence against them. Later, as you're thinking about what you'll do in your oral or written presentation, formulate mini-arguments that respond to the various arguments you expect. Then when your opponent presents arguments, you are prepared to respond to them instead of being caught off guard.

In other words, "thinking like your opponent" in advance and coming up with possible responses to opposing arguments, in advance, can enable you to seem like a very quick thinker—it can maybe even make you appear to be a little brilliant!

One final general suggestion: if your opponent's case has a truly "huge" problem, and that problem is painfully obvious to you, I wouldn't wait until the end to bring it up. Why? Because audiences are often eager to figure out what the "truth of the matter" is with respect to a particular issue—they usually don't simply take in all the information, suspend judgment, and wait until the end to determine their opinion. Therefore, you often want them to start thinking "your way" as quickly as possible—if they do, then every opposing argument that follows becomes a little bit "tainted." Say for example that your opponent advocates that the federal government should require all states to ban lawn signs for political candidates. In such a situation, my very first response might be: "Regardless of whatever merit there might be in eliminating lawn signs--and I don't think there is, by the way--such a decision is not allowed by the U.S. Constitution. Legally, these types of decisions are and should be left to the states. People who live in Ohio ought to be able to determine whether candidates in Ohio can advertise on people's yards—that's their business, not the business of the federal government. So whatever you may like about the regulation of political advertising, such a plan is simply not Constitutional, and should be rejected on that basis alone." Again, what you are trying to do is provide an initial argument that raises significant doubts about the opponent's case that kind of "hang over it" throughout the discussion. Or, put another way, you want the receivers to keep reminding themselves that despite whatever merit the opponent's case may have, there are one or two significant problems with it that just won't go away. In other words, try to start strong; don't save your best or most "devastating" arguments for the very end.

That can be accomplished by providing a brief reference to this obvious weakness at the outset, promising to develop it in even more depth as you proceed.

STEPS IN REFUTATION

There is a natural sequence of steps in refutation. Although two of the four steps are potentially "optional," in a lengthy, detailed argument, all four are probably needed:

Step 1 (required): State the opposing argument, clearly and fairly.

This step might seem self-evident, but people have a tendency to "just start talking." It's their moment to refute the opposing case, and they say something like, "Inflation has not increased significantly in recent years, and the unemployment rate has remained steady." The listeners are thinking, "Say what? What does this statement *relate* to? *What* are they trying to refute?" So, the first step is always to clarify for the receivers what opposing argument you are dealing with—in this case, it might be something like, "Bob has argued that the U.S. economy is faltering." Then, once we know that, we can better appreciate what you are saying and why. Just remember that although you may know what you are responding to, the audience may not unless you tell them.

Notice that this step asks you to state the opposing argument clearly and fairly. The "clearly" part is probably self-evident. But why "fairly"? The answer to that question is perhaps a little less obvious, but worth noting. You do not want to be perceived as someone who "twists" the opposing argument; misrepresenting the opposition's case can have a detrimental effect on your credibility. So, do not put words in the mouth of your opponent, so to speak.

Step 2 (optional, but often helpful): Preview your response.

Now that you have identified the particular argument that you will be responding to, it's often helpful to give the receivers some idea of how you will proceed. In contest debate, one of the most common such previews will be something like, "I would respond in three ways." Essentially, this tells the audience that you are, in this case, going to have three separate points that you are going to make. But there are obviously other types of previews as well. Hypothetically, for example:

- "I will demonstrate that Bob's sources are biased and lack expertise."
- "I will show that Bob's proposal is unworkable and undesirable."
- "I will argue that Bob's evidence is irrelevant to the central issue here."

Of course, if you have a very simple point to make, and your response is not going to be especially lengthy, a preview may be unnecessary. But, even with a brief response, it's often helpful to give receivers an idea of where you are going.

Step 3 (obviously required!): Do the refutation.

Once you have clarified what argument you are responding to, and how you will proceed, then you can do the actual refutation. For now, let's leave it at that—for most of the remainder of this chapter, I'll provide a variety of responses that you might use.

Step 4 (optional, but very helpful): Show the impact of what you've done.

After you've made your points, people might still be asking themselves, "So what? So what does this mean?" You often need to tell them. And usually you will *want* to tell them, because you want your responses to matter, to have impact. Say, for example, that you are able to seriously discredit both of your opponent's main sources of evidence. If you have, do you want to stop there? I don't think so. You may want to conclude with something like, "So, Bob relies on only two sources, and I have shown you that both of those sources have obvious biases. This means [here's the "impact" part] that Bob really has *no* unbiased sources to support his position; on that basis alone, we should reject it." What you are doing here is showing the importance of your response. Step 4 is especially helpful when you have, for instance, undermined a central premise of the opposing case. Maybe an entire case in favor of lowering the drinking age is built around the premise that kids can get alcohol right now anyway, so we might as well not make them criminals for doing so. However, if you can show that in fact, teenage drinking has gone down since 21 became the legal drinking age, then this very premise is put into question—that is, the legal age can indeed have an impact on drinking behavior. Or, maybe the case is built around a fallacy in reasoning—Bob states that the number of violent crimes went up right after the new President was elected, meaning his whole argument is based on a *post hoc ergo propter hoc* fallacy, assuming that the first caused the second. Whenever you can, you want to put your responses into a "bigger perspective," in terms of what damage they have done to the overall argument.

THE FOUR MAIN REFUTATIONAL RESPONSES

When all is said and done, there are really only four main ways to refute a claim. The first way is the one that people most commonly relate to:

1. The claim is not true.

It is very tempting for people to make this their main—even their only—type of refutation. And of course, there are many situations where this response is the best and the most appropriate. If I say that the population of the United States is six billion, so we need more highways for all those people, I can simply say that you, my friend, are way way off on that population figure—it just isn't true. Or, you might say that obesity is totally unrelated to genetic factors, and I might say, no way—there's a wealth of scientific evidence that suggests otherwise. So, I am by no means against saying that the opposing claim is untrue; however, for some people, that is the only refutational response they can envision. In their mindset, if the other person says "up," then I should respond by saying "down." If they say "black," then I say "white." And if they say "yes," then I should say "no." However, the other three responses operate from a different starting point—namely, that there is something "true" about what the other person is saying.

2. The claim is true, but insignificant.

Let's suppose that a student comes in to see me, complaining about their final grade in my course. They have a 3.9 GPA, and I wound up giving them a "B." Their claim is, "You have ruined my GPA!" In such a situation, can I really say that their GPA will not go down, that what they are saying is "not true"? Of course not—that's a "mathematical reality," if you will. So in this situation, it does me no good to say they are incorrect. However, what I can say is that the overall effect of this "B" on their GPA is so slight as to be unimportant. And, frankly, I have actually been in this situation from time to time, and I have done the calculations—over a four-year college career, that one "B" would have an extremely minor impact on a GPA near 4.0—probably a reduction of about .03. In the end, does it really matter if your GPA is 3.90 or 3.87? I'd contend that it doesn't matter.

There are a variety of other situations where the "true, but insignificant" response is probably in order. Sometimes a policy change, for example, might produce a benefit, at least in theory—but the costs involved in getting that benefit, or other disadvantages that might accrue, make the benefit seem insignificant. Certainly if you told me that I could save 4 percent on my energy bills by changing all the light bulbs in the house to some other type, I might respond that even if that is true, it's not worth the hassle and the expense involved in changing all the bulbs. Again, there is no need here to dispute that an energy savings might be possible; rather, I will take issue with the significance of some aspect of the claim.

A final illustration: yahoo! News (2007) reports that the elderly are "most at-risk in suicide." This article states that "the elderly are the highest risk population in the country for suicide." Knowing such information, one is tempted to create special programs to prevent suicide by the elderly, spend tax money on an anti-suicide education program, or even change our laws regarding euthanasia, or "mercy killing." But wait. Reading further down, one learns that according to 2004 data from the Centers for Disease Control and Prevention, the overall U.S. suicide rate is 11 per 100,000 people. But for those 65 and older, "that figure rises to 14 per 100,000." Now, consider those numbers. Consider a huge football stadium, such as the one in Ann Arbor, Michigan, with 100,000 "non-senior citizens." Out of those 100,000, about 11 will commit suicide in their lifetime. Now fill the stadium with 100,000 people over 65, and you find that a whopping 14—three more, total—would have committed suicide. Three more out of 100,000: does that sound like a "suicide epidemic" to you? If I were to respond to an argument based on those figures, I would not want to sound callous, but I would want to make it clear that this difference, even if "true," is not significant. I can say that no one wants our citizens to commit suicide, and that we need to pay attention to this problem as it related to the elderly, but we simply do not have the evidence to support the idea that turning 65 also turns one into a significantly more depressed, suicidal individual.

3. The claim is true, but irrelevant.

Here we have an even more powerful response. In this situation, you can fully agree with your opponent, but still deny their overall claim because what they are saying is irrelevant in some way. Take that disgruntled student who complained about getting a "B" in my class. She might say, "Professor Lapakko—I worked so hard in your class. I read the textbook every night, made elaborate review sheets, wrote three drafts of every paper, and never missed a class. Don't I deserve an 'A'?" Now, in this situation, imagine where it would get me to simply deny her claims: "No, I thought you were extremely lazy. I've never seen these review sheets you're talking about. And I'm not sure that you even had perfect attendance!" What we have now is a person plotting to get even—this type of response, a direct denial, is not persuasive in such a case. Rather, I need to find a way to agree with her, but in a sense disagree as well. How about this:

"I don't doubt for a moment that you worked hard in this course. In fact, I wish I had more students with your kind of work ethic. Trying hard is important, and I encourage you to keep up the good work. Unfortunately, I'm really not allowed to give a grade based solely on effort—even if you showed more effort than anyone else, which you did. Your exam scores were in the 80 percent range, and at least a dozen students had higher point totals in this class. So, as much as I might like to give you an 'A,' I have to remember that grades in college are not purely based on effort." Will this response automatically make her happy? Of course not—but it offers a way to embrace her points and still make a "negative" final conclusion.

Remember from chapter 3 (evidence) that relevance is the first and most important test for any type of support material. So if the evidence is not relevant to the claim, that's important to stress. A prospective college student takes a campus tour. The tour guide says, "We have the best collegiate dance line in the region!" You say—assuming that you are not a dancer—"even if you're right, it's not relevant to my decision-making with respect to a college."

4. The claim is true, but leads to a different conclusion.

This final type of response can be especially disarming to an opponent, because not only are you agreeing with them, but you are sometimes even "happy" to do so. In its most potent form, this response starts with agreement, and then turns the idea in an entirely different direction. One form of this is often called "turning the tables." With such a tactic, you actually make the opposing argument a reason to support *your* position. Take the campus tour guide mentioned immediately above. You could conceivably say in response, "If your school has the best dance line in the region, that tells me exactly why I would *not* want to go here. Any school that puts that much stress on such a silly activity is not my kind of school." To the student with the near-perfect GPA who complains about that "B," one could say: "It's really a *good* thing that you're getting a 'B' in this course. Potential employers are often suspicious of students with 'perfect' academic records. They figure such people are 'perfectionists' and have never learned how to struggle with a problem. So, thank goodness there's at least one 'B' on your transcript."

Salespeople are very good at this tactic. In the world of sales, this type of response is sometimes called the "boomerang technique." The most obvious example is when people complain about the price of a product or service. The salesperson can indeed try to minimize the initial cost, but another reaction is to say, "Certainly you've heard of the adage, 'You get what you pay for.' In this case, by purchasing the best, you get the best quality and the best performance. In fact, because our dicer and slicer is of such high quality, it will last you many more years than cheaper brands. So, over time, you will actually *save* money!" My, my—suddenly spending more seems like a real virtue.

Another example of table-turning from a Presidential debate involved President Ronald Reagan's handling of the "age" issue in the 1984 election. Now, Ronald Reagan was not exactly a "spring chicken" when he first ran for President; in fact, when he ran for re-election in 1984, he was already 74 years old, and some people thought that 74 was simply too old for a sitting President. Mr. Reagan could have tried to deny that he was 74, but that would be a difficult "sell"; it would be neither logical nor persuasive. So, instead, Reagan refuted his critics in a nationally-televised debate with his opponent, Walter Mondale. Rather than denying that he was 74, he made his age a *virtue* instead by saying, "I will not exploit for partisan advantage my opponent's youth and inexperience." That is a clever way to try to disarm an opponent.

By now, I hope you see the potential value of this response with regard to more "significant" social issues as well. If Bob says that we shouldn't pursue a particular policy because it will increase gasoline prices, I could potentially say, "Good—less gasoline consumption is exactly what this country needs. Thank goodness we might move in the direction of more energy conservation."

Of course, this response does not have to be a complete exercise in "table-turning." Sometimes you may simply want to say that the opponent's information leads to *another* claim, not necessarily the "opposite" claim. Suppose Bob says that there are too many handgun crimes and so we must ban handguns. I can agree with him that there are too many such crimes, but say that this should lead us to better enforce and prosecute current handgun laws, which are fully capable of addressing this problem. In other words, I am saying that the logical conclusion of his points can and does lead in another direction.

It's worth stressing that of these four major refutational responses, an arguer might select more than one of them for a particular opposing argument. One such option, for example, is what I would call the "even-if" response. Suppose your opponent claimed that her school's soccer program was a failure and that therefore the soccer coach should be replaced. I might respond that (a) such a claim is not true, providing evidence to refute that idea, but also (b) even if it *is* true, it leads to a different conclusion—maybe in this case that the school needs to provide more support to the soccer program and less to football and basketball. So, in essence, I think you are "wrong," but even if you are "right," there is a better way to interpret the situation and deal with the problem. The basic goal is to "cover yourself" either way. Similarly, I might say that the increase in losses by the soccer team is not really significant, but I might also say that even if it *is* a significant difference, it's irrelevant to whether the coach should be retained, since athletic coaches need to be evaluated by more than simply tallying up the wins and losses.

OTHER TYPES OF REFUTATIONAL RESPONSES

With these four general responses as a foundation, we can now look at more specific refutational tactics. In some ways, we have already been dealing with refutation—at least indirectly—when you see some of the suggestions below:

1. Point out weak or faulty evidence.

Chapters 3 and 4 dealt with evidence. In those pages, you should've learned what the key tests for various types of evidence are. Does your opponent's evidence pass these various tests? Chances are the support material provided by your opponent is vulnerable in some way. Maybe it's outdated. Maybe the statistics are misleading. Maybe the evidence lacks specificity. Maybe the evidence does not pass the test of "external consistency" (see chapter 3). But whatever the problems with their evidence might be, you want to point them out. And with respect to "step 4" in refutation—showing the impact of what you've done—in some argumentative spheres (law, for example) not having sufficient or appropriate evidence is about the same as not having any sort of case whatsoever; therefore it can be a critical deficiency to identify.

2. Point out weak or faulty reasoning.

Check chapters 5 and 6 of this text, where reasoning and fallacies in reasoning are discussed. Is your opponent engaging in a hasty generalization? Perhaps a fallacy of composition? Maybe a "straw man" argument? Whatever you do, pay close attention to how your opponent arrives at claims; in the process, you may well find fault with the reasoning involved. Do keep your audience in mind, though: now that you are familiar with the various fallacies, you have some specialized knowledge that some others don't have. So, you will often need to explain very carefully why a particular argument is fallacious—you might not simply be able to say, "She's begging the question" and expect even an intelligent lay audience to grasp what that means.

3. Identify misleading or exaggerated language.

As discussed in chapter 7, arguers will often try to manipulate language to their advantage, not always using words in a fair and accurate way. You need to pay close attention to their word choices and make sure that they don't take liberties with language. If your opponent uses words in a way that is either unfair, unclear, or misleading, it will weaken their credibility--even if on more "substantive" grounds they have a strong case. But words are chosen strategically to influence our view of things, and you need to be mindful of how your opponent's word choices may be misleading and self-serving.

4. Note inconsistencies.

As you consider the opposition's case, you need to take a look at the "big picture"—does everything fit together in a consistent way? Inconsistencies weaken an argument, and you should be on the lookout for them. Maybe in one part of your opposition's case, they claim that "government bureaucracy" is hindering small businesses—but then, you see that their solution is equally "bureaucratic," and so you'd want to seize upon that. Or maybe your opponent favors "the right to self-determination" in all nations of the world, but this same person is irritated because one particular country happened to favor a less democratic form of government than we have in the U.S. Or maybe your opponent has gone on record in favor of "freedom of speech," but is disturbed because some people are saying what he regards as "offensive" things that shouldn't be tolerated. In each of these cases, there are potential inconsistencies that you should be alert to.

5. Note "dropped" or avoided arguments.

Refutation is not only focusing on what people *do* say, but also what they *don't* say. Many times, an opponent will tend to steer away from certain issues because these issues are their "weak points." They hope that by not talking about these weak points, that they will magically go away. You don't want to let that happen. So if you make a very good point about the lack of funding for your opponent's program, and your opponent doesn't respond to that concern, you want to make sure we realize that he or she is dodging this rather important issue. And, for instance, if someone is making a case for more families to "home school" their kids, you'd want to note any obvious omissions—possibly issues involving quality of instruction, or kids' social development, or greater difficulty in being involved in extracurricular activities. Just because *they* don't talk about it doesn't mean that *you* shouldn't.

6. Pre-empt the opposing argument—deal with it before your opponent does.

To pre-empt an argument means to bring it up first, before your opponent has a chance to; this is sometimes referred to as "anticipatory refutation." If you know, for example, that your opponent, a nuclear power advocate, is going to tell us how reliable nuclear power is, then you can consider dealing with the "reliability" issue before your opponent ever has a chance. Why? Because such an approach can take the wind out of their sails, so to speak. Now when your opponent actually gets to the reliability issue, you have already cast some doubt upon it, putting your opponent in a more "defensive" position. In the academic world of persuasion, this tactic is often connected to "inoculation theory." The analogy here, to getting a shot in your arm to develop resistance to some disease, is quite fitting. In this case, by getting a "shot" of the opposing argument and then discrediting it in some way, sort of "immunizes" the receivers to the opposing argument when they actually hear it. So, there can be value in "beating your opponent to the punch," if you will. (However, you do want to be absolutely certain that your opponent will indeed be bringing up this particular point; otherwise, you could be accused of being unfair, or "rushing to judgment" about a case that we have yet to even hear.)

7. Formulate a dilemma.

Creating a dilemma for your opponent is a more sophisticated refutation tactic, and it does take some thought and insight. Essentially, a dilemma is a situation where two alternatives exist, and both are undesirable—a "damned if you do, damned if you don't" situation. Now, as noted in chapter 6, there is a fallacy in reasoning called a *false* dilemma. With a false dilemma, you are misleading the receiver into thinking there are only two options, when in fact there are more—but that is not what you are trying to do here. Rather, your goal is to show that there really are only two basic alternatives, and both are undesirable—so, either way, we should reject the opponent's case. Say, for example, that your opponent is in favor of capital punishment. One issue that comes up here is how to deal with the possibility of error—that is, to be sure that someone who is about to be executed is actually guilty of a capital crime. So, some believe that all convicted murderers in capital punishment states should have an automatic review/appeal of their case to a higher court—again, to guard against error. However, reviewing criminal cases of this sort is both expensive and time-consuming. So, if you were opposed to capital punishment, you could construct the following dilemma:

- If we DON'T have an automatic appeal/review of all death penalty cases, we run the risk of convicting and executing innocent people. Clearly, that is not good.
- On the other hand, if we DO have an automatic appeal/review of all death penalty cases, that too is undesirable—because it's expensive, time-consuming, and can clog up the court system. In fact, the appeals process can end up costing as much as it would cost to simply imprison that person for life. So, either way, capital punishment is a bad idea.

Or, let's suppose that a local community—Hicksburg—wants to install parking meters on Main Street to generate some revenue for the town. If you are opposed to such a plan, you can put your opponent in a dilemma: on the one hand, if Hicksburg installs these new meters and strictly enforces their use, people will go to neighboring Vicksburg to shop because they don't have to worry about parking meters there. Not only that, but people will develop an overall negative attitude about Hicksburg, and stay away from the city whenever they can. On the other hand, if Hicksburg installs the meters but doesn't enforce them very strictly, that too is bad, because then the city will not get the revenue it desires—people won't be motivated to "plug the meters" if they know the meters are not really monitored. Either way you look at it, new parking meters are a bad idea.

8. Turn the tables.

As noted earlier in this chapter, turning the tables—agreeing but arriving at the exact opposite conclusion—can be a very effective way to refute an opposing argument:

You say: "This program is unwise because the federal government doesn't oversee its operation."

I say: "That's the very reason why it's such a good program! It promotes local involvement and control."

You say: "Passing 'conceal and carry' laws for handguns will
                simply put more guns out on the street."
I say: "That's exactly why we'll be more secure! More
                law-abiding citizens will be armed and able to pro-
                tect themselves."

You say: "The passage of this law will lead to an increase in
                the price of gasoline."
I say: "Good! Perhaps people will finally be motivated to
                use our excellent mass transit systems."

9. "Praise motives, but......"

This tactic has the virtue of seeming tactful—even kind. Basically, you start out by praising your opponent for her concern—for
example, "I commend Sheila for her deep and abiding concern for
our public schools. Clearly she cares about what's best for our
students." By starting in such a positive way, you help establish
good will between you, Sheila, and your audience. Then, of course,
you will take the discussion in a different direction—for example,
"Despite Sheila's sincere desire to improve our schools, I think
we can examine the standardized testing that she advocates and
see that there are better ways to reach these important goals," or
some such thing. Don't be afraid to say something nice about your
opponent—it does not make you seem weaker, but rather, more
fair, credible, and likeable. Again, effective refutation is not based
on coming off like a jerk.

10. "Wrong time, place, or occasion" (for policy issues).

This approach is also a very appealing one, since it enables you
to agree in some way with your opponent. Yes, you say, it would
be nice to build a new park system in our community, as we would
all like to see beautiful parks. Unfortunately, you say, we are currently facing a massive budget deficit in the city, and if we don't
take care of the toxic landfill on the north end of town, it will haunt
us for years. So, even though it's a wonderful idea, now is not the
right time or place for it. Maybe in just a few years it will be. With
this approach, you can come off as a reasonable and sympathetic
individual—and, often, this sort of response is very much in keeping with the "hard realities" of the particular situation. (Hint to
parents: this tactic can sometimes work with your kids, too. "Gee,

Jimmy, going to the zoo is a great idea, but it's supposed to rain this afternoon and daddy has to mow the lawn before it rains—let's not go today.")

11. Propose "minor repairs" in the status quo (for policy issues).

Remember that the stock issue of inherency involves whether the alleged problem is built in to the current system in such a manner that the only way to address the problem is to change policies. With this refutational tactic, you are saying, in essence, yes there may be a small problem, but we can address that problem without going to an entirely new policy system. Instead, we can "tweak" the current system to make it more responsive to the problem. That's a minor repair. So, rather than abandoning our city's bus system in favor of light rail, we can simply improve the bus system that we have—maybe through more efficient routing, or through better economic incentives to ride the bus. In other words, we can deal with this problem through the status quo—with a few adjustments. Many "real world" arguments on politics are essentially issues of whether the current system can be altered a bit, or whether a whole new system needs to be put in its place. If you're arguing against such a policy change, your refutation will push for the minor alterations.

12. Propose a counterplan (for policy issues).

A counterplan is a more "extreme" refutational tactic, but sometimes both necessary and effective. It's especially appropriate when everyone knows, or seems to know, that there are significant problems, and the status quo seems incapable of handling them. Therefore, from a "stock issues" perspective, when you present a counterplan, you are essentially conceding the stock issues of "significance" and "inherency"—that is, you admit that there is a significant problem, and that the status quo is incapable of ever solving it. But where you differ is in regard to the solution, and your solution is quite different from your opponent's. But it's a "better" solution, and that's why we should reject the opponent's case and adopt yours instead.

For example, let's suppose that your opponent—let's go back to "Bob"—believes the current educational system is failing. Kids, he says, are not doing as well as they should do in school, and the current educational system is incapable of doing anything about it. Therefore, Bob advocates that all states should have "minimum competency tests" for all students—and if you can't pass the test as a senior, you can't graduate from high school, period. In this situation, I could, for example, respond to Bob by saying: "I agree that our schools have not totally fulfilled their goals, and that in their present form, they may not be able to. But having artificial, culturally-biased competency tests will not promote higher achievement. Rather, what *will* promote achievement is greater competition among schools. That's why I propose the following counterplan: that all 50 states implement a school *voucher* system, where each family has a set amount of public money to spend. They can choose to send their kids to a public school, or a charter school, or a parochial school. But it is the choice, and the competition, that are inherent to the voucher system that will improve the overall educational opportunities for our kids—not testing. Therefore, we should reject a system of mandatory minimum competence tests in favor of a voucher system for public education."

Or, suppose that Bob makes a convincing case that the health care system in the U.S. needs to be revamped, so he advocates that the U.S. adopt the Canadian system of health care. If I were to propose a counterplan, I would say something like, "Bob's point is well-taken that our health care system isn't working as well as it should—but the answer is not to adopt the Canadian health care system, but the *British* system." Then, if I can show that the British system is comparatively better than the Canadian system, I have still provided a reason to reject the policy proposal—i.e., I have given convincing reasons why we should not adopt the Canadian model of health care. But again, both implicitly and even explicitly, I am conceding the stock issues of significance and inherency—so I'd better be darn sure that I can show the British system is really better!

One variation of this approach would be to present what is often called a "conditional counterplan." Using the minimum competency testing example above, I would not necessarily concede that our schools can't handle things, but **IF** such is the case, then I would say that we **COULD** adopt the voucher system to improve our schools rather than relying on comprehensive exams. I'm not necessarily advocating this, mind you—I simply mean to say that if indeed my opponent can demonstrate the problem, there is still, in theory, a better solution, and you should choose that solution over my opponent's. So my proposal is conditional—upon whether my opponent can really show a significant, inherent problem. Of course, if you use this approach, your opponent may push you to take a stand one way or the other: are you proposing a voucher system, or not? You'd be well-advised to have a persuasive answer to that question.

DEBATE JUDGING PARADIGMS

OK, so two (or more) people have been making arguments, refuting each other's arguments, and trying to rebuild their own case in light of opposing refutation. For a critical receiver, the question still remains, how do you decide who has the better case? How do you determine who has "won"? In contest debate, a judge or panel of judges literally gives a "win" to one of the two teams, and debaters obviously strive to maximize their win-loss percentage. And although contest debate is an "artificial" environment, the notion of "wins" and "losses" applies just as much to the "real world." Every time there is a Presidential campaign debate, every time a "pro-life" person debates a "pro-choice" person, every time a "creationist" debates an "evolutionist," someone is out there listening and asking, "Who won this thing?"

As with many other issues discussed in this text, if you are looking for a simple answer to the question, it just ain't gonna happen. "Winning" and "losing" are very human judgments, somewhat subjective judgments, and judgments that are based on what criteria one employs to evaluate an argumentative dispute. There simply is no "magic formula" to arrive at an incontrovertible "right" answer. Therefore, depending on what evaluation criteria are used, one could draw very different conclusions as to who had the better case. In the contest debate world, certain "judging paradigms" have been advanced that can help us understand the different ways in which arguments might be judged or evaluated in any situation. Those include a tabula rasa perspective, a skills perspective, a stock issues perspective, a legislative perspective, and a hypothesis-testing perspective:

• **Tabula rasa perspective.** More Latin for you—in this case, "*tabula rasa*" literally means "blank slate." If you evaluate a debate from this perspective, you try not to have any preconceptions about the issue, or the debaters—you simply try to evaluate the discussion based solely on what you hear at that time. Even if someone makes a very silly or ignorant statement (e.g., "Eating dead mice can cure glaucoma"), if the opponent does not respond to this point, the *tabula rasa* evaluator decides that even though it seems like a dumb point, there wasn't a response, and so based solely on what was heard, they may deserve to "win" that particular point. Perhaps needless to say, to be a *tabula rasa* judge in its most complete form is not only very difficult, but perhaps not even wise. Yes, as a receiver one should avoid having a lot of preconceived biases, but "common sense" would dictate that arguments do not exist in a total vacuum—to use the "dead mice" example above, the opponent might have regarded it as such a ridiculous point that they simply ignored it and would expect any sane listener to do the same.

• **Skills perspective.** From this perspective, a receiver pays a lot of attention to matters of form. Did she sound confident? Was he well-organized? Did she say "um" too much? Did he seem friendly and have good eye contact? Did she have an extensive vocabulary? Did he respond to each of her points directly? For better or worse, many people are drawn to this way of evaluating a debate. One could certainly make the case that many national Presidential debates are assessed in this manner. Part of our national folklore, for example, is the belief that in the first televised Presidential debate in 1960 (between Richard Nixon and John F. Kennedy), that Kennedy just plain looked and sounded better—JFK was perceived as more relaxed, more handsome, more confident, more vigorous, and even more "Presidential." In the 2008 Presidential campaign, many observers believed that Democrat Barack Obama had a gift for public speaking that his opponent, Republican John McCain, did not. (Although in a very clever sort of refutation, candidate McCain argued at times that Obama's perceived "eloquence" was a *negative* trait, because his "smoothness" as a speaker enabled Obama, in McCain's view, to be deceptive! The essential argument, a form of "turning the tables," was that Obama had the potential to fool people with his rhetorical skills.) In one sense, a skills perspective can seem rather trivial from an argumentation perspective—after all, content should matter more than form. But, at some level, the form issues always seem to come up, and if we are talking about who should represent the nation from the White House, maybe matters of form are relevant. However, at the very least, I hope we do not embrace this perspective to such a degree that we wind up choosing our political office holders by the color of their shirt or the tone of their voice!

Of course, a skills perspective does not need to be totally superficial. Providing quality evidence, being able to support one's argumentative warrants, using language effectively, and being able to refute an opposing case point-by-point are also "skills"—but perhaps skills that are a little more sophisticated and important than delivery style or tone of voice.

• **Stock issues perspective.** By this point in the text, this framework should look awfully familiar, although check chapter 2 for a little review. A stock issues evaluator will determine if someone calling for change has identified a significant and inherent problem in the status quo and has offered a workable a desirable solution to that problem or set of problems. If one or more stock issues is in doubt, such an evaluator will probably decide to stay with the policy system (or value claim or factual claim) that aligns with "presumption." Such a critic will pay less attention to matters of delivery and form, concentrating instead on the issues.

• **Legislative perspective.** Using this orientation, a critic will essentially assume the role of a member of Congress or some other legislative body; for that reason, this is also often referred to as a "policymaker" perspective. From this orientation, the question becomes, if this were a "real life" proposal, would I be willing to vote for it? Although this perspective overlaps with a stock issues orientation, it probably puts a little more emphasis on "pragmatic" issues involving any proposal for change—for example, how a plan is funded, or the specific mechanics of its implementation. Suffice it to say that people who use this evaluative framework are more likely to take the discussion rather seriously, as if it were a "real" piece of legislation.

• **Hypothesis-testing perspective.** Finally, within the world of academic debate, a hypothesis-testing perspective has also been advanced. (It is also the most *abstract* perspective, the most *difficult* one to explain, and the one that is treated in several different—and *inconsistent*—ways in the debate literature.) I will address it in this manner: From this perspective, the debate resolution is basically a verbal statement that is being intellectually tested in an academic setting. For example, if the debate resolution is "That executive control of U.S. foreign policy should be significantly curtailed," the judge will tend to view the resolution as simply a statement that must be either affirmed or denied. The judge's orientation is to regard the debate as a critical thinking activity that examines this statement as an intellectual proposition. With this mindset, the definition of each term in the resolution becomes more important; for example, if someone calling for a "significant" reduction cannot clearly define what the word means, that makes the statement one that must be rejected. Similarly, if "executive control" remains an ambiguous term by the end of the debate round, this is problematic for an advocate who wants us to agree with such a statement. And if giving the President too much control over U.S. foreign policy is regarded as "undemocratic" or "unethical," such claims—even if they are impossible to "measure" from a policymaking perspective—become more relevant because they deal with important intellectual concepts. Regardless of whether in the real world an affirmative stance is advisable—which is important from a "legislative" perspective—this orientation treats debate as an "academic game." The game is not entirely divorced from the "real world," but the proposition is, in the end, just a statement—a declarative sentence—to be accepted or rejected.

Freeley & Steinberg (2005, 310) contend that "the hypothesis-testing judge does not seek to compare two policy systems. He or she is testing the hypothesis—that is, the affirmative case—alone. . . . If the negative demonstrates that no need exists for the proposition, the hypothesis-testing judge will conclude that the hypothesis is not true and should not be affirmed." Freeley & Steinberg also note that "The hypothesis-testing judge tends to be receptive to hypothetical counterplans"—again, mainly because the topic is simply being debated "in theory," and so a detailed, carefully laid-out counterplan is not as critical.

As with many sets of categories in this text, there is no "pure" form of any one of these perspectives. Chances are that critical receivers will employ two or more of them as they analyze and evaluate an argumentative dispute. And the lines between each of the five perspectives can get a little fuzzy. Still, these paradigms provide a useful framework for considering how people react to the cases and the arguments that they encounter.

CONCLUSION

Overall, refutation is an important skill to learn, and it is a skill that is best learned through actual practice. But once you have mastered it, you will feel a little more secure—sort of like having your own can of "rhetorical mace" to fend off potential attackers. Refutation normally consists of four steps, with four possible main responses. But there are a variety of ways to try to weaken an opposing case; this chapter includes a number of specific strategies that can be considered. Finally, once the argument has been concluded, there are at least five different ways to evaluate whose position should be favored.

REFERENCES

Freeley, Austin J. and David L. Steinberg. *Argumentation and debate: Critical thinking for reasoned decision making,* 11th ed. Belmont, CA: Thomson-Wadsworth, 2005.

McBurney, James and Glen Mills. *Argumentation and debate: Techniques of a free society,* 2nd ed. New York: The Macmillan Company, 1964.

Verlinden, Jay. *Critical thinking and everyday argument.* Belmont, CA: Thomson-Wadsaworth, 2005.

Ziegelmueller, George W., Jack Kay, and Charles A. Dause. *Argumentation: Inquiry and advocacy,* 2nd ed.. Englewood Cliffs, NJ: Prentice Hall, 1990.

Yahoo! News (2007). Experts: Elderly Most At-risk in Suicide. Retrieved September 18, 2007 at http://news.yahoo.com/s/ap/20070918/ap_on_he_me/elderly_suicide

Chapter 11

SPHERES OF ARGUMENT

After reading this chapter, you should understand:

- What a "sphere" of argument is
- How arguments are constructed in the scientific sphere
- How arguments are constructed in the legal sphere
- How arguments are constructed in the religious sphere
- How arguments are constructed in the business sphere
- How arguments are constructed in the political sphere
- Common value premises within U.S. culture that influence argument

Specialized terms to know:

- empirical data
- *stare decisis*
- *de novo* argument
- grounding text
- apocalyptic rhetoric
- paradox
- majoritarianism
- middle-of-the-roadism
- quasilogical style

You may remember that in chapter 1, I noted that one can consider argumentation as "field-invariant" or "field-variant." Basically, to this point, I have treated the subject from a field-invariant perspective, meaning that I have simply tried to categorize the kinds of evidence, reasoning, language, and so on that characterize argument in general. However, it is now time to consider the field-variant perspective by examining several specific contexts in which argument occurs.

As also noted in chapter 1, because a field-variant approach to argument pays attention to the specific context in which arguments occur, it is a little closer to the topic of "persuasion"—it asks us to consider the audience for our argument, and the context in which it is taking place. Yet this is important, insofar as one's argumentative success is connected to one's ability to adapt to the context. Part of this chapter will offer suggestions as to how to be "successful" within each sphere, but a significant portion will also simply try to analyze and identify the characteristics of argument within each sphere.

The inspiration for this chapter, and many of the ideas that are in it, comes from the one text in the field of communication studies that has really paid close attention to the field-variant aspects of argument. That text is *Argumentation and Critical Decision Making* by Richard D. Rieke, Malcolm O. Sillars, and Tarla Rai Peterson. Rieke, Sillars, and Peterson devote a full five chapters to the topic, one for each of five different fields. In some ways, my analysis is freely borrowed from theirs, although in every case, I have attempted to refine some of their ideas, as well as adding my own perspective and voice to the discussion. Their analysis focuses on five fields, and I shall use the same five: the scientific sphere, the legal sphere, the religious sphere, the business sphere, and the political sphere. Finally, to the extent that one's own national culture is a "sphere" of argument—that is, a context in which arguments take place—I would also like to examine common values within U.S. culture that have a bearing on how arguments are perceived and evaluated.

THE SCIENTIFIC SPHERE

People in the academic and scientific sphere make arguments all the time, even if they are not necessarily called "arguments." But of course they are arguments in the sense that they involve claims, data, and assumptions, and because they ask us to see the world in a particular way, What's important to realize is that in the scientific world, some ways of constructing arguments will "fly" better than others. So, what things characterize arguments in the scientific/academic world?

1. Scientific arguments follow a prescribed form.

Check any journal in the physical or social sciences and you will find that virtually all of the research studies follow a very predictable pattern, which we can call: **problem, literature review, methodology, results, and discussion.** First the study will lay out the nature of the issue or problem being examined, and its importance. Then the article will review the previous literature (previous studies) that have been done on this topic and explain why the current study needs doing in light of all this previous research. Next, the researchers will explain their research method: how did they collect data in this study? Then, they will provide the results of the study—the hard data, the actual statistics. Finally, research papers and articles will attempt to draw conclusions from all this, including what questions remain unanswered and thus require additional research. This general progression is so common that if a research article, or master's thesis, or doctoral dissertation were organized in some other manner, people might be confused or even irritated!

It is also worth noting that in the academic world, claims, data, and warrants are expected to be **documented** in a clear and systematic way. College students who turn in essays and research projects need to realize that any quotations, statistics, ideas, and/ or language that are used as information need be cited in the *body* of the paper—each separate passage that relies on the work of others needs to be identified as you go. (Rather than seeing this as something that detracts from the paper, documenting the various things you say with specific sources is a way to impress the academic reader that you have done your research!) There are standard ways to provide such in-text source citations; two of the most common are the APA and MLA styles—if you are not familiar with them, there are plenty of resources available with just the click of a mouse. But the big idea is that "good" academic writers demonstrate a willingness and ability to cite sources.

2. Scientific arguments rely on empirical data.

In some spheres—religion, for example—people are allowed to make claims based on personal beliefs or even intuitive impressions. However, for better or worse, the scientific world places great stress on empirical data. The word "empirical" means that one has actually observed the phenomenon that one is studying and has collected data. For example, I may have a personal belief about whether a particular reading program will help young children learn to read, but if I don't actually try it out on a bunch of kids and see the results, I do not have empirical data—merely a hunch, or a belief. In the academic/scientific world, people need and want to see the data that supports conclusions that are made.

3. Scientific arguments deal primarily with factual claims.

It's not that scientists don't ever concern themselves with policy matters, such as what we should do about global warming, or value questions, such as the ethics of stem cell research, but the predominant focus of scientific argument tends to be in the factual realm. Whether in the physical or the social sciences, questions about causality prevail: what causes what? Typically, in the social sciences, the issues will involve the connection between one variable (say, height) and another variable (say, perceived credibility), so that the factual question becomes, are tall people more credible than short people? Factual claims are at the heart of scientific argument.

4. Scientific argument downplays the role of ethos.

As discussed in chapter 1, ethos involves source credibility—in essence, the perceived image and appeal of the source. In politics, for example, having high ethos is critical; voters are influenced by a candidate's appearance, and likeability, and perceived competence. However, in the academic world, the importance of the source is somewhat diminished. I can say that "Albert Einstein believed in the theory of relativity, and therefore so should you," but in the end, it is the data that must support Einstein's theory. In other words, "name-dropping," if you will, has limited value in the scientific arena. One cannot simply cite a well-known source and leave it at that.

5. Scientists operate from an assumption of order.

Underlying almost all scientific and academic inquiry is the idea that somehow, the world has an orderly quality to it that only needs to be discovered. Maybe you've seen one of those horror or sci-fi movies where strange things are happening, people are being killed, and monsters are running around. Usually it's the scientist who says, "There has to be a rational explanation for all this!" And indeed, that is how scientists usually think: that the universe has an underlying order, and that their task is to discover what that order is. That's why, within the scientific community, *theories* are important—because theories are intended to explain and predict how things happen. Of course, those who work in the academic and scientific worlds need to remember that the word "theory" does not have the same denotative or connotative meanings within some segments of the general public. When scientists use a term such as the "theory of relativity" or the "theory of evolution," they mean more than "just a guess or an idea"—in the academic context, a theory really offers a meaningful explanation, one that may not necessarily be "true" but is based on extensive study, data collection, and research. By contrast, some in the general public see the term "theory" as representing a type of "mere speculation."

6. Scientific claims are made with considerable caution.

In some argumentative spheres—politics, for example—you will often hear rather "wild" claims about how the current President has "wrecked the environment" or "ruined the economy" or "destroyed the welfare system." In the academic world, what Toulmin calls "qualifiers" and "reservations" are much more common. Arguers in the academic sphere avoid making "rash" claims, preferring instead to qualify their conclusions. In academic writing, expect to see words and phrases such as "it would appear" or "all else being equal" or "tendency in the direction of" or "unless other variables are operating." In academia, advocates must generally carry themselves with a degree of humility; those of us in colleges and universities are often fond of saying "the more you know, the less you know"—it's a way of saying that absolute understanding of just about anything is hard to come by.

THE LEGAL SPHERE

1. Legal arguments are concerned with four main questions that are embodied by the acronym "IRAC."

In legal arguments, there are really four main concerns. The first involves identifying the **issue (I)**—what is the issue of law to be decided? In this phase, the question becomes, what are the relevant considerations in this case? What "facts" are connected to this case? In essence, what has happened, and what has to be decided? The second element involves **rules (R)**—what are the relevant laws, previous rulings, or principles that are connected to this issue? The third step, **analysis (A)** involves carefully considering how the relevant rules might apply to this particular situation. Finally, **(C) a conclusion** is drawn based on this analysis. In other words, the way in which issues are resolved in a legal context is a somewhat methodical process of revealing the issue, showing what rules are relevant to it, analyzing those rules vis a vis the issue, and drawing the correct conclusion. In that sense, legal argument deals more with "factual" claims than value or policy claims insofar as the most important question frequently becomes, what does the law say, and how does it relate to the matter at hand? Put another way, legal argument is analytical and fairly explicit. Dernbach & Singleton (1981, 7) reinforce this idea when they write:

> Although judicial opinions can contain many things, five components are of great importance. These are a description of the facts, a statement of the legal issues presented for decision, the relevant rules of law, the holding (the rule of law applied to the particular facts of the case), and the policies and reasons that support the holding.

Generally speaking, courts of law are not places where the great values of the day are debated, nor is legislative action the main concern. The central questions are based on the issue of, what happened? Was she in the room on the night of the crime? Did he know that his actions would hurt someone else? Was she the one who embezzled $50,000 from the company? And then, rules of law are applied. Did she commit the crime, given the facts and relevant statutes and rules? Was this business in violation of employment laws, or environmental laws, or antitrust laws?

2. In the legal sphere, rules for evidence are rather strict and definite.

If you are going to make a legal argument, you'd better be sure that you have all of your facts right, and that you've collected the information in a careful manner. All you need to do is watch an episode of "CSI" to realize that evidence in a criminal trial, for example, has to be gathered very carefully. Not only that, police must follow certain rules of evidence—they cannot, for instance, simply walk into your home and start dusting for fingerprints. Any incriminating evidence they might find in such an investigation would very quickly be thrown out of court, having been obtained illegally. Even if you are fighting a parking ticket, you'd be well-advised to document everything carefully—which parking meter was it? What was the number of the meter? At what exact street address? When, precisely, did you arrive and leave the parking spot? Other claims made in court may require some sort of notarized document, or some letter of substantiation from, say, a physician or an attorney. Do not take these matters lightly—courts are rather "fussy" about how evidence is collected and presented. Of course, within the legal community, such rules are often regarded as serving an important purpose—there is a substantive principle involved. That principle, in essence, is that "good rules" lead to a "good conclusion"—that is, if one follows procedures for evidence carefully, then the outcome will be more reliable. After all, if I beat a confession out of you, that could be very misleading; if I rely on hearsay evidence, I may be fooled. So, despite some occasional complaints in the "real world" that "those criminals are getting off on technicalities," the rules of evidence are designed to ensure that the best decision and most correct decision is made.

3. Legal precedents of various sorts are important.

You've probably seen it on a TV show: the prosecutor or the defense attorney wants some sort of special ruling, and to make their case, they will cite a legal precedent for such a ruling—that is, some other case where such a ruling was made. The fact of the matter is that if one can show a previous case where a particular ruling was handed down, then the same or a similar ruling could be justified in the matter at hand. As Romain (1997, 252) explains, "Legal reasoning typically starts with a previously decided case, called a precedent, whose acceptance is fixed by the legal doctrine of *stare decisis*, which means 'let the decision stand.'" As Shapo et al. (1989, 7) explain,

> Precedent becomes "binding authority" on a court if the precedent case was decided by that court or a higher court in the same jurisdiction. Cases decided by other courts, such as a court of another state, are persuasive authority only. When an authority is persuasive, the court deciding a dispute may take into account the decision in the precedent case, but it need not follow that decision. If precedents exist that are binding authority on the particular point of law, however, then those precedents constrain a judge to decide a pending case according to the principles laid down by the earlier decisions or to repudiate the decisions.

If, for example, courts in the "home jurisdiction" as well as other courts have consistently ruled that an accused criminal has a right to silence, guaranteed by the 5th amendment to the Constitution, then any attempt to argue or rule otherwise would violate the stare decisis principle. Put another way, stare decisis is really much like the concept of "presumption" discussed in chapter 2—that is, we should stay with current rulings based on their presumed wisdom and/or legitimacy. Still, to be precise, the issue of stare decisis is not what you would call a "black and white" issue. As Dernbach and Singleton (1981, 22) observe,

> In theory, the concept of binding precedent seems abso-lute. In practice, precedent and stare decisis are flexible rather than static concepts. The inherent ambiguities of judicial opinions and varying levels of interpretation allow judges significant latitude even when dealing with binding precedent. The interplay between the stated holding of a case, its underlying reasons, and its factual situation per-mits these differing interpretations.

Also, although precedent often involves the "strict legality" of a particular ruling, judges like to be "consistent" in a more gen-eral sense as well. Case in point: many years ago, I had as a guest speaker in my Persuasion class a woman named Sarah Wedding-ton. You probably don't know the name, but you probably have heard of a famous Supreme Court ruling called *Roe v. Wade*—the decision that essentially legalized abortion in the United States. Sarah Weddington was the attorney who successfully argued *Roe v. Wade* before the Court. One of the points she made in her pre-sentation to my class involved her research on each of the nine Supreme Court justices. She wanted to know what their opinions had been and how they had ruled in similar or related cases in the past. Then, she was able to use those previous positions to help make her case—because judges, like most people, do not want to be inconsistent. In other words, the precedents they had set in the past as jurists were used to justify a particular stance on the issue of legalized abortion. Legal precedents are carefully monitored, because judges want to stay within the established rules of law, not outside of them. And now that *Roe v. Wade* is the Supreme Court's decision, it stands as "authoritative," whether one likes it or not, which influences any future cases dealing with abortion.

4. Lacking legal precedents, attorneys can make a *de novo* argument.

Yes, legal precedent is relevant and often important in legal argument. Even so, there are other warrants for legal arguments. In a *de novo* argument, one is "starting fresh," not using precedent as a warrant but some more "new" idea. For example, besides past court decisions that have set precedents (*stare decisis*), other common warrants in legal argument revolve around what has already been legally decided or established in the legislative arena. Rieke, Sillars, and Peterson (2005, 228) cite a book by former U.S. Supreme Court Justice Benjamin N. Cardozo that indicates the importance of Federal and state constitutions; Federal, state, and local statutes or codes; and legislative intent. In other words, besides previous court rulings, the meaning and intent of current laws become an important premise for legal claims. Further, as Rieke et al. note through the Cardozo book, "history, custom, or tradition" along with "the pragmatic effect of decisions" are also viable premises for legal argument. What this means is that a "persuasive" case in the legal sphere may also need to be consistent with our general cultural practices, and the consequences or effects of a particular ruling must be taken into account. Overall, the big idea is that although legal precedent is hardly "sacred," legal arguments must still be mindful of the judicial and legislative history of the issue; an argument that is not grounded in some way to our past practices, our cultural values, and the potential consequences of a particular ruling will not carry as much weight. Put still another way, a "good" legal argument does not necessarily have to be grounded in "precedent," but it still has to make sense. Indeed, one could say that both of these goals are important. According to my guest speaker Sarah Weddington of *Roe v. Wade* fame, a good legal argument not only makes sense in terms of the law itself, but it also makes good sense independent of the law—in essence, in a world with *no* laws, it would still be the "right" decision.

5. Argument by analogy is quite common and important.

As noted above, the issue of stare decisis is not a fixed, black-and-white issue. Some situations are different than others. New technology comes along. Unprecedented events occur. Therefore, there is no obvious legal precedent, and attorneys must argue by analogy—that is, they must be able to show similarities between the current case and other cases to make the other cases seem relevant. This is especially relevant where there simply are no precedents. Take, for example, the new technology of "thermal scanning." It's now become possible for the police, from the outside of a building, to do a thermal scan of the interior and to determine if anyone is inside. As "21st century" as this technology is, back in the 18th century, when the Constitution was written, the 4th amendment states that people should not be subjected to "unreasonable searches and seizures." So, is taking your thermal image and using it to apprehend you a violation of the 4th amendment? From a legal perspective, the answer involves other analogous but not identical situations. How were those similar types of cases—perhaps using some other form of "high-tech" crime detection—resolved? Are the similarities relevant to the current situation? In some ways, reasoning by analogy is the "heart and soul" of many legal arguments; comparing one case to another, one law to another, one ruling to another becomes a critical thought process.

6. Trials are more "argumentative" from start to finish than you might think.

A simplistic view of the legal process would suggest that a jury of one's peers is selected, they listen to evidence about the case, and then consider the evidence and render a verdict. But the "arguing" that occurs in a trial begins long before each attorney makes an opening or a closing statement. Say, for example, that I am defending a supermarket. One of the shoppers slips on a lettuce leaf on the floor of the produce aisle and breaks her leg. Is the store legally responsible? If I'm selecting jurors, I would want to do more than simply get information. I might want to ask something like, "As a prospective juror in this case, do you think you could separate your natural sympathy for an injured woman from the legal issue of whether my client is responsible for her injury?" This obviously is more than a question—it's a veiled argument that reveals where the defense may be going.

Similarly, cross-examination is more than a casual "Q and A" session. Attorneys will order questions in such a way that they are doing more than simply getting information—they are making an argumentative point. To use the supermarket example above, I might, as the defense attorney for the store, ask the injured woman a series of seemingly innocent questions that will lead the jury to a particular conclusion:

Me: "Do you shop at SuperFoods often?"
She: "Well, yes, at least once or twice a week."
Me: "When you go to the produce section there, are there a lot of shoppers?"
She: "Oh yes, sometimes it gets very busy."
Me: "So at any given time, how many people are buying produce?"
She: "Well, maybe 10 or 15."
Me: "Regarding the lettuce leaf you slipped on: how long was it on the floor?"
She: "Gosh, I don't know."
Me: "Is it possible that it was only on the floor for a few minutes?"
She: "I suppose."

Well, this may not be the most brilliant defense in the world, but you get the idea. From these rather "innocent" questions I can begin to build my defense: that "SuperFoods" is a busy place, that it's inevitable that a few grapes or lettuce leaves might make their way to the floor, and that it's unrealistic to expect a supermarket to monitor all of this minute-by-minute. Generally, attorneys are not going to ask a question in cross-examination if they don't have a pretty good idea of how the witness will answer—they don't want surprises, and they want to build an argument off of the responses they know they are likely to get.

It is also worth stressing that this treatment of legal argument is most definitely brief and oversimplified. As Rieke et al. (2005, 223-224) contend,

> argumentation in law can vary according to the kind of case. Criminal cases call for argumentative practices that are different from those in civil cases. In criminal cases, for example, the argument must meet a greater burden of proof (beyond a reasonable doubt) than that required of arguments in civil cases (by a clear preponderance of evidence).

And even within these broad concepts, argumentation in, say, a murder case can be different from that in a narcotics case. And argumentation in patent law, tax law, estate law, divorce law, labor law, environmental law, and torts (such as acts of negligence leading to personal injury) are quite different in many respects. Arguments at the trial level are profoundly different from that before appellate courts. . . . It is only through experience that lawyers learn the subtle differences.

Overall, legal argument has its own written and unwritten rules, and one of the main reasons why people go to law school in the first place is to learn how to make a convincing argument within this world.

THE RELIGIOUS SPHERE

For some, the idea that "arguments" are part of religion may seem odd, but of course, any claim made by someone—including claims about the nature of God, or the universe, or what's moral or immoral—constitutes an argument. What are some common characteristics of religious argument?

1. Religious claims are often based on interpreting a "grounding text."

One special form of evidence that seems to pervade religious discourse is the presence of a "grounding text"—that is, a particular source that is considered to be the "ultimate authority" on various matters. Within the Christian world, that text is the Holy Bible; within Islam, it's the Qur'an; within the Hindu world, it is the Vedas. In each case, there is an implicit assumption (essentially, what Toulmin would call a "warrant") that this text can be consulted whenever an issue of fact or value comes into play. In some parts of the Christian world, that underlying assumption is so strong that *only* scripture can provide an ultimate answer to the issue or problem. Somewhat ironically, because "interpretation" is always an obstacle to understanding scriptural meanings, different religious groups, relying on the same Bible, often come to radically different conclusions about what the Bible is really saying. Nonetheless, it is more or less assumed that with the "proper" interpretation, the grounding text can and will provide a definitive answer.

Some uses of scripture for argument are, shall we say, fairly controversial. For example, there is a group of people who believe that the book of Isaiah foreshadows a series of events that have happened on or near Interstate Highway 35 in the U.S. In recent years, there has been a bridge collapse on I-35 in Minneapolis; President Kennedy was assassinated in Dallas, near I-35; and there have been a series of kidnappings and murders in Laredo, Texas—also near I-35. Isaiah 35:8 states: "And a highway shall be there, and it shall be called the Holy Way; the unclean shall not pass over it, and fools shall not err therein." Now exactly what this passage means is unclear to me and to *Star Tribune* reporter Chao Xiong (2007, B1), but according to Xiong, a group of Christians believes that this Biblical verse has special meaning. These believers suspect that Isaiah 35:8 is a sort of warning, leading them "to pray for the overall betterment of the country, forgiveness of personal and collective sins and closeness with God." In fact, worshipers in this group prayed nonstop for 35 days from late October to early December; some of them belong to the "Light the Highway" movement, founded by a woman named Cindy Jacobs. Jacobs says, "It's amazing that there's a scripture that talks about the highway of holiness and there's an actual one." And, churches in 17 cities participated in the Light the Highway campaign, "praying along with a guide that outlined 'sins' to address, including poverty, racism, abortion and homosexuality" (B3). All of this activity stems from 27 words in the Bible, but it is characteristic of the prominence that scripture has within religious argument.

Indeed, one of the most interesting forms of religious argument that has been around for centuries, but has been especially prominent as we have entered a new millennium, is "apocalyptic rhetoric," in which the Bible is used as evidence to predict events such as the "rapture" and/or the second coming of Christ. As Barry Brummett (1991, 31) has observed:

> As rhetoric, what is most important about apocalyptic is that it is a system of order. As a system of order, it replaces the received systems of explanation that an audience has lost. To an audience that thought that it was adrift amidst chaos, apoca-

lyptic reveals a grand plan underlying all of history, a plan that was in place all along.

And so, by "properly" interpreting the grounding text—in this case, the Bible—those who make apocalyptic arguments have determined, as Brummett notes, that "History is moving relentlessly toward its culmination in a perfection, and the plan that underlies this progress is the guiding master force behind events" (34)—and further, that apocalyptic rhetoric "is a mode of thought and discourse that empowers its audience to live in a time of disorientation and disorder by revealing to them a fundamental plan within the cosmos" (9). Because this type of argument has become quite prominent in our culture—especially among people who might be described as "fundamentalist Christians"—we would be well-served to consider whether such arguments are grounded appropriately, because as we all know, the Bible is used as "evidence" for a wide variety of claims by theists, atheists, agnostics, and everyone in-between!

2. Reasoning in religious discourse is often more "deductive" than in the sciences, or in law.

Remember that in the scientific world, general claims and theoretical statements need to be based on the data—that is, the information collected by the researcher. As such, academic argument has a strongly inductive flavor—one does not generalize before getting the specific evidence. On the other hand, perhaps because religious discourse has been around for quite a while, religious argument often begins with some sort of generalization and then makes inferences from it—the very definition of deductive reasoning. Consider, within the Christian paradigm, for example, some of the generalizations you have probably heard:

- God has a plan for your life.
- God works in mysterious ways.
- God will forgive you for your sins.

Now, with these types of generalizations, we often make inferences to specific situations. If you believe that God indeed has a personal plan for your life, then you will tend to interpret particular events as being part of that plan. Similarly, if something happens that seems totally confounding to you, you might use the generalization that "God works in mysterious ways" to interpret the situation. This is not to say that all religious argument is deductive in nature—merely that it is a more distinctive and common form of reasoning than in some other spheres.

3. Sign reasoning is common in religious argument.

For better or for worse, observable signs and symptoms are often linked in religious discourse. The very concept of a "miracle" is, in essence, a type of sign reasoning. For example, Little Jimmy has a terrible disease. The family prays for little Jimmy. And then, miraculously, Little Jimmy is cured. In such a situation, the inference is often made that prayer was what led to his recovery. Of course, I am not here to say that such thinking is either wrong or muddled—I merely mean to point out what type of reasoning is involved. Having said that, you should know by now that sign reasoning—because it can't explain why two things are connected—should be considered less convincing than causal reasoning, where a causal link is demonstrated. When your favorite NFL running back points toward heaven as he crosses the goal line, it is tempting to conclude that God wanted him to score and beat the Dolphins. (Exactly why God favors the Raiders over the Dolphins we'll probably never know.) However, we would hope to keep such sign relationships in check. At their "worst," people have concluded, for example, that because AIDS is prevalent in the gay community, that this is a sign from God that He disapproves of homosexuality. Hmm. You can see that we are in some pretty awkward places here. Again, sign reasoning is not inherently incorrect, but one should pay close attention to how it is used, whether it's in the religious context or in some other context.

4. Religious arguments make distinctive use of parables and paradox.

Unlike, say, the business sphere, where stories and paradoxical statements would be greeted with looks of bewilderment, religious arguments can be based and often are based on parables and/or paradox. Obviously, there are many parables or stories in the Bible; they are often-cited and often instructive. Parables such as the stories of Lazarus, The Good Samaritan, the Fig Tree, and the Mustard Seed (and many, many more) are all designed to serve as "evidence" for certain spiritual truths. Like examples as evidence (see chapter 3), these parables have emotional appeal and a sort of argumentative "clout" as a result.

Besides the use of parables, religious argument does at times make distinctive use of paradox. A paradoxical statement, on the surface, seems to be internally contradictory or inconsistent. However, within this contradiction, the arguer is trying to make a point. Consider, for example, the notion of "becoming free by being a slave to God." [Romans, 6:22-23] Initially, such a phrase seems to make no sense: how does one become free by being a slave? But of course, the "real" point is that by being devoted to God (a "slave" to God) that one can experience the freedom of not worrying about the future. Similarly, the idea that "He that loveth his life shall lose it; and he that hateth his life in this world shall keep it unto life eternal" [John, 12:25] conveys the paradoxical idea that "loving" life (meaning the everyday things, such as DVD players and microwave ovens) will have an empty, shallow existence—while those who "hate" life (read: are spiritually aware and not driven by materialism) will live eternal life.

THE BUSINESS SPHERE

Many of you will pursue careers in business. Trying to convince others—that is, to persuade and to argue—is an important part of many corporate positions. Therefore, it's important to realize what counts as a "good" argument within this sphere.

1. Business claims place a heavy reliance on statistical evidence.

Imagine making a presentation in a business setting with a parable—like the tenacious mustard seed, you say, my new product line will start small, but stubbornly grow. Why? Because you have faith in your new product line. Such an argument, although potentially OK in the religious sphere, is likely to die a very quick death in the business realm. You need the numbers to make your case—market research demographics, per unit costs, start-up costs, expected profit margins, and so on. This is not to say that businesses are totally rational decision-makers—only that businesses like arguments that have the *appearance* of rationality. And statistics help provide that sense.

2. The business sphere gives special credibility to (a) the boss, and (b) expert consultants.

For better or worse, not all opinions in the business sphere are equal. Because management has the resources to make things happen and the ability to reward and punish—and, more charitably, because management often has special expertise and experience—the boss's opinion often counts for quite a bit. Even at the college where I work—not exactly a profit-driven business—if I can show that the President of the college and the Academic Dean both favor my proposal, I'd normally be wise to mention it. If management is in favor of it, that's usually helpful to stress.

Additionally, many businesses hire expert consultants to come in and try to address various problems in the company, whether those problems involve efficiency, productivity, low morale, or poor communication skills. Because the firm is paying good money for these services, and because consultants are often perceived as having special, unbiased knowledge, their views are often carefully considered. So, if the consultants are on your side, it's probably worth mentioning. (I should add, though, that some corporate people have a more cynical view of consultants, and don't think that they—consultants—could find a particular part of their body with two hands and a flashlight. So you should not just assume that any consultant has credibility with an organization.)

3. Common warrants in business argumentation revolve around "more," "bigger," or "better."

Businesses seem unwilling to plod along at the same pace. There are pressures and expectations to keep improving. Even if a firm's profits are up 10 percent over the same quarter last year, there is always the belief that they can and should do better. Higher profits, more efficiency, greater market share, improved on-the-job safety record—whatever it is, if you can show that there will be *more* of it, it's usually a persuasive warrant in the Toulmin sense. Again, if the Catholic Church found that they could increase the number of Catholics by 10 percent if they changed certain church doctrines, it's unlikely that would be a persuasive premise in the religious sphere—but in the business sphere, more is usually assumed to be better.

4. Business argumentation must sound and look "professional."

In some spheres—the academic arena, for example—people can look and sound pretty goofy and still fit in. (Check any photo of Albert Einstein!) We all know that professor who looks a little rumpled, whose personal hygiene leaves a bit to be desired, who uses frayed notes and seems helpless in the face of technology, and who seems a little absent-minded. In fact, to some extent, people who fit this profile in the academic world can be perceived at times as rather charming, even wise in their own way. However, in the business world, I think one's image needs a little more polish. You need to look and dress like a successful corporate member. Your paper resources, such as proposals and handouts, need to look flawless. And visual aids—certainly PowerPoint comes to mind here—have to be used in a state-of-the-art fashion. And so, you should be sure that you are polished and sophisticated in matters of image and style, because people will notice.

THE POLITICAL SPHERE

Within the realm of politics, arguments have their own distinctive characteristics.

1. Policy claims dominate political argument.

Not surprisingly, a lot of the focus of political argument involves, what should we do? Should we expand capital punishment? Should we have a "flat tax" in place of a graduated income tax? Should marijuana be legalized for medical purposes? Should the federal government give tax credits for those who buy hybrid cars? In the end, that's what the political sphere is all about. Of course, issues of fact and value are always there as well—it's just that they don't usually become the focal point of discussion.

2. The use of "qualifiers" in political argument is more limited.

As noted in the section on scientific argument, political arguments tend to be rather "lean" when it comes to Toulmin's "qualifiers." Remember, qualifiers reflect the degree of certainty that one has in a claim, and both office holders and candidates don't like to be perceived as "weak," or "uncertain," or "indefinite." Therefore, qualifiers can be hard to find. The President is not likely to say that her Social Security reform package "might" have a beneficial effect—she is more likely to say, "This revision in Social Security will ensure the viability of Social Security into the 22nd century." Period.

3. Two common warrants are "majoritarianism" and "middle-of-the-roadism."

In a republic such as the United States of America, we believe that "the majority should rule." Of course, there are probably some issues where the majority should *not* rule (such as protecting individual rights against what is sometimes called "the tyranny of the majority"), but nonetheless, what the majority wants is a persuasive premise in most political argument. So, if I can show you that a majority of the residents in Metropolis are opposed to a new publicly-funded football stadium for their professional team, I have provided evidence that many will regard as persuasive. In short, we like to do things, politically, which the majority favors.

Additionally, American society over the years has been rather resistant to "extremism." We like the concept that a "good" solution will find "middle ground" between two extremes. Political candidates who have positioned themselves as "extremists" have usually gone down in flames, so to speak—a notable example in my lifetime was Senator Barry Goldwater, who in the 1964 Presidential election embraced the word "extremism" and then got creamed by Lyndon Johnson in November. (Specifically, Goldwater said, in his acceptance speech at the Republican National Convention that "extremism in the defense of liberty is no vice" and "let me remind you also that moderation in the pursuit of justice is no virtue.") Generally, we like compromises—solutions that are neither too radical nor too conservative. If you can position your solution as a middle-of-the-road reasonable compromise, you'll have a better chance of success in many situations.

4. In political campaigns, "leave no shot unanswered."

Much as we might like to think otherwise, politics is riddled with charges and countercharges. Political campaigns include all kinds of accusations about the opponent—that he's "too soft on terrorism," "morally unfit for office," "someone who constantly flip-flops on the issues," "a person who was born into a rich family with a silver spoon in his mouth," and so on. In some campaigns, candidates have attempted to "take the high road" and ignore those accusations about them when they regard the charges as either too personal, or factually incorrect, or irrelevant to the election. Unfortunately, not talking about these charges will not make them go away, and in the political arena, an unanswered charge leaves some lingering suspicion: is there some substance to this charge, perhaps? How come this person is not defending himself? As Rieke et al. (2005, 315) contend, "Some negative campaigning backfires, but it always has to be refuted."

5. In political discourse, stories have become increasingly important.

Many rhetorical theorists would argue that the power of narratives or stories is significant. People are moved by stories, because they bring big ideas down to earth in a way that is appealing and understandable. Within the political sphere, stories as a form of evidence are enjoying a resurgence. Some believe that with the election of Ronald Reagan in 1980, narratives gained a new popularity. Indeed, one of my old college debate partners, Bill Lewis, has written an excellent analysis of Reagan's use of stories as evidence (Lewis, 1987).

But you don't need me or Bill Lewis to realize the importance of stories in our political heritage. Surely you know the story of George Washington and the cherry tree, or the story of Abe Lincoln walking some ungodly distance simply to return a library book. These stories, we seem to believe, tell us something important about the person. In the modern era, there have been other stories: President John F. Kennedy as the commander of a PT boat in World War II, Dwight Eisenhower as a celebrated war hero, and even Jimmy Carter as a humble peanut farmer from Plains, Georgia. In the 2008 Presidential campaign, much attention (*too* much attention, in my view!) was devoted to the story of a man who became known as "Joe the Plumber"—the media kept asking, what was Joe's situation, and who would better address his problems: John McCain or Barack Obama? (For those of you with short attention spans, Joe the Plumber was Joe Wurzelbacher, an Ohio man looking to buy a plumbing business. By the end of the 2008 campaign, both McCain and Obama claimed that Joe would be better off voting "their way." For better or worse, Joe made *his* way into the 2008 Presidential debates as a concrete example of how each of the candidates would formulate national economic policy.)

Of course, not all of these stories have been entertaining or complimentary; "negative" stories have been used against candidates. In the 1988 Presidential campaign, Democratic candidate Michael Dukakis was accused of being "soft on crime" because Willie Horton, an inmate in his home state of Massachusetts, murdered someone while he was on a release from prison. In the 2004 Presidential campaign, opponents of John Kerry implied that his military record was not as favorable as he claimed. Bill Clinton was victimized by stories of his infidelity. The story about Richard Nixon was that his secretary deleted 18 minutes of in-house tape recordings that might have implicated Nixon in the Watergate scandal. And former President George W. Bush has been on the receiving end of some uncomplimentary stories about his behavior as a college student and his military record. In short, people pay attention to stories, and they have become commonplace in political discourse.

FOR ALL SPHERES

Further, it is worth stressing that regardless of the argumentative context, it is important for people to do what Lyne (1990, 183) calls learning to "'talk like' a member of the profession—to learn the 'code,' so to speak." Lyne observes that lawyers must learn to speak "legaleze," and that an economist must "talk like an economist." Being able to use the jargon of one's group, he writes, "is a way of proving one's membership in the relevant community." Put another way, learning the specialized language of a given field is one important way to establish your credibility.

Some people, of course, would contend that the specialized vocabularies of different groups are not really necessary, and that they are a way to give "experts" the appearance of power—after all, if your physician says that you have "an upper respiratory infection," that sounds more authoritative than simply saying that you have "a cold." On the other hand, as Lyne notes, specialized language is "simply a necessary part of technical and precise thought. A chemist needs a language apart from everyday language that is adequate to the things chemists study."

Therefore, learning specialized terminology and using it, judiciously, is helpful in any sphere of argument, whether it be business or politics or religion, for instance. In each case, there are "linguistic cues" that will tell members of that rhetorical community that you are informed, and that you belong.

U.S. CULTURE AS A SPHERE OF ARGUMENT

Finally, any discussion of the contextual dimensions of argument would not be complete without some consideration for our national culture generally. Although it is always problematic to generalize about a culture, it is nonetheless the case that observers of U.S. culture have identified certain values that almost transcend the specific contexts (law, religion, politics, etc.) that have been discussed to this point. These "American" cultural values play out to some extent in all of the contexts examined previously. And even the most "rational" person must acknowledge that the values embedded within national cultures influence our assessment of arguments that are connected to those values. What, then, constitute dominant American cultural values, and how do they influence argument?

Americans tend to value freedom, individuality, and independence. As mentioned in chapter 7, "freedom" is a "God term" in U.S. culture. We celebrate people's individuality and ability to choose; ours is not a culture where people generally try to conform to the group and "fit in." As a result, arguments in all spheres that promote these values tend to be better received. For many in the U.S., anything that smacks of "socialism"—for example, "socialized medicine"—violates a cultural belief that people ought to be free to choose their own health care options. Americans tend to dislike "collectivistic" answers to problems that reduce personal freedom. Even an argument for mandatory uniforms in the public schools is likely to be met with some resistance, because conformity in dress is not something we promote or celebrate. We are willing to support arguments that ensure "independent living" for our senior citizens, because we believe that people at all ages should be as independent and self-reliant as possible.

Americans believe in equality. Unlike cultures where "hierarchy" is important—including titles and positions such as "king" that have ultimate authority—Americans believe, at least in principle, that everyone is created equal. As Bosrock (1999, 50-51) observes,

The concept of equality as it has evolved in the United States does not mean that everyone is entitled to an equal station in life or that equal results are guaranteed. Rather, Americans believe that each person is born with the same rights and freedoms as everyone else. Everyone should be given the opportunity to compete with everyone else according to his or her abilities and talents. . . Americans are very uncomfortable with any class distinctions. They dislike anyone who acts superior or tries to "pull rank." Even important and influential people attempt to appear approachable.

An argumentative case that would call for preferential treatment for one group over another tends to be a difficult case to make in the U.S. That is one reason why "affirmative action" laws, which attempt to provide job opportunities on the basis of race, are often resisted in the U.S.

Americans focus on the future and are more "striving" than "fatalistic." In some cultures, the dominant belief is that there are limits to what people are able to do about problems; things simply are as they are, whether they be good or bad. And in many more traditional societies, the past is revered and history really matters. On the other hand, U.S. culture is geared toward the future— planning for the future, predicting the future, and controlling the future. And the cultural belief is that if people work hard enough and "apply themselves," they can achieve just about anything. As Bosrock (1999, 67) argues, "Because Americans do not feel burdened by the past, they look with hope to what lies ahead. Americans believe this forward-looking vision has served them well, so they are usually optimistic about the future." Indeed, an argument about some aspect of U.S. foreign policy that was focused on our past indiscretions might seem irrelevant and inappropriate—to the typical American, the issue is, "where are we now, and where do we want to go in the future?"

Americans are competitive. Obviously, any culture promotes cooperation to some degree. However, U.S. culture puts great emphasis on competition. In order to have a competitive mindset, one must first compare oneself to others—Americans, for example, try to "keep up with the Joneses." To the American, if one is "falling behind the Joneses," that becomes a concern and a source of motivation. As Stewart and Bennett (1991, 79) observe, "Competition is the primary method among Americans for motivating members of groups. Americans, with their orientation toward individualism and achievement, respond well to this technique." So, what does this cultural tendency have to do with argumentation? To the American mind, if we are "losing to the competition," then doing something about that becomes a compelling argumentative stance. Indeed, the U.S. has spent hundreds of billions of dollars trying to keep up with its adversaries, both in terms of the "space race" and the "arms race." (It is interesting in itself that we have typically used a competitive "racing" metaphor to describe these issues.) And some have been convinced that more money needs to be spent on education because the U.S. rates low on certain achievement tests compared to students from other industrialized nations. In short, Americans like to be "number one" and are quite willing to entertain arguments that ensure our competitive position in the world. Even a college football program can be resurrected if those in a position of authority can be convinced that the home team is falling behind the competition, especially other schools in the same athletic conference.

Americans value efficiency and practicality. Those who have closely observed U.S. culture believe that Americans are "doers" and "problem-solvers" who are interested in what "works," and what works most efficiently. As Jandt (1995, 218) explains, "We are perceived as placing such a high value on time that we even have 'efficiency experts.' Our emphasis on getting things done on time causes us to organize our lives for efficiency so that we can get the most done." In the typical American mindset, having a solution that works is more important than its theoretical elegance, or its philosophical appeal. For example, although some Americans might support arguments to fund our space program to support "the wonder of human exploration," many more might be inclined to support the space program because of its practical benefits and applications. In other words, they believe the space program has provided new technology and important advances in science, medicine, communication, and so on—in short, it has practical value. Even college students are not immune to this mentality—some would never consider majoring in something like philosophy or history because these fields, they believe, lack a practical connection to the world. "What's the point in studying *that?*" some might ask. So, arguments that promote practicality and efficiency tend to resonate well with U.S. Americans.

Americans like to think they are being "rational," but they are also wary of "intellectuals." At first glance, this statement may seem inconsistent or contradictory, but the basic idea is this: Americans do not like to think of themselves as irrational decision-makers, but they are suspicious of "intellectuals," who only have "theories" and "book knowledge." On the one hand, Americans—like members of most "Western" cultures—prefer a type of discourse that could be described as "quasilogical." As Lustig and Koester (2006, 245) note, in a quasilogical style

> .... the preference is to use statistics and testimony from expert, objective witnesses as evidence. The evidence is then connected to the conclusion in a way that resembles formal logic. . . In the quasilogical style, the speaker or persuader will connect the evidence to the persuasive conclusion by using such words as thus, hence, and therefore. The form or arrangement of the ideas is very important.

On the other hand, American culture has historically been wary of people, ideas, or arguments that seem too "abstract," "academic," or "theoretical." As Stewart (1972, 22) proposes,

> Americans are distrustful of theories which seem remote from some type of application. The role of concepts and ideas in American life is to provide direction for instrumental activity. . . The role of the American intellectual over the span of American history is precarious. He has been consistently pressed to show the utility of his ideas and theories—unlike the intellectual in many countries of Europe who earns respect for his work distinct from its practicality.

So in U.S. culture, one must appear to be "rational and intelligent" but not too out of touch with "common sense." Larson (2007, 195) refers to the "anti-intellectual" aspect of this cultural belief as the "wisdom of the rustic," implying that "common sense" and the "simple wisdom of the backwoods" are favored over advocates who are perceived as "intellectuals," who are often "the brunt of jokes." Indeed, college professors are often not even considered part of the "real world," which apparently exists across the street from campus. These professors sit in "ivory towers," looking down on the rest of the world with no real understanding of how it operates. They only have "book smarts," and throw out a bunch of "theories." So, if you can live with this apparent inconsistency, the point is that Americans sometimes tread a very fine line: they want arguments to seem objective and rational, but they resist arguments and arguers who seem too abstract, too theoretical, or too out-of-touch with the rest of the world. In short, an effective advocate in the U.S. must seem sensible yet pragmatic, rational but not "stuffy."

Americans are materialistic. Often when people encounter the word "materialistic," they take it to mean, "wanting to have a lot of things." And that indeed is one dimension of being materialistic. Bosrock (1999, 70) contends that

> Americans gain a feeling of well-being and identity from their possessions. Religious and social taboos against excessive consumption have deteriorated. People constantly see images of wealthy people living amid luxury through the television screen or in catalogs and ads that promote indulgent lifestyles.

Therefore, any argument that promotes material welfare tends to be regarded as persuasive. A "shoes for needy kids" drive will appeal to many people, because it's giving kids something tangible that they need. A program to ensure that all public schools have computers would be considered a "no-brainer" to many, since schools must have good facilities to provide a proper education.

However, "materialism" as a way of thinking runs deeper than simply wanting a lot of consumer goods. Materialism can be contrasted with an "aesthetic" or "spiritual" approach to life in which the "things" of life become less important and less valuable. In the U.S., we tend to focus on the tangible, material aspects of life. Thus, an argument to improve the "infrastructure" of our society— its roads, bridges, sewers, etc.—will be regarded as convincing. Similarly, if we want our local sports teams to be "successful," they need to have modern, state-of-the-art practice facilities and arenas. Those of you who are college students may have been convinced to attend a particular school because of its wonderful facilities. Put another way, not many prospective college students are presented with the argument that "this institution is a haven of fine minds who share important values"; rather, they are shown the new library and are invited to marvel at the material "look" of the place. Even our thinking about foreign policy over the years has been geared quite a bit to its material dimensions—for decades, a central issue in the U.S. was, how big is our pile of missiles compared to the Russian pile? If the two piles were about the same size, we felt more secure; if we thought our pile was smaller, then arguments were presented to make our pile bigger.

CONCLUSION

In the end, then, there are really two "layers" of culture that any arguer must consider—the more "narrow" layer which is the occupational context in which the argument takes place, and the "broader" layer of the culture as a whole. Both of these layers help to shape what is considered a "good" or a "convincing" argument. In some ideal world, perhaps the context of an argument should not matter—but in the more "real" world, arguments must be tailored to the context in which they are presented. A sophisticated student of argument realizes that arguments are made in a particular social, professional, and cultural context, and that these "spheres" affect how arguments are made and evaluated.

REFERENCES

Bosrock, Mary Murray. *Put your best foot forward—USA*. St. Paul, MN: International Education Systems, 1999.

Brummett, Barry. *Contemporary Apocalyptic Rhetoric*. New York: Praeger, 1991.

Dernbach, John C. and Richard V. Singleton. *A practical guide to legal writing and legal method*. Littleton, CO: Fred B. Rothman & Co, 1981.

Jandt. Fred. *Intercultural communication: An introduction.* Thousand Oaks, CA: Sage, 1995.

Lewis, William F. 1987. Telling America's story: Narrative form and the Reagan presidency. *Quarterly Journal of Speech,* 73: 280-302.

Lustig, Myron W. and Jolene Koester. *Intercultural competence: Interpersonal communication across cultures,* 5th ed. Boston: Pearson, 2005.

Lyne, John R. Argument in the Human Sciences in *Perspectives on argumentation: Essays in honor of Wayne Brockriede.* Prospect Heights, IL: Waveland Press, 1990.

Rieke, Richard., Malcolm O. Sillars, and Tarla Rai Peterson. *Argumentation And critical decision making.,* 6th ed. Boston: Pearson, 2005.

Romain, Dianne. *Thinking things through: Critical thinking for decisions you can live with.* Mountain View, CA: Mayfield, 1997.

Shapo, Helen S., Marilyn Walter, and Elizabeth Fajans. *Writing and analysis in the law.* Westbury, NY: The Foundation Press, Inc., 1989.

Stewart, Edward C. *American cultural patterns: A cross-cultural perspective.* Society for Intercultural Education, Training, and Research, 1972.

Stewart, Edward C. and Milton J. Bennett. *American cultural patterns: A cross-cultural perspective.* Yarmouth, ME: Intercultural Press, 1991.

Xiong, Chao. 2007. I-35 is Road to Salvation, Say Some Christians." *Star Tribune,* December 31, 2007, pages B1-B3.

Chapter 12

EFFECTIVE ORAL DELIVERY AND WRITTEN PRESENTATION

After reading this chapter, you should understand:

- How matters of form relate to one's credibility
- The differences between oral messages and written messages
- The nature of "stagefright" and possible remedies for it
- What the classical canons of rhetoric involve
- Four general guidelines for effective speech delivery
- Four common audience complaints about speech delivery
- Why a "rulebook" approach to delivery is discouraged
- The difference between a "loosener-upper" and a "tightener-upper"
- Basic keys to effective writing
- Common writing problems involving grammar and usage
- Common writing problems involving punctuation
- Common writing problems involving spelling
- Common writing problems involving style

Specialized terms to know:

- invention
- disposition
- elocution
- vocalized pauses

To this point, I have dealt largely with the "hard, structural" aspects of argument—the Toulmin model, for example, or tests for evidence, or fallacies in reasoning. And obviously, it's important to be competent in the way you use these various ideas. But, there are also matters of form—the "soft" side of argument, if you will. And like it or not, these less "logical" aspects of argument do make a difference.

238

Indeed, a variety of ancient orators argued, in so many words, that "wisdom without eloquence is impotence." Logically, I suppose it shouldn't matter how one speaks or writes when one presents an argument—after all, it's the content and substance that should matter. However, the reality is, you can be a very wise person, but if you can't express yourself in an eloquent way, you will be impotent (the rhetorical variety of impotence, of course!). So, we must pay attention to the kind of impression we make when we speak, and when we write. People will judge your argument as much on "form" as they will on "content." To make matters even a little more challenging, we must always remember that one's credibility or ethos is what would be considered a "receiver-based construct," which is a fancy way of saying: you cannot determine your own credibility—it's all about what the *receivers* think! Even if you have a Ph.D. and believe that you are a "noted authority in your field," you only have as much credibility as people are willing to give you. Not only that, but credibility has a fluid and dynamic quality—it changes over time. At one moment you can sound brilliant, and then a few moments later you mispronounce a word or make a factual misstatement and your credibility can suffer. Therefore, the first half of this chapter will deal with presenting an oral argument, and the second half will focus on writing—always with the goal of credibility in mind.

Before dealing with each, it would be good to consider how oral and written messages can and should differ. **Oral messages need to be different than written messages, in a variety of ways:**

1. Oral messages need to be relatively brief. With a written essay, if I get bored or distracted, I can pick it up again later and read it again. Not so with speaking! People have limited attention spans, and you need to respect that. All speeches have "time limits" in the sense that the audience has an expectation of how long you will speak; violating that expectation in an oral message is particularly problematic.

2. Oral sentences need to be shorter. If you have a written work that you are trying to convert to a speech, you will need to be on the lookout for wordy sentences, compound sentences, and complex sentence construction. In a speech, words must be processed aurally by the audience, and long sentences are difficult to comprehend. In a speech, even grammatically incomplete sentences—or sentence fragments, if you will—are potentially useful and effective.

3. Oral messages need more repetition and more explicit structure. As mentioned in chapter 9, in a speech, the audience is highly dependent on you the speaker to put things in an organizational framework for them. Tell them where you are going, where you are, and where you have been.

4. Oral messages should use fewer different words, fewer technical words, and more simple words. If, in a speech, you start using words like "epistemology" or "hermeneutics" and assume that the audience will automatically know what you're talking about, you are inviting confusion and disinterest. With a written essay, a receiver could take a little time to "look up" the meanings of a word, but not so in an oral context.

5. Oral messages should use more informal language. In a speech, audiences do *not* want to feel as if they are listening to someone "read a paper." They want to feel as if they are in a mutual transaction with a real person. The best speeches tend to have what might be called a "heightened conversational style"— not like chatting in the kitchen with a friend, but personable and not distant and stuffy. One way that you accomplish this goal is to be OK with a few personal pronouns—an occasional "I" or "my" is not usually inappropriate. You can use a few contractions—rather than saying "I do not believe," consider "I don't believe." And even a well-chosen colloquial or slang expression, provided that it's not x-rated, can be helpful.

ORAL PRESENTATION SKILLS

People often dread giving speeches. One reason for this apprehension may be that most people don't have the opportunity to give very *many* speeches. Like writing, speaking takes preparation and practice, and it takes more than three or four performances to truly develop the skill. In that respect, your college courses which have oral assignments are a good start, but they are only the beginning of a lifelong quest to become fully competent.

People who speak to others often experience what we used to call "stagefright" but now call "communication apprehension."

Whatever you call it, it's those butterflies, or beads of sweat, or internalized discomfort that go along with speechmaking. What makes people feel nervous when speaking in public? As Beebe and Beebe (2006, 12) note,

> A study by two communication researchers found that among the causes were fear of humiliation, concern about not being prepared, worry about one's looks, pressure to perform, personal insecurity, concern that the audience wouldn't be interested in oneself or the speech, lack of experience, fear of making mistakes, and an overall fear of failure.

So, all of these feelings are normal and perhaps almost inevitable. But there is a good side to nervousness as well: you can take some of that nervous energy and transform it into a more animated, interesting speech. Believe it or not, nervousness can work in your favor if you can "get those butterflies to fly in formation," if you will. As Zarefsky (2005, 24) emphasizes,

> Being nervous is normal. You believe that what you have to say is important, and you value your listeners' judgment. Wanting to please your audience and to make a good impression, you may worry about making some innocent but colossal mistake. In response to this emotional state, our bodies undergo numerous chemical changes. More blood sugar becomes available; insulin is secreted; blood pressure, respiration, and the conductivity of nerves all increase. . . . Interestingly enough, though, [these] same chemical changes that cause extreme anxiety in some people bring others to a higher state of readiness and confidence. Many speakers get a boost of energy that, properly channeled, causes them to feel "psyched up" for the speech and hence in a position to do well.

Additionally, it's worth noting that **you will likely feel more nervous than you actually look**; most stagefright is "internalized" and is not readily observed by the audience, even if you may feel otherwise. **Having a realistic view of the audience** will also help—it's been my experience that 99 percent of audiences want you to succeed and are really not out to get you. Also, **more speak-**

ing experience will help alleviate those fears. In fact, many schools have forensics or contest speaking programs that enable students to give literally scores of speeches at weekend tournaments; such experience is invaluable. But most important, **careful preparation** will help alleviate stagefright. If you are prepared, and you know exactly what you will be doing, then the actual speech will tend to take care of itself.

Classical views of speechmaking tend to reinforce the idea that methodical preparation is very helpful. The so-called "classical canons of rhetoric," which date back to antiquity but are still being used today, include five steps in speech preparation:

1. **invention** – You need to do your research, brainstorm about various topics, consider what possible lines of argument you might make.
2. **disposition** – Once you know what you will discuss, you need to put it into a structure that is clear and coherent (essentially, chapter 9 of this text).
3. **elocution** – Now that you have the ideas and the structure of the message, what sylistic touches can you add to make the speech more memorable? Humor? Interesting metaphors? Visual aids? A startling statement in the introduction?
4. **memory** – Now that you have prepared the speech, you need to "internalize" it and get to know it. Many people do oral rehearsal. Others just keep going through the speech in their mind. But you need time to get comfortable with the material.
5. **delivery** – Here's the part that the audience actually sees and hears—the actual speech.

The point of all this is that if you can do a careful job in steps 1-4, then step 5—the actual speech—will tend to go much better. Just like papers, speeches are better when they are prepared.

With respect to the nonverbal aspects of speech delivery, certain general guidelines come to mind:

1. *Seem* **natural.** Note that this is not the same thing, necessarily, as *being* natural. For example, I test out as a natural "introvert" on the Myers-Briggs test, but in speaking situations, I need to be more animated and outgoing than I would otherwise be. In

general you want to appear to be comfortable—not overly stiff and formal.

2. **Vary the stimuli**. A constant stimulus won't keep our attention. Even if you wear a bright orange sweatshirt, if you wear it every day, people will get used to it and not notice it as much. The key is to vary things. That includes your vocal volume, your vocal rate, the pitch of your voice, who you make eye contact with, what gestures you use, and so on. If your delivery is too "predictable," audiences will tend to either tune out or become painfully aware of the pattern you've fallen into; in either case, the message gets lost.

3. **Make sure the verbal and nonverbal messages are congruent**. If you are interested in your topic, you need to *seem* interested. If you are concerned about something, you need to *sound* concerned. If you are confused, then you need to sound confused— not angry or sarcastic. As you probably realize, when the verbal and nonverbal messages are not consistent, people tend to believe the nonverbal, simply because they sense that it is out of our conscious awareness and thus more "revealing."

4. **Don't do anything that is distracting**. When you ask people what things speakers do that can be distracting, they usually have lots of immediate answers: When they pace aimlessly around the room! When they jingle change in their pockets! When they chew gum! When they are holding a pen in their hand! When they take that pen and tap on the lectern! When they keep rubbing their nose! Suffice it to say that there are a wide variety of nonverbal behaviors that can "get in the way." If you have a well-meaning friend or instructor, or if you have the ability to videotape your presentations, you have the opportunity to discover what you do that may be distracting.

Further, it seems to me from my experience that there are certain predictable "pet peeves" that audiences have regarding speakers. These complaints, which are things you should avoid, would include:

1. **Lack of eye contact**. Audiences need and want to be included in the speech transaction. If you as a speaker do not look at them,

they will feel excluded—as if they are witnessing someone talking, not participating in communication. Look around the room; find four or five friendly faces; and look at individual people.

2. A monotone voice. People's voices can be very dreary, almost inviting the audience to tune out. You need to learn to listen to yourself—again, an audio or video recording of your presentation can be very helpful.

3. Speaking too softly. A first prerequisite of any speech is that people have to be able to hear you. If they can't hear, they'll get nothing out of the experience. Even in a small room, if people can hear you if they try, that's not good enough. You want to have sufficient volume so that they *have* to hear you, whether they want to or not. Think in terms of projecting your voice to the people in the last row.

4. Vocalized pauses—"ums," "OKs," "you knows." Speakers are often uncomfortable with silence—even a few nanoseconds of silence between sentences. And so, they fill those moments with "ums" and "you knows" and the like. Again, start to listen to yourself—a few "ums" and "you knows" are tolerable, but if listeners start being distracted by them, you have a problem. Learn to pause silently—with practice and a lot of self-monitoring, you really *can* do it. But it takes some work and attention.

Two final thoughts about speechmaking

First, be aware of the general principles and issues cited above, but **don't fall into a "rulebook" mentality.** What I mean by that is that some people seem to think that there are absolute rules (almost "laws") about public speaking—rules that are written down *somewhere*, and rules that they must be *violating*! But it's usually OK to put your hand in your pocket once in a while, as long as it isn't distracting. The audience will not probably care if you have a bottle of water near the lectern because you tend to get "cottonmouth." If you are reading a direct quotation from a source, your eye contact may intentionally (and quite appropriately) be on your notes for a while. A few "ums" and "ahs" are totally natural; it's only when they occur every five seconds that you have a problem. And you can in fact rest your hand on the lectern now and then—nothing will explode and nobody will die if you do! (It's a **lectern,** by the way, not a "podium"—a podium is a platform to stand on; a lectern is anything that holds your notes, even if it goes to the floor. Many people in communication studies with a Ph.D. erroneously call a lectern a "podium.")

Second, try to avoid being a "loosener-upper" or a "tightener-upper." (These two terms are my creation; for better or worse, you will not find them in any other communication textbook.) Sometimes when I hear people speak, they seem a little "anal," for lack of a better word. They are often very well prepared, very carefully organized, and their delivery is very much in control. But, they are often very boring as well. They lack vitality. They need to take a few more chances with language, be a little more colorful and creative, and have a little more dynamic and animated style. In short, they need to *loosen up*! On the other hand, some speakers seem incredibly "random" and disorganized. Their language seems imprecise. They have all kinds of nervous mannerisms. They don't seem at all prepared. They wander aimlessly around the lectern—sometimes around the whole room. They make you feel as if you are listening to maybe Robin Williams on either amphetamines or barbiturates, or both. And to these speakers, everyone in the audience wants to say, *tighten up your act*!

Over the years, I've found that almost all speakers tend to gravitate to one of these two poles. So ask yourself, are you someone who in general needs to move in the direction of tightening up, or loosening up? Overall, the goal is to arrive somewhere at the "middle" of this continuum—that is, trying to seem orderly and in control, yet somewhat lively and spontaneous.

WRITING SKILLS

There was a time when I thought writing might become less important—after all, we are now in many ways an "oral, electronic" culture. However, it turns out that the ability to write competently has become even more important. What, after all, is the Internet but an extremely vast typing pool? If you can't write well on your personal computer, everyone on the web will know it. And sometimes, people just don't seem to get it—some of my own advisees, communication studies majors who should know better, will send me notes that are riddled with spelling errors, vague phrasing, run-on sentences, and the like. People will judge your speaking by cosmetic factors, and so too will they judge you based on your writing—I am sorry to be the bearer of bad news about this, but e-mail is really not the same as text-messaging on a cell phone.

As with effective speaking, effective writing takes work. Just as you can't "wing" a speech, you also have to work hard to make your writing polished. As a faculty member who has been reading student papers for roughly thirty years, I can say that far too many read like "first drafts." In other words, people cobble together some material, often at the last minute, spend some time at the keyboard, print it out, and turn it in (often not stapled, and often without page numbers!). **One key to effective writing, plain and simple, is re-writing.** Any writer—even a seasoned professional—needs to be able to write a first draft, let it sit for a while, come back to it and make improvements, and then do all that again, possibly many times, until it's really good. When writing is polished, it really looks polished—one can tell from the look of the paper, the word choices, the number of errors, and the level of research. In general, it's hard to fake a good paper; you need to agonize over it a bit.

Additionally, I would say that **many problematic aspects of your writing will reveal themselves if you would get in the habit of reading what you have written out loud.** Like anything else, this is not a "magic cure" for one's writing deficiencies, but there are problems that you ear will pick up very quickly that your eye would never notice. So, read it aloud—to yourself, and/or to someone else—it will tell you a lot about what needs changing.

Clearly, this chapter is not meant to be an exhaustive discussion of writing. You should and most likely will take a composition course as part of your complete education. However, over the years, I have seen certain patterns in people's writing that I would like to identify here. These patterns are discussed below; I've numbered the comments for ease of reference.

ISSUES INVOLVING GRAMMAR / USAGE

#1   DO NOT WRITE IN SENTENCE FRAGMENTS.

Learn how to write in complete sentences. Generally, sentence fragments will become more obvious if you read your writing aloud. Remember that complete sentences have, among other things, both a subject and a verb. Remember also that a subordinate clause is not a sentence. Examples of sentence fragments:
- Such as candy, cookies, and ice cream.

- Although I had never been on a college campus.
- Anything from writing a poem to writing a novel.
- Which is something that everyone should do.

#2　DO NOT USE THE RELATIVE PRONOUNS "WHICH" OR "THAT" TO REFER TO PERSONS. USE THE WORD "WHO" INSTEAD.

- Incorrect: I wondered how a boy that was so small could play football.
- Correct: I wondered how a boy who was so small could play football. Better still: I wondered how such a small boy could play football. [Sentences with which/that/who constructions are often wordy and lack punch.]

#3　SUBJECT-VERB AGREEMENT: THE SUBJECT OF A SENTENCE IS NEVER IN A PREPOSITIONAL PHRASE.

- Incorrect: High levels of air pollution **causes** damage to the respiratory tract.
- Correct: High levels of air pollution **cause** damage to the respiratory tract. ["Levels" is the subject in this sentence; "of air pollution" is the prepositional phrase.]
- Incorrect: The number of school-age children **are** declining.
- Correct: The number of school-age children **is** declining. ["Number" is the subject.]

#4　KNOW THE DIFFERENCE BETWEEN "LESS AND FEWER," "AMOUNT AND NUMBER."

- "Less" and "amount" are for things that *can't* be counted-- e.g., "less trouble" or "a smaller amount of rice."
- "Fewer" and "number" are for things which *can* be counted-- e.g., "fewer calories" or "a smaller number of people."

#5　OTHER MATTERS OF USAGE:

- **Affect** is usually a verb meaning "to influence." **Effect** is usually a noun meaning "result." Example: The drug did not affect the disease, but it had several adverse side effects.
- **Loose** is an adjective meaning "not securely fastened." **Lose** is a verb meaning "to misplace." Example: Did you lose your only loose-fitting pants?

- **Who's** is a contraction of who is; **whose** is a possessive pronoun. Example: Who's ready for more popcorn? Whose coat is this?
- The *sender* of a message **implies**; the *receiver* **infers**. Example: George implied that he knew all about computers, but the interviewer inferred   that John was inexperienced.
- **Everyday** [one word] is an *adjective*: e.g., people and their everyday problems. But if you are discussing what you do each day, it's *two words*--every day. Example: I run three miles every day because it's part of my everyday routine.

#6   KNOW WHEN TO USE "A" AND "AN."

The article "a" is for words that, when spoken, begin with a consonant sound. The article "an" is for words that, when spoken, begin with a vowel sound. For example:

a discussion	an article
a hamburger	an herb
a historic moment	an illogical argument
a European hotel	an hour

ISSUES INVOLVING PUNCTUTATION

#7   COMMAS AND PERIODS GO <u>INSIDE</u> QUOTATION MARKS.

When you are quoting something, commas and periods go inside the quotation marks. For example:

   The article notes that such ideas are "impractical."

   "Easy writing," the professor said, "makes for hard reading."

Check any newspaper or magazine in the U.S., and you will see that this is how the punctuation is done. Incidentally, colons and semicolons go *outside* quotation marks--e.g., He said this was "impossible"; I tend to disagree.

#8   DO NOT JOIN TWO SENTENCES WITH A COMMA. (This is called a "comma splice.")

Examples of comma splices: "The current was swift, he could not swim to shore," or "Hiking is great fun, you should try it." In both cases, the two independent clauses should be either:

(a) joined by a semicolon. [The current was swift; he could not swim to shore.]
(b) made into two separate sentences, with a period in between. [The current was swift. He could not swim to shore.]
(c) joined by a "connective" such as "and" or "or." [The current was swift, and he could not swim to shore.]

#9 TITLES OF ARTICLES ARE IN QUOTATION MARKS; TITLES OF PUBLICATIONS AND BOOKS ARE UNDERLINED.

So, for example, an article titled "Faculty Responses to Academic Dishonesty" would appear in the <u>Chronicle of Higher Education</u>.

ISSUES INVOLVING SPELLING

#10 THERE IS <u>NO SUCH WORD</u> AS "ALOT."

It is two words (a lot). But be careful not to overuse these two words--there are often better alternatives.

#11 TO MAKE A NOUN PLURAL, EITHER ADD AN "S" OR "ES"--DO <u>NOT</u> ADD AN APOSTROPHE.

For some unknown reason, more and more people are making nouns plural by adding an apostrophe--e.g., "three idea's," "five argument's." [The worst case I've seen: a beautiful hand-painted sign reading "Noon lunch'es."] Apostrophes have only two uses: to indicate possession [Bob's idea] or to indicate that letters are missing [tons o' fun, didn't, wouldn't].

#12 "IT'S" ONLY HAS AN APOSTROPHE IF IT MEANS "IT IS."

- Correct: It's only human to have such emotions.
- Incorrect: I will discuss the camera and it's uses. [no apostrophe]

#13 KNOW YOUR LATIN ABBREVIATIONS!

The letters **"e.g."** mean **"for example."**
The letters **"i.e."** mean **"that is."**

[I have used "e.g." frequently here to save space, but you should not make a habit of cluttering your sentences with either abbreviation. Use them sparingly.]

#14   NOW YOUR LATIN SPELLINGS! (Distinction between singular and plural)

Singular	Plural	Singular	Plural
criterion	criteria	alumnus	alumni [men]
phenomenon	phenomena	alumna	alumnae [women]
medium	media		

[Note that the word "media" is plural—for that reason, it is most correct to discuss what the media *are* doing, not what the media *is* doing. Remember, the *medium* of television is one of the mass *media*.]

#15   COMMON SPELLING ERRORS TO AVOID:

Incorrect	Correct	Incorrect	Correct
speach	speech	alright	all right
persuation	persuasion	catagory	category
recieve	receive	seperate	separate
alot	a lot	buisness	business
arguement	argument	sophmore	sophomore
orientate	orient	untill	until
tendancy	tendency	aquire	acquire
should of	should have	room to *breath*	room to *breathe*
more then	more than	employee *moral*	employee *morale*

#16   HUGE SPELLING NO-NOs! Whatever you do, do NOT mess up on these:

two   the number which comes after one
to   a preposition--e.g., going to the store
too   means *very* (too cold, too difficult) or *also* (she's here, too)

there   a *place*--over there
their   involves *possession*--their idea, their sandwich

they're a contraction for "they are"

your   also involves *possession*--your idea, your sandwich
you're is a contraction for *you are*--e.g. "you're wrong," "you're driving me crazy"

When you make mistakes on these very simple words, you make a very poor impression. There is absolutely no excuse for misspelling these. None. Zero. Zip. Don't do it, period.

#17   *PROPER NOUNS ARE CAPITALIZED. COMMON NOUNS ARE <u>NOT.</u>*

Common noun	Proper noun
school (could be any school)	Augsburg College (a particular school)
religion (could be any religion)	Buddhism (a particular religion)
beverage (a generic term)	Pepsi-Cola (a particular beverage)

ISSUES INVOLVING STYLE

#18   *BE CAREFUL WHEN USING "ETC.".*

"Etc." should only be used if the other elements of a list are **entirely** self-evident [e.g., 2, 4, 6, 8, etc.]. Do not use "etc." as an excuse for incomplete or sloppy thinking [e.g. there are many reasons for this--poverty, lack of education, etc.]. And if you do use the term, please remember that it is **not** spelled "ect."--it stands for et cetera.

#19   *WATCH USE OF THE WORD "AREA."*

• This is another term that tends to be misused, or overused. "Area" should usually be confined to things geographical--e.g., areas of the world. Consider alternatives such as "aspect," "topic," "respect," or "regard." Example:
• Troublesome: I want to examine three areas of the problem. Preferable: I want to examine three aspects [or dimensions or facets] of the problem. [Or: I want to examine the problem in three respects.]

#20   SOME OTHER WORDS TO THINK ABOUT:

- **Firstly** sounds stilted, and it leads to the awkward series firstly, secondly, thirdly, fourthly, and so on. Use first, second, third instead.
- **Utilize** means "to make use of." However, it is seldom, if ever, necessary to "utilize" this word. Utilize sounds pretentious; in most cases, **use** is preferable.

#21   USE THE ACTIVE VOICE RATHER THAN THE PASSIVE VOICE.

Using the active voice will give your writing more "punch."
- Passive: A staff meeting was called by the district manager.
- Active: The district manager called a staff meeting.
- Passive: Investigations were made, and conclusions were arrived at.
- Active: I investigated the issues and reached several conclusions.

#22   CUT OUT EMPTY WORDS AND PHRASES.

Be on the lookout for unnecessary words. Many sentences can profit from this kind of "pruning." For example:

in order to.........	to	with reference to..........	about, as for
prior to..............	before	for the reason that........	since, because
inasmuch as.......	since	at the present time.......	at present
in the event that...	if	increasing amounts of...	more

#23   KEEP SENTENCES TO A REASONABLE LENGTH.

Modern composition texts tend to favor using shorter sentences. As a general rule of thumb, be careful about writing sentences which are longer than, say, 25 or 30 words.

#24   AVOID EXCESSIVE FORMALITY, HIGH LEVELS OF ABSTRACTION, AND NEEDLESS JARGON.

Especially in academia, some people write to impress others rather than to communicate. Don't fall into the trap of being excessively "highbrow." Good writing has vigor, strength, and precision. Do *not* write paragraphs of this sort:

> It may be concluded that multivalued decision problems are so common in economics that the objectives and criteria of conservation decisions are best formulated in a way that takes uncertainty explicitly into account; this can be done, for example, by subjecting the economic optimum to the restriction of avoiding immoderate possible losses, or by formulating it as minimizing maximum possible losses.

I'll leave it to you to figure out how to re-write *that* to make it communicate!

In summary, remember that writing takes work. *Nobody*--myself included--can write a polished first draft. Start by writing *something*--no matter how bad it seems--and continue to work with it. Read it aloud, show it to friends, let it sit for a day or two and then come back to it. Just remember the motto that "easy writing makes for hard reading."

A final note regarding spelling: just as mowing your front lawn is the quickest and easiest way to improve the appearance of your yard, making sure that all words are spelled correctly is the quickest and easiest way to improve your credibility as a writer and the overall "feel" of the paper. Like it or not, people will judge you on the basis of your spelling. They will draw conclusions about your effort, your attention to detail, and even your competence and your intelligence. Therefore it is critical to make your writing look "correct" on this superficial level. Having every word spelled correctly will not magically take care of many problems, but it will tell the reader that you are not illiterate. These days, of course, various "spell check" programs are a common part of computer software; you should use these spell check applications but not worship them. Realize that they will not catch everything; extra "human checking" is normally needed. Also, do a websearch for "commonly misspelled words"—many electronic sites have lots of lists of words that often give people problems.

CONCLUSION

Whether it be speech or writing, what we are dealing with is how you present yourself to the world, and how to establish your credibility. So, you ought to be concerned about effective speaking and writing, not for someone else's sake, but for your own. And whether it be speaking or writing, like a lot of things in life, the key to becoming better is investing real time and real energy in making it better—in the end, there is no substitute for hard, sustained work.

REFERENCES

Beebe, Steven A. and Susan J. Beebe. *Public speaking: An audience-centered approach*. Boston: Pearson, 2006.

Zarefsky, David. *Public speaking: Strategies for success*. Boston: Pearson, 2005.

ANSWERS TO THE FALLACY QUIZ ON PAGE 127

1. *argumentum ad verecudiam* – it's an appeal to tradition
2. begging the question – "smart" is just another word for "intelligent"
3. *non sequitur* – it's not at all clear how the first half of the sentence relates to the second half
4. equivocation – the word "liberal" is being used in two ways— one "political," one not
5. *argumentum ad hominem* – clearly a case of name-calling here
6. fallacy of division – what's true of the team as a whole may not be true of each part
7. *argumentum ad lazarum* – mud huts *may* make you wiser, but not necessarily
8. slippery slope argument – in real life, we can only hope that this is not the case!
9. hasty generalization – Biff may have you fooled here by his one annual trip to the library
10. *argumentum ad populum* – the majority can be "wrong"
11. *reductio ad absurdum* – this is twisting the argument in a way that's misleading
12. gambler's fallacy – "Lady Luck" is not predictable at that level!
13. *argumentum ad misericordiam* – especially if Jimmy has a lousy "skill set"
14. *argumentum ad ignorantiam* – the pro-avocado person is ignoring her burden of proof
15. *argumentum ad baculum* – surely no student would actually do that, would they?
16. perfect solution fallacy – the vast majority of people have no interest in such deviousness
17. red herring – get back to whether Maria is a good actress! That's the issue
18. two wrongs make a right – we can't excuse our behavior with such a rationalization
19. false dilemma – certainly there are more than two possibilities here
20. fallacy of composition – let this be a lesson to you!
21. line-drawing fallacy – at some point, too much is simply too much
22. straw man argument – it makes Mr. Windbag look bad, but it's a relatively minor issue

23. *post hoc ergo propter hoc* – I also got *older* after I met you! So what?
24. historian's fallacy – no weather forecast could help the Petersons in this case
25. *argumentum ad crumenum* – you wouldn't hold the low price against me, would you?

Of course, as discussed in chapter 6, sometimes good people might not agree on what fallacy is the most relevant, or whether there even is a fallacy in the first place—again, this is not mathematics. But I think the interpretations above are reasonable.

GLOSSARY OF KEY TERMS

Absolute percentage
The actual difference between two percentages; for example, an increase from 1 percent to 2 percent is an absolute increase of 1 percent

Abstract language
Words that can refer to many different things and do not have a concrete referent—for example, "wealth" or "independence"

Access
The standard for evidence that deals with whether the source really has first-hand knowledge of the subject

Apocalyptic rhetoric
In its religious form, rhetoric which argues that the "rapture" and/ or the second coming of Christ is imminent, as revealed by scripture

Argumentation
The process of advancing, examining, and responding to claims, primarily through the use of reasoned discourse.

Argumentum ad baculum
An inappropriate appeal to force or the threat of force

Argumentum ad crumenum
A fallacy that falsely assumes that there is a direct relationship between "cost" and "quality"

Argumentum ad hominem
A fallacy in reasoning in which a personal attack takes the place of a substantive argument

Argumentum ad ignorantiam
Involves either (a) assuming something is true because it has not been proven false, or (b)
assuming something is false because it has not been proven true

Argumentum ad lazarum
A fallacy that assumes something is necessarily a better value because it costs less, or that
someone of little means is "wiser" or "more intelligent"

Argumentum ad misericordiam
An inappropriate appeal to pity

Argumentum ad *populum*
The fallacy that because the majority of people believe something it must be correct or true

Argumentum ad verecundiam
A fallacy that involves either an inappropriate appeal to tradition or an inappropriate appeal to authority

Begging the question
A fallacy in reasoning that involves "proving" an assertion by simply repeating it or rephrasing it

Blame/inherency
In policy discussions, the stock issue that involves whether a problem is of such a nature that a new solution is necessary

Burden of proof
The need to make a convincing case to overcome presumption

Causal organization
A type of organization where each main point becomes a "cause" for the next main point—for example, "kids watch a lot of TV," "watching TV leads to obesity," and "obesity leads to heart disease"

Causal reasoning
Reasoning that establishes a definite link between two things; for example, a study that shows taking a daily baby aspirin thins the blood and reduces heart attacks

Circumstantial evidence
Evidence that relates indirectly to the claim being made

Comparative advantage organization
A type of organization that is built around a list of future advantages or benefits to a proposal rather than an indictment of the status quo

Concrete language
Language that is specific, down-to-earth, and can be mentally pictured—for example, "car" or "hamburger"

Connotative meaning
The "feelings" that a word inspires; for example, "thrifty" has a more favorable connotation than "cheap," even though they both denote the same idea

Correlation
The idea that two things vary together in a predictable way; for example, that as student alcohol consumption increases, student grades decrease

Cost/desirability
In policy discussions, the stock issue that involves whether on balance, the advantages of a proposal outweigh potential disadvantages

Counterplan
A refutation strategy (for policy issues) in which you concede that there is a significant and inherent problem but propose a "new" solution that is substantially different than your opponent's solution

Criteria-based organization
An organizational format that proposes certain criteria for evaluating options and then uses those criteria to arrive at the best option

Critical thinking
The careful, deliberate determination of whether we should accept, reject, or suspend judgment about the truth of a claim or a recommendation to act in a certain way

Cumulativeness
The standard for evidence which considers whether all the available evidence "adds up" to support the claim

Cure/solvency
In policy discussions, the stock issue that involves whether the proposed plan of action is workable and practical and will actually solve the problem

Data
In the Toulmin model, any evidence that is used to support a claim

Deductive reasoning
Reasoning from the general to the specific; involves taking a generalization and applying that generalization to a specific case or situation

Defining by authority
Defining a word by citing the definition of an authority figure

Defining by etymology
Defining a word by its linguistic roots; for example, that "euthanasia" is derived from the Greek for "easy death"

Defining by function
Defining a word by what it does; for example, an amphetamine is a drug that stimulates the central nervous system

Defining by negation
Defining a word by indicating what it is *not*

Denotative meaning
The "dictionary definition" of a word—what a word denotes or stands for; for example, "chair" denotes a piece of furniture to sit on, or the head of a committee

Dilemma
A refutation strategy in which you formulate two possible outcomes or aspects of an opponent's position, and both are undesirable

Direct evidence
Evidence that relates directly to the claim being made

Disposition
The classical canon of rhetoric that involves organizing ideas into a coherent form

Dramatism
The idea that humans think about issues and events in theatrical terms, with heroes and villains, victims and allies, a particular stage and a particular plot line

Dualistic thinking
Sometimes called "either/or" thinking; a type of thinking that is "black and white" and tends to oversimplify an issue

Dysphemism
The opposite of a euphemism—purposely using a more "emotional" and "biased" word in place of a more neutral word. For example, "propaganda" rather than "information."

Elocution
The classical canon of rhetoric that involves providing stylistic touches to the message

Ethos
Source credibility; persuasion that is the result of finding the source to be credible

Euphemism
Taking the emotional "sting" out of a word by using a more "polite" or less "emotional" word; for example, saying "restroom" rather than "toilet"

Equivocation
A fallacy that involves using the same word or term in two different ways so as to mislead

External consistency
The standard for evidence that involves whether the evidence is consistent with other available evidence

Factual claim
A statement that involves a "true or false" issue and has the potential to be verified

Fallacy of composition
Falsely assuming that what is true of the parts is also true of the whole when the parts are put together

Fallacy of division
Falsely assuming that what is true of the whole is also true of each part of the whole

False dilemma
A fallacy that involves presenting two possible alternatives (an either/or situation) in a way that is inappropriate or misleading

Fantasy theme
Ernest Bormann's term for a story about something which has a dramatic element that people identify with, share, and "chime into"

Fantasy type
Ernest Bormann's term for two or more fantasy themes dealing with different subjects that have common thematic elements

Fiat
(Latin for "let it be done") is a theoretical construct which focuses on whether a proposal is **desirable**, rather than whether it is likely to be **enacted** in the "real world."

Field-invariant approach to argument
A "generic" approach to argument that pays no real attention to the social or cultural context of the argument

Field-variant approach to argument
An approach to studying argument that considers the social and cultural context in which the argument is made

Figurative analogy
Comparing two things that are from different classes or categories; for example, comparing the United States to a flower garden

Gambler's fallacy
A fallacy that assumes the laws of probability must "balance out" in the short run; for example, the mistaken belief that three coin flips in a row that are "heads" means that the net flip is more likely to be "tails"

God and devil terms
Words that are so strongly positive or negative in connotation that they are normally unchallenged—for example, "freedom" (God term) and "terrorism" (devil term)

Hasty generalization
An inductive generalization made on the basis of two few cases

Historian's fallacy
A fallacy that assumes decision makers in the past could see things from the same perspective and with the same information when later discussing the decision

Historical analogy
Comparing two things from different time periods; for example, comparing the war in Iraq to the Vietnam War

Hyperbole
Language that is extremely exaggerated—for example, "he is the worst leader in the history of the universe."

Ill/significance
in policy discussions, the stock issue that involves whether there is a significant problem that needs to be addressed

Inductive reasoning
Reasoning from the specific to the general; sometimes called reasoning by generalization

Internal consistency
The standard for evidence which asks if the evidence is internally consistent within itself

Invention
The classical canon of rhetoric that involves research, brainstorming for ideas, and developing possible lines of argument

Line-drawing fallacy
A fallacy that suggests if it's difficult to draw a line between two things, then one simply shouldn't even draw a line; the fallacy is in thinking that "one more doesn't matter"

Literal analogy
comparing two things in similar categories; for example, comparing the crime rates of two states

Logos
That part of a message that appeals to the intellect or reason

Mean
The type of average that involves adding up all the scores and dividing by the number of scores in the distribution of numbers

Median
The type of average that involves finding the point at which half of the numbers are greater and half are less than that point

Metaphors
Implied comparisons, not using "like" or "as"

Method of residue organization
An organizational format in which the possible alternative policies are refuted, one-by-one, leaving your preferred policy as the one "left standing"

Minor repair
A refutation strategy for propositions of policy which argues that problems in the status quo can be alleviated by making changes that are smaller and qualitatively different than the opponent's solution

Mode
The type of average that involves finding the most common or frequent number in the distribution of scores

Negative evidence
The lack of evidence used as evidence for a claim

Non sequitur
A fallacy where one thing does not seem to follow from another

Operational definition
Defining a word with a practical way to operationally measure it; for example, "obesity" is a Body Mass Index of more than 30

Oral signposts
Language in a message that indicates when you are moving from one major point to the next

Pathos
That part of a message that appeals to our needs, drives, or emotions

Perfect solution fallacy
A fallacy that occurs when an argument assumes that a perfect solution exists and/or that a solution should be rejected because some part of the problem would still exist after it was implemented; essentially, the fallacy is in thinking that any problem can be totally eradicated, and that if it can't be, there's no reason to try

Persuasion
A type of influence that relies on both logical and psychological strategies

Persuasive definition
A "loaded" definition that is not objective or neutral—for example, a "politician" is "someone who wants to take as much of your tax money as possible"

Policy claim
A statement that says something should be done

Positive evidence
The presence of evidence to support a claim

Post hoc ergo propter hoc
A fallacy in causal reasoning that falsely assumes that if A happens, and then B happens, that A necessarily caused B

Presumption
The idea that we should stay with what we do or know until someone can prove otherwise; presumption lies with the status quo

Primary evidence
Evidence that comes from the original source who gathered the data

Prima facie case
A case that is strong enough on its face to require a response from an opponent

Problem-solution organization
An organizational format that first defines the problem and then identifies a solution

Rebuttal
Attempting to rebuild your case in light of opposing refutation

Red herring
A fallacy that involves bringing in a clearly irrelevant point to distract people from the "real" issue

Refutation
Any attempt to weaken an opposing case

Relative terms
Terms that have no absolute meaning but only have meaning in relation to something else—for example, words such as "rich" or "intelligent"

Rhetorical vision
Ernest Bormann's term for any broad, overarching dramatization that explains any number of specific fantasy themes and fantasy types—for example, a "liberal" or "conservative" rhetorical vision

Qualifier
In the Toulmin model, any language that indicates the degree of certainty that one has of the claim

Reasoning by analogy
reasoning by comparing two things; analogies can be literal, historical, or figurative

Reductio ad absurdum
A fallacy that involves taking an opponent's idea to an extreme, to an absurd level, in a way that is inappropriate and misleading

Relative percentage
The percentage that relates one percentage to another; for example, an increase from 1 to 2 is an increase of 100 percent

Reluctant evidence
When a source presents a point of view or position that would not seem to be in their best interests—for example, a Republican endorsing a Democrat

Reservation
in the Toulmin model, any circumstance or set of circumstances under which one would want to withdraw the claim, frequently preceded by the word "unless"

Secondary evidence
Evidence in which some sort of intermediary has interpreted the original, primary evidence

Sign reasoning
Making a causal connection between two things by use of observable signs or symptoms; for example, believing that you will have bad luck if a black cat crosses your path

Similes
Implied comparisons which use "like" or "as"

Slippery slope fallacy
A fallacy that falsely assumes once we go in a particular direction in a "small" way that we will inevitably go much further down the "wrong path"

Stare decisis
In legal argument, a concept that is similar to presumption; it literally means "let the decision stand" because of an established legal precedent exists

Statistical significance
When a difference in means between two groups is so large that it is highly unlikely that such a difference is due to random chance

Stock issues
Standard, universal, generic issues that are potentially relevant to any controversy

Straw man argument
A fallacy in which an arguer misrepresents an opponent's position to make it easier to attack

Syllogism
A formal expression of deductive reasoning which includes a major premise, a minor premise, and a conclusion

Symbolic convergence theory
Ernest Bormann's idea that people share dramatizations about issues and events and make connections to one another based on commonly-held dramatizations

Tabula rasa perspective
Literally means "blank slate." If you evaluate a debate from this perspective, you try not to have any preconceptions about the issue, or the debaters—you simply try to evaluate the discussion based solely on what you hear at that time

Topical organization
Organizing a message around a list of separate and discrete ideas or arguments

Turning the tables
A refutation strategy in which you make the opponent's counter-argument a reason to support your position—for example, saying that an "expensive" solution is desirable because it will provide more quality and fewer long-term problems

Two wrongs make a right
A fallacy in which someone defends a "wrong" by pointing out that others, or their opponents, have acted in the same (equally bad) manner

Validity
within social scientific *research*, validity involves whether you are really measuring what you claim to be measuring. Within the world of logical *syllogisms*, validity involves whether the major premise, minor premise, and conclusion are properly constructed.

Value claim
A statement that involves an issue of "good" or "bad," "right" or "wrong"

Villain
In Jensen's heuristic, who or what is responsible for a problem

Vocalized pauses
The "ums," "OKs," or "you knows" that can function as "fillers" in speech delivery and are potentially distracting

Warrant
In the Toulmin model, an assumption that enables one to make a particular claim from particular evidence

Willing evidence
Evidence that is given freely by an advocate, sometimes with a vested interest in mind

BIBLIOGRAPHY

Bassham, Gregory, William Irwin, Henry Nardone, and James M. Wallace. *Critical thinking: A student's introduction*, 3rd ed. Boston: McGraw-Hill, 2008.

Beebe, Steven A. and Susan J. Beebe. *Public Speaking: An Audience-Centered Approach*. Boston: Pearson, 2006.

Best, Joel. *More damned lies and statistics: How numbers confuse public issues*. Berkeley, CA: University of California Press, 2004.

Bierman, Arthur K. and Robin N. Assali. *The critical thinking handbook*. Upper Saddle River, NJ: Prentice-Hall, 1996.

Bloom, Benjamin S., Max D. Engelhart, Edward J. Furst, Walker H. Hill, and David R. Krathwohl. *Taxonomy of educational objectives: the classification of educational goals*. New York: Longman, Green, and Co., 1956.

Bormann, Ernest. *Communication theory*. New York: Holt, Rinehart, and Winston, 1980.

Bosrock, Mary Murray. *Put your best foot forward—USA*. St. Paul, MN: International Education Systems, 1999.

Brummett, Barry. *Contemporary Apocalyptic Rhetoric*. New York: Praeger, 1991.

Burke, Kenneth. *A grammar of motives*. Berkeley, CA: University of California Press, 1969.

Carey, Stephen S. *The uses and abuses of argument*. Mountain View, CA: Mayfield Publishing, 2000.

Chaffee, John. *Thinking critically*, 5th ed. Boston: Houghton Mifflin, 1997.

271

Dernbach, John C. and Richard V. Singleton. *A practical guide to legal writing and legal method*. Littleton, CO: Fred B. Rothman & Co, 1981.

Elder, Paul and Linda Elder. *The miniature guide to critical thinking*. Dillon Beach, CA: Foundation for Critical Thinking Press, 2007.

Fearnside, W. Ward. *About thinking*, 2nd ed. Upper Saddle River, NJ: Prentice Hall, 1997.

Freeley, Austin J. and David L. Steinberg. *Argumentation and debate: Critical thinking for reasoned decision making*, 11th ed. Belmont, CA: Thomson-Wadsworth, 2005.

Gass, Robert and John Seiter. *Persuasion, social influence, and compliance gaining*, 3rd ed. Boston: Pearson, 2007.

Govier, Trudy. *A practical study of argument*, 3rd ed. Belmont, CA: Wadsworth, 1992.

Haiman, Franklyn S. 1949. An Experimental Study of the Effects of Ethos in Public Speaking. *Speech Monographs* 16: 90-202.

Hayakawa, S. I. *Language in thought and action*. New York: Harcourt, Brace & World, 1964.

Inch, Edward S., Barbara Warnick, and Danielle Endres. *Critical thinking and communication: The use of reason in argument*, 5th ed. Boston: Pearson, 2006.

Jandt. Fred. *Intercultural communication: An introduction*. Thousand Oaks, CA: Sage, 1995.

Jensen, J. Vernon. *Argumentation: Reasoning in communication*. New York: D. Von Nostrand, 1981.

Kahane, Howard and Nancy Cavender. *Logic and contemporary rhetoric: The use of reason in everyday life*, 10th ed. Belmont, CA: Wadsworth, 2006.

Lapakko, David. 1997. Three Cheers for Language: A closer examination of a widely cited study of nonverbal communication. *Communication Education*, 46: 63-67.

Lakoff, George and Mark Johnson. *Metaphors we live by*. Chicago: University of Chicago Press, 1979.

Larson, Charles U. *Persuasion: Reception and responsibility*, 11th ed. Belmont, CA: Thomson-Wadsworth, 2007.

Lewis, William F. 1987. Telling America's story: Narrative form and the Reagan presidency. *Quarterly Journal of Speech*, 73: 280-302.

Lustig, Myron W. and Jolene Koester. *Intercultural competence: Interpersonal communication across cultures*, 5th ed. Boston: Pearson, 2005.

Lyne, John R. Argument in the Human Sciences in *Perspectives on argumentation: Essays in honor of Wayne Brockriede*. Prospect Heights, IL: Waveland Press, 1990.

McBurney, James and Glen Mills. *Argumentation and debate: Techniques of a free society*, 2nd ed. New York: The Macmillan Company, 1964.

McKibben, Bill. 2007. Carbon's New Math. *National Geographic*, 212: 33-37.

Merriam, Alan. 1990. Words and numbers: Mathematical dimensions of rhetoric. *The Southern Communication Journal*, 55: 337-354.

Moore, Brooke Noel and Richard Parker. *Critical thinking*, 8th ed. Boston: McGraw-Hill, 2007.

O'Keefe, Daniel. 1977. Two concepts of argument. *Journal of the American Forensic Association* 13: 121-128.

Reichenbach, Bruce. *Introduction to critical thinking*. Boston: McGraw-Hill, 2001.

Rieke, Richard., Malcolm O. Sillars, and Tarla Rai Peterson. *Argumentation and critical decision making*. 6th ed. Boston: Pearson, 2005.

Romain, Dianne. *Thinking things 7hrough: Critical thinking for decisions you can live with.* Mountain View, CA: Mayfield, 1997.

Rottenberg, Annette T. *Elements of argument: A text and reader,* 2nd ed. New York: St. Martin's Press, 1988.

Rudinow, Joel and Vincent Barry. *Invitation to critical thinking.* Belmont, CA: Thomson-Wadsworth, 2008.

Ruggiero, Vincent. *Beyond feelings: A guide to critical thinking,* 7th ed. Boston: McGraw-Hill, 2004.

Rybacki, Karyn Charles and Donald J. Rybacki. *Advocacy and opposition: An introduction to argumentation.* Boston: Pearson, 2005.

Schmickle, Sharon. 2001. A Life Expectancy of 100? Not in Our Lifetimes. *Star Tribune,* February 19, 2001, pages A1/A10.

Shapo, Helen S., Marilyn Walter, and Elizabeth Fajans. *Writing and analysis in the law.* Westbury, NY: The Foundation Press, Inc., 1989.

Stewart, Edward C. *American cultural patterns: A cross-cultural perspective.* Society for Intercultural Education, Training, and Research, 1972.

Stewart, Edward C. and Milton J. Bennett. *American cultural patterns: A cross-cultural perspective.* Yarmouth, ME: Intercultural Press, 1991.

Stossel, John. 1995. "Fact or fiction? Misleading statistics." ABC News, 1994.

Toulmin, Stephen. *The uses of argument.* Cambridge, England: Cambridge University Press, 1964.

Verlinden, Jay. *Critical thinking and everyday argument.* Belmont, CA: Thomson-Wadsworth, 2005.

Walton, Douglas. *Appeal to pity: Argumentum ad misericordiam.* Albany, NY: State University of New York Press, 1997.

Weaver, Rrichard. *The ethics of rhetoric*. Chicago: Regnery, 1953.

Whately, Richard. *Elements of rhetoric*. Carbondale, IL: Southern Illinois University Press, 1963.

Wilson, David C. *A guide to good reasoning*. Boston: McGraw-Hill, 1999.

Wolff, Alan. 2002. Old Black Magic. *Sports Illustrated*, January 21, 2002, 50-62.

Xiong, Chao. 2007. I-35 is Road to Salvation, Say Some Christians. *Star Tribune*, December 31, 2007, B1-B3.

Yahoo! News (2007). "Experts: Elderly Most At-risk in Suicide." Retrieved September 18, 2007 at http://news.yahoo.com/s/ap/20070918/ap_on_he_me/elderly_suicide

Zarefsky, David. *Public speaking: Strategies for success*, 4th ed. Boston: Pearson, 2005.

Ziegelmueller, George W., Jack Kay, and Charles A. Dause. *Argumentation: Inquiry and advocacy*, 2nd ed. Englewood Cliffs, NJ: Prentice-Hall, 1990.